The Complete Guide to Photorealism for Visual Effects, Visualization and Games

This book offers a comprehensive and detailed guide to accomplishing and perfecting a photorealistic look in digital content across visual effects, architectural and product visualization, and games.

Emmy award-winning VFX supervisor Eran Dinur offers readers a deeper understanding of the complex interplay of light, surfaces, atmospherics, and optical effects, and then discusses techniques to achieve this complexity in the digital realm, covering both 3D and 2D methodologies. In addition, the book features artwork, case studies, and interviews with leading artists in the fields of VFX, visualization, and games. Exploring color, integration, light and surface behavior, atmospherics, shading, texturing, physically based rendering, procedural modeling, compositing, matte painting, lens/camera effects, and much more, Dinur offers a compelling, elegant guide to achieving photorealism in digital media and creating imagery that is seamless from real footage.

Its broad perspective makes this detailed guide suitable for VFX, visualization and game artists and students, as well as directors, architects, designers, and anyone who strives to achieve convincing, believable visuals in digital media.

Eran Dinur is an Emmy and VES award-winning VFX supervisor, artist, and author of *The Filmmaker's Guide to Visual Effects* (2017). His film and TV work includes: *The Trial of the Chicago 7*, *Hereditary*, *The Greatest Showman*, *Uncut Gems*, *The Wolf of Wall Street*, *Boardwalk Empire*, *Star Trek*, and *Iron Man*. He is an adjunct professor at the School of Visual Arts and the author of several popular VFX courses at fxphd.com.

The Complete Guide to Photorealism

For Visual Effects, Visualization and Games

Eran Dinur

Routledge
Taylor & Francis Group
NEW YORK AND LONDON

First published 2022
by Routledge
605 Third Avenue, New York, NY 10158

and by Routledge
2 Park Square, Milton Park, Abingdon, Oxon, OX14 4RN

Routledge is an imprint of the Taylor & Francis Group, an informa business

© 2022 Taylor & Francis

The right of Eran Dinur to be identified as author of this work has been asserted by him in accordance with sections 77 and 78 of the Copyright, Designs and Patents Act 1988.

All rights reserved. No part of this book may be reprinted or reproduced or utilised in any form or by any electronic, mechanical, or other means, now known or hereafter invented, including photocopying and recording, or in any information storage or retrieval system, without permission in writing from the publishers.

Unless otherwise noted in the captions, all photographs and artwork © Eran Dinur.
All illustrations © Ben Zylberman.

Trademark notice: Product or corporate names may be trademarks or registered trademarks, and are used only for identification and explanation without intent to infringe.

Library of Congress Cataloging-in-Publication Data
Names: Dinur, Eran, author.
Title: The complete guide to photorealism for visual effects, visualization and games / Eran Dinur.
Description: New York, NY : Routledge, 2021. | Includes index.
Identifiers: LCCN 2021012600 (print) | LCCN 2021012601 (ebook) | ISBN 9780367199258 (hardback) | ISBN 9780367199265 (paperback) | ISBN 9780429244131 (ebook)
Subjects: LCSH: Rendering (Computer graphics) | Photo-realism. | Digital images—Editing. | Digital cinematography. | Architectural rendering—Technique. | Video games—Design. | Cinematography—Special effects.
Classification: LCC T385 .D585 2021 (print) | LCC T385 (ebook) | DDC 776—dc23
LC record available at https://lccn.loc.gov/2021012600
LC ebook record available at https://lccn.loc.gov/2021012601

ISBN: 978-0-367-19925-8 (hbk)
ISBN: 978-0-367-19926-5 (pbk)
ISBN: 978-0-429-24413-1 (ebk)

DOI: 10.4324/9780429244131

Typeset in Avenir
by Apex CoVantage, LLC

Dedicated to my father, Ouri Dinour, 1934–2020

CONTENTS

Acknowledgments...XV
Introduction..1
   A Note about Animation..2
   A Quick Overview of the Book..3

PART 1: CORE CONCEPTS...7

Chapter 1: Reality and Photorealism..9
   Human Vision and Cameras..9
      The Similarities..10
      Field of View...10
      Seeing with the Mind..11
   The Uncanny Valley...14
   The Detail Conundrum...15
   The Role of Imperfections..16
   Case Study: Detail and Imperfections in Man-Made Objects...................17
   The Reality of the Unreal..18
   Image Quality and Photorealism...19
   2D and 3D Workflows..20

Chapter 2: Photorealism in Digital Media....................................22
   Visual Effects...22
   Games..24
   Visualization..25
      Architectural Visualization...25
      Product Visualization...28
   Case study: Exterior Architectural Renders.................................29

Chapter 3: Color 31
The Six-Layer Approach 33
Thinking Additive 35
Subtractive Color 35
Additive Color 36
Hue, Saturation, and Brightness in RGB 37
Color operations 40
Gain (exposure) 41
Offset 42
Lift 42
Gamma 42
Saturation 44
Bit Depth and Dynamic Range 45
The Low End 46
The High End 47

PART 2: THE REAL WORLD 49
Chapter 4: Light Essentials 51
Light as Waves 51
Light as Particles 52
Light Decay 53
Direct and Indirect Illumination 54
What Is "Ambient Light"? 55

Chapter 5: Light Interaction 57
Absorption 58
Reflection and Scattering 59
Specular Reflection 59
Diffuse Reflection 62
Scattering 63
Subsurface Scattering 63
Transmission and Refraction 64
Albedo 66
Case Study: Side by Side Comparison 67

Chapter 6: Daylight 69
The Sun 69
The Atmosphere 71
Reflection and Absorption 72
Atmospheric Scattering 74

    Rayleigh Scattering 74
    Mie Scattering 75
    Volumetric Light 76
Aerial Perspective 76
    Air 77
    Water Droplets 78
    Haze 79
Case Study: Natural Environment in Clarisse IFX 79

Chapter 7: Nighttime and Artificial Lighting 82
Natural Nighttime Light 82
    The Purkinje Effect 82
Artificial Lighting 83
    Color Temperature 83
    Light Intensity 84
    Common Lamp Types 84
    Light Modifiers 85

Chapter 8: Shadows 87
Shadow Softness 88
Shadow Color 91
Overlapping Shadows 92
Nested Shadows 92
Contact Shadows 93

Chapter 9: Basic Material Properties 94
Dielectric Materials 94
    Dielectric Diffuse/Specular Balance 94
    Fresnel Effect 95
Metals 97

Chapter 10: Lens and Camera Characteristics 99
Defocus 99
    Depth of Field 99
    Bokeh 102
Lens Distortion 103
Chromatic Aberration 104
Lens Flares 105
    Simple Glow 106
    Diffraction Spikes 106

    Additional Flare Elements 107

    Dirt and Imperfections. 107

    Anamorphic Lens Flares. 108

    Lens Bloom 108

Motion Blur 109

Grain 110

PART 3: THE CG WORLD 113

Chapter 11: Rendering and Lighting 115

From Scanline to Path Tracing. 115

    Scanline/Rasterized Rendering 116

    Raytracing 116

    The Challenge of Global Illumination 118

    Path Tracing 120

    Unbiased vs. Biased Rendering 121

Traditional Light Emitters. 122

    Point/Spot Lights 122

    Directional Light. 123

Contemporary Light Emitters 123

    Area and Mesh Lights 123

    Image-based Lighting 124

    Procedural HDR Environments. 126

    Photometric Lights. 126

Essential Strategies for PBR Lighting. 128

    Scale Matters. 128

    Natural Daytime Lighting. 128

    Skylight Color 129

    Ambient Occlusion for Outdoor Scenes 129

    Daytime Interior Scenes. 130

    Man-made Lighting 131

Case Study: Rendering Interiors in Unreal Engine. 131

Chapter 12: Shading 133

A Brief Overview of Shader Evolution 133

The BRDF Shading Model. 134

    Diffuse 135

    Dielectric/Metallic Toggle 135

    Specular. 136

    Coat 137

  Transmission. 138

  Subsurface Scattering 139

  Emission. 140

  Additional BRDF Features 141

 Other Common Shaders 142

  Car Paint Shaders 142

  Volumetric Shaders 142

  Hair/Fur Shaders 143

 Case Study: CG Portraiture 144

Chapter 13: Texturing 146

 PBR Texturing 147

  The Linear Workflow 148

  Base Color Map. 148

  Roughness Map. 150

  Metallic Map 150

  Bump (Normal) Map 151

  Ambient Occlusion (AO) Map 152

  Displacement (Height) Map. 153

  Transparency Map vs. Opacity Map 153

 Texture Generation Workflows 154

 Image Textures 154

 Shooting and Prepping Photos for Texturing 155

  Resolution 155

  Baked-in Lighting. 155

  Angle, Perspective, and Focus 156

  Exposure 156

  Optimizing Photographs for Tiling 157

 Procedural Textures 157

 Combining Workflows. 159

 Case Study: Creating Bark Textures for SpeedTree. 160

Chapter 14: Modeling 163

 Modeling for Lighting 163

 Procedural Modeling. 164

  Terrain Modeling 165

 Case Study: Erosion Algorithms in Gaea. 167

  Plant Modeling 168

PART 4: THE 2D WORLD 171

Chapter 15: Integrating 2D Elements 175

Color Matching 175

Edges: Problems and Solutions 176

    Matching Background Luminosity 177

    Spill Suppression 178

    Edge and Core Extractions 178

    Edge Reconstruction 179

    Matte-less Extractions 180

    Edge Blur and Edge Color 182

    Light Wrap 182

Chapter 16: Integrating CG Elements 183

Compositing with Render Passes 183

    Lighting Passes 183

    Utility Passes 186

Deep Compositing 189

Improving CG in Comp 190

    Render Resolution 191

    Hazing Effect 191

    Highlights Bloom 191

    Albedo Pass and Contrast 191

    Edge Treatment 192

Chapter 17: Lighting in 2D 193

Relighting with Color 193

The Challenge of Reflections 193

    Fresnel Effect 196

    Breaking up Reflections 196

Creating Shadows 197

    Shape, Angle, and Stretching 197

    Shadow Softness and Falloff 198

    Breaking up Shadows 198

    Shadow Color 198

    Contact and Proximity Shadows 200

Case Study: Matte Painting Integration in Film 200

Atmospheric Depth 202

    Referencing the Footage 202

Chapter 18: Lens and Camera Effects 205
Defocus 205
Lens Distortion and Chromatic Aberration 206
Lens Flares 207
Motion Blur 208
Grain 208

Epilogue: The Future 210
Realtime Rendering 210
Photorealism on the Cloud 211
LED Screens and Virtual Environments 211
Machine Learning 212
Procedural Environments 213
Will Photorealism Disappear? 213

Appendix A: Glossary of Abbreviations 215

Appendix B: Software list 217
All-round 3D Software 217
Specialized 3D Software 217
    Sculpting 217
    Terrain and Landscape Creation 217
    Plant Modeling 217
    Other Specialized 3D Software 218
Game engines 218
Render Engines 218
Image editing 218
Compositing 218
Texture Authoring 218

Index 219

ACKNOWLEDGMENTS

Writing this book was a true journey for me, and I would like to thank all the people who supported me along the way, and shared their expertise, insight, and talent.

Many thanks to Dr. Amodsen Chotia of the University of Paris for his invaluable help in clarifying complex physical concepts of light and light-surface interaction, and to my friend Dr. Ariel Lindner for connecting us.

A big fat thank you to my colleague Ben Zylberman for creating the book's superb illustrations, and for being ever so patient toward my never-ending requests.

I would like to thank all the talented artists from around the world who kindly contributed some of their brilliant artwork to this book: Benjamin Bardou, Carlos Colorsponge, Christoph Schindelar, David Edwards, Gregory Smith, Hadi Karimi, Javier Wainstein, Jeff Heral, Jose Iuit, Liam Cramb, Luke Panayiotou, Marvin Funke, Massimo Righi, Maxchill Patiphan, Raphael Rau, Robert Berg, Tamas Medve, and Terje Hannisdal. Thanks also to Brainstorm Digital's artists and founders Richard Friedlander and Glenn Allen for allowing me to use images from our demo reels, and to John Montgomery and Eduardo Abon for allowing me to use footage from my fxphd compositing course.

I owe special gratitude to a unique group of artists who offered not just their artwork, but also words of wisdom that shed light on their own creative process: Aron Kamolz, Daniel Bayona, Dax Pandhi, Julian Sadokha, Pasquale Scionti, and Sarah Scruggs.

Many thanks to Jimmy Calhoun, Jesse Flores, and the anonymous peer reviewers for providing their thoughtful and illuminating feedback. To Nick Constandy and Manuel Riedl for all those fascinating discussions about reality, CG, and photorealism.

Many thanks to the Routledge editorial and production team, and in particular: Simon Jacobs and John Makowsky for helping me take the first steps of the journey, Katherine Kadian for overseeing the entire process, Alyssa Turner for her continuous assistance and advice every step of the way, copy editor Jane Fieldsend, and production editor Helen Evans.

To my amazing family – how can I ever thank you enough? Karin, my partner in life, and Ayala, my daughter, for your patience, wisdom, and understanding, and Yotam, my son, for helping me all along the way as an advisor, an editor, a games expert, and a sharp-eyed critic. I love you all so much!

Finally, to my dear father: Aba, I featured your sunset photographs in the book, just like I told you I would! I wish you could be here with us to see how it all came out.

I dedicate this book to your memory.

Introduction

Photorealism is a vital component in digital visual media: in visual effects, seamless integration with live action footage is crucial for telling a believable visual story, and photorealism lies at the core of all successful VFX magic. In architectural and product visualization, photoreal CG renders are now the norm, and often replace photography in advertisements, presentations, and catalogues. Photorealism in video games is constantly evolving along realtime rendering technologies, with new games consistently raising the bar. Recent developments in virtual and augmented reality bring new challenges for synthesized realism and immersive experiences.

Yet despite the technological advancements and the wealth and quality of tools available to digital artists, achieving photorealism in digital media remains a complex, challenging, and often elusive goal. Multiple factors come into play, and these factors stretch across different crafts, from modeling, texturing, and shading, to lighting, matte painting, and compositing. Think about creating photoreal content, and numerous questions come to mind: how do you generate imagery that is indistinguishable from real photographs? How do you successfully emulate light and its interactions with surfaces? How much detail is needed to make digital visual content convincingly real? How to avoid the dreaded "CG look"? How to achieve realistic daylight and atmospheric depth? How to get the best out of physically based renderers? What are BRDF shaders? How can render passes help in compositing? How to seamlessly blend 2D elements? And so on, and so on …

This book provides a comprehensive guide to achieving photorealism in digital media. It approaches the subject through a broad perspective that spans various crafts and caters to digital artists working in a variety of fields. The key to photorealism lies in plain sight: it is everywhere around us. To produce convincingly realistic digital imagery, artists must expand their knowledge beyond the specific software tools and techniques of their craft and study the real world: the way light interacts with different materials; how Rayleigh and Mie scattering in the atmosphere transform the light of the sun; the way dirt and grime form on surfaces; the differences between human vision and cameras; the complex structure of plants; how the aperture of a lens affects defocus; or the different characteristics of metallic and dielectric surfaces (to mention just a few of the subjects discussed here).

In writing this book, I set myself two goals: the first is to provide an in-depth study of real-world light, the physical interaction of light and surfaces, material properties, atmosphere, depth, and cameras. These topics are vital for digital artists, yet much of the available information about them is explained in hardcore scientific jargon and through complex equations. In this book, I approach

Freestyle by Tamas Medve. Built in 3D Studio Max, rendered with V-Ray.
© Tamas Medve.

these subjects from an artist's point of view – focusing on their visual (rather than mathematical) aspects.

The second goal is to address the tools and techniques that digital artists can use to visually emulate reality and produce photoreal content. This includes both CG approaches (path-tracing, BRDF shaders, PBR texturing, procedural modeling, etc.) and 2D workflows (seamless integration, extraction techniques, working with color, render passes, etc.). While these topics focus on particular 3D and 2D crafts, I have intentionally avoided software-specific discussions, knowing that readers rely on a wide variety of different applications and tools. So, whether you use Maya or Unreal Engine, V-ray or Redshift, Substance Painter or Mari, After Effects or Nuke, this book provides the general knowledge that can complement software-specific books, courses, or tutorials.

A Note about Animation

I am of course completely aware of the importance of animation in the context of realism. Clearly, even the most photoreal modeling, texturing, shading, and lighting cannot salvage a poorly animated character, a lack of a proper sense of weight and inertia, or bad timing and gesturing. But the subject of animation is too vast to be covered in this book in any meaningful way, and it stands independent from other subjects discussed here. Moreover, there are already many excellent books devoted to animation and motion capture. Therefore, this book remains focused on the visual rather than kinetic characteristics of realism (with only a few minor exceptions in discussing motion blur and lens flares). In other words, this book is about how things *look*, and not about how things *move*.

A Quick Overview of the Book

The book is divided into four parts: Part 1 (Core Concepts) addresses fundamental aspects of photorealism and color; Part 2 (The Real World) is an artist-friendly exploration of the physical characteristics of light, materials, the atmosphere, and lenses; Part 3 (The CG World) examines photoreal CG topics in reverse order, starting with rendering and lighting, then shading, texturing, and modeling; Part 4 (The 2D World) is dedicated to the 2D aspects of photoreal content in compositing, matte painting, and image manipulation.

Here is a short description of each chapter:

Chapter 1: Reality and Photorealism

A discussion of the fundamental aspects of photorealism, such as the difference between human vision and photography, detail and imperfections in simulated reality, the uncanny valley, and more.

Chapter 2: Photorealism in Digital Media

This chapter compares the different roles, methodologies, aesthetics, and challenges of photorealism in three main categories: visual effects, games, and visualizations.

Chapter 3: Color

Understanding color is crucial for achieving photorealism – and this chapter offers a methodological look at essential color subjects like color perception, additive color theory and operations, black and white levels, and dynamic range.

Chapter 4: Light Essentials

The fundamental physical properties of light are explained here from a visual perspective. Subjects covered include the particle/wave duality, photons and the electromagnetic spectrum, light decay, and direct/indirect light.

Chapter 5: Light Interaction

What happens to photons when they hit an obstacle? This chapter explores the principal light/surface interactions: diffuse and specular reflection, absorption, and transmission.

Chapter 6: Daylight

Daylight is explained by studying the interaction of sunlight with atmospheric elements and the effect of Rayleigh and Mie scattering. This chapter also covers the principles of aerial perspective.

Chapter 7: Nighttime and Artificial Lighting

An overview of common emitters and fixtures, luminance and temperature measurements, and natural nighttime light.

Chapter 8: Shadows

Analysis of shadows: softness and color, nested and overlapping shadows, contact, and proximity shadows.

Chapter 9: Basic Material Properties

This chapter expands the subject of light–surface interaction by examining material properties like diffuse/specular balance, large and small-scale roughness, the Fresnel effect and the difference between metallic and dielectric materials.

Chapter 10: Lens and Camera Characteristics

This chapter provides a discussion of depth of field, Bokeh, lens distortion, chromatic aberrations, lens flares, lens blooms, motion blur, and grain.

Chapter 11: Rendering and Lighting

A brief overview of rendering and global illumination methods followed by a close look at path tracing and physically based rendering. This chapter also focuses on various CG lighting tools like area lights and image-based lighting, and discusses physically based lighting practices for varying scenarios.

Chapter 12: Shading

This chapter starts with a glance at the evolution of shader technologies, then moves on to the various attributes of BRDF and how they contribute to photoreal renders. Additional shaders like hair/fur and volumetric are also discussed.

Chapter 13: Texturing

This chapter offers an overview of the PBR texturing workflow and discusses best practices and techniques for image-based lighting and procedural textures.

Chapter 14: Modeling

The focus in this chapter is on aspects of modeling that relate to photorealism, like modeling for light and procedural generation of complex natural elements such as plants and terrains.

Chapter 15: Integrating 2D Elements

This chapter provides a thorough examination of different techniques for 2D integration and edge treatment, such as color matching, edge keying, matte-less extractions, and motion blur reconstruction.

Chapter 16: Integrating CG Elements

An overview of lighting and utility render passes and their use for improving the integration and realism of rendered elements, followed by additional techniques for "sweetening" the CG look.

Chapter 17: Lighting in 2D

This chapter examines different techniques of using color to modify the lighting, create atmospheric depth, shadows, and reflections in 2D.

Chapter 18: Lens and Camera Effects

In this chapter we look at tools and techniques for simulating lens and camera effects like depth of field, distortion, chromatic aberrations, and grain.

Epilogue: The Future

A brief discussion of some of the emerging trends and technologies that may shape the way we approach photorealism in the future.

PART 1

CORE CONCEPTS

The Signal by Gregory Smith. Created and rendered in Blender.
© Gregory Smith.

Chapter 1

Reality and Photorealism

Human Vision and Cameras

What is the definition of photorealism? Here is a common one: "If it looks like a photo, it is photoreal". This is a short, clear, and straight-forward answer, but it raises two essential questions: First, what does a photo "look like"? And second, why "look like a photo"? Why not just "look real"? Let me start by addressing the second question. The reality we see through our own eyes cannot be recorded and played back. We have no way (not yet, at least) to connect a person's brain to a monitor and see the world through that person's eyes. Everything we see on a screen or a monitor that we consider real (as opposed to animation, cartoons, or motion graphics) must first be captured by a camera. From the earliest printed photos of the 19th century to today's phones and tablets, the only way we can watch "transported reality" (any reality that's different from what we see around us) is through the mediating assistance of a camera. Our perception of reality in movies, videos, and still photography is very tightly tied to a "photographic look", because essentially, it is the only look we have ever seen on a screen. Therefore, if we wish to create convincingly realistic digital content, we need to emulate the characteristics of photography and cinematography, rather than the way we see the world with our own eyes. This leads to the first question: What does a photo look like? In other words, if we could literally hook up a person's brain to a monitor and compare that person's vision to the camera's, would they look different? And in which ways?

This is of course a tricky question, exactly because we cannot perform this hypothetical comparison. If we think of "seeing" as a single process, then viewing photographs (or movies) is a double process: we are seeing through our own eyes reality that was "seen" (captured) by the camera. Take, for example, focus. Just like a camera, our eyes can dynamically shift focus. But we cannot possibly "view" our vision's out-of-focus areas. On the other hand, a photo on paper or on screen allows us to view areas that are in or out of focus equally well. So, while human defocus forever lies at the periphery of our vision, photographic defocus is an observable, meaningful part of the picture and a crucial artistic and narrative aspect of photography and cinematography. This is but one example that shows why, without the ability to observe our vision in the same way we observe footage, the comparison is somewhat flawed. Yet despite these limitations, it is still worth exploring, if only for the purpose of identifying those specific characteristics of photography that are distinctly different from human vision. Understanding those characteristics is crucial to making our digital content "look like a photo".

The Similarities

On a superficial level (and without digging too deep into anatomy or optometry) our eyes operate very much like a camera. The cornea and lens form the optical assembly that is the biological equivalent of a camera lens. The cornea acts like the static outer glass, while the inner lens is flexible and controllable to allow focus changes (much like the inner glass in a camera lens, which moves back and forth when the focus is adjusted). Our iris functions as the diaphragm, and controls the size of the opening (the aperture) through which light comes in. The purpose is the same as in a camera: to restrict the amount of light that reaches the retina in a brightly lit environment and let more light in when the environment is dark. Although the retina is structurally different from a camera sensor (it is curved, and its receptive cells are not evenly distributed along its surface) it still performs a similar task, sensing different light frequencies and intensities, and passing that information through the optic nerve to the brain. However, despite the initial similarities, there are some critical differences between cameras and human vision, and those differences define the characteristics of photographed material.

Field of View

The sensitivity of a camera sensor is balanced across its entire surface, and good lenses maintain a consistent sharpness and quality from edge to edge. The correlation between the focal length and the field of view is thus easy to measure and define. Human vision, on the other hand, has a distinct sharpness falloff from the focal center toward the fringes of the viewing field. If you gaze forward while waving your hand near your left ear, you can still see the hand – but it is quite blurry. To see the hand in focus, you must either bring it closer to the center of your vision, or instead turn your eyes hard left (which then makes everything at the front blurry). The nature of our peripheral vision means that unlike lenses, there is no precise definition of our field of view. Should we measure the entire width of the vision field, or only the sharpest area? And where exactly do we draw the line between sharp and blurry? So, while precise numbers are debatable, it is generally agreed that our overall

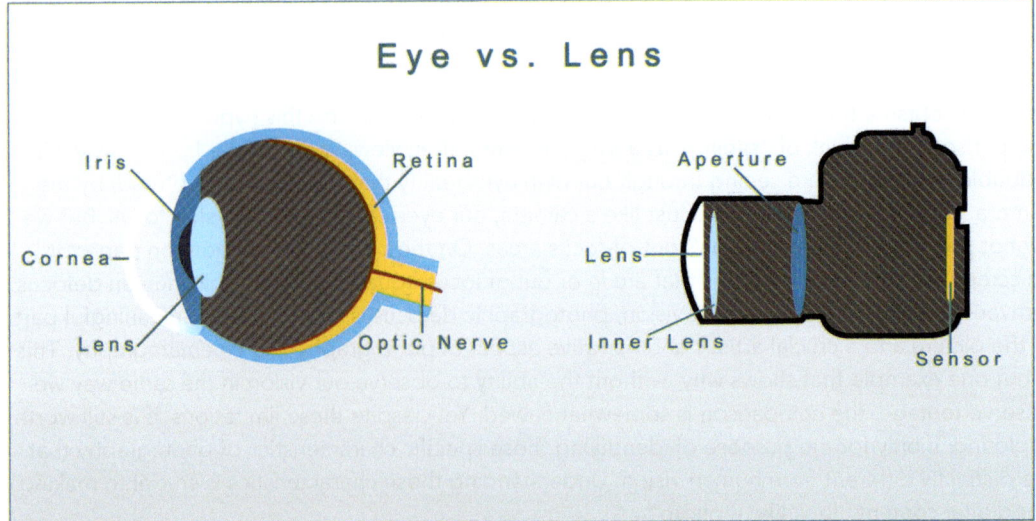

On a fundamental level, our eye and the camera are very similar.

CORE CONCEPTS

Left: an approximate depiction of human vision (roughly 22mm center-focused). Notice how odd and "unreal" it feels when viewed as a photograph. Right: a 43mm equivalent of our effective viewing area.

field of view is roughly comparable to a 22–24mm lens on a full-sensor camera, and our effective (relatively sharp) field of view is comparable to a 43mm lens. Medium lenses are thus traditionally used to convey human vision, although they clearly do not mimic our wider peripheral vision.

The most important difference in relation to field of view, however, is the fact that we cannot change our focal length. In photographic terms, we are forever limited to a single prime lens – no switching lenses, no adjustable zooms. This does make sense if you think of our eyes as a spatial navigation tool (it would be very hard to properly assess distance if we constantly changed our focal length), but it also means that the wide variety of perspectives that characterizes photography, from the exaggerated depth of wide lenses to the compressed perspective of long lenses, is simply not available to us. Yet even though changeable perspective is foreign to our vision, we completely embrace the rich perspective vocabulary of photography and cinematography and accept it as "real". We have no problem watching footage shot with a 12mm or 250mm lens, even though both lenses show the world in a way that we can never see with our own eyes. To achieve photorealism, we must treat field of view in photographic terms, and all but ignore the fixed-perspective, peripheral nature of our own eyes. Interestingly, tilt-shift effects and other photographic techniques that somewhat simulate human vision are often perceived as artificial and strange. This is but one example that shows how accustomed we have gotten to the language of photography and to viewing the world through a lens.

Seeing with the Mind

We think, and cameras don't – this is an important difference between human vision and cameras, and an essential concept for photorealism. To illustrate this difference, let us examine two scenarios that should feel familiar to anyone who's ever used a camera:

1. On a trip to the mountains, you are standing on a high overlook, admiring the breathtaking landscape of tall peaks and deep valleys. Inspired by the beautiful view, you pull out the camera and take some photos. But to your disappointment, the photos convey none of the sense of depth and grandeur you experienced.
2. While on an apartment hunt, you find a place you really like – spacious, well-lit, and with a nice view outside. You take some photos, but they don't do the apartment justice. If you expose for the interior, the windows blow out and you cannot see the view outside, and if you expose for the windows, the interior looks dark and depressing. Either way, the pictures of the apartment do not look and feel like what you've seen with your own eyes.

In the actual photograph (left), the camera records light exactly as it reaches the sensor, including haze and humidity that severely flatten the image. But we "see through" the haze with our mind, intuitively reconstructing detail and depth (right).

The extreme luminance difference between the interior and exterior are captured as muddy blacks and blown-out highlights by the camera (left). But our mind balances the exposure, lifting the shadows and toning down the highlights.

The camera merely records light that enters the lens and hits the sensor, and produces an objective snapshot of the environment. Whether that snapshot conveys anything meaningful is completely up to the photographer – indeed, the art of photography and cinematography is explained, debated, and taught in thousands of books, courses, and tutorials, because it involves so much more than just point-and-click. But there are no books about the "art of seeing" – maybe because we are all unrecognized masters of this art. While our eyes record light just like the camera, our brain constantly interprets and enhances that recording. We cannot separate the two processes, and they happen simultaneously (and mostly subconsciously). In the first example, you experience the beauty and grandeur of the landscape because you have knowledge and understanding of the scale and the depth of the view. You know that the mountains are tall, and the valleys are deep. You can see through the haze and make out the tiny houses of the distant villages. You are taking in the grand view while at the same time zooming in (mentally, not physically) on the smallest detail. The subjective snapshot captured by our eyes is simultaneously augmented by our memories, knowledge, experience, and emotions, and this augmentation becomes an inseparable part of the viewing process.

In the second example, as you observe the apartment, your mind instantly compensates for the extremities of bright light and darkness. It brings out detail in the shadows and at the same time tones down the highlights, which allows you to experience both the interior and the exterior with an optimal exposure. This constant real-time exposure balancing act is simply not possible with a camera and can only be achieved as a post process. However (and this is the important part) when we look at photographs or footage, we seem to be more at ease with the typical single-exposure look of photography, than with any attempt to emulate the way we see. Take, for example, HDR (High Dynamic Range) photography: The process of merging several different exposures generates an image that mimics our vision quite closely. Yet HDR photography never quite caught up as a popular mainstream style. Most likely, because the typical HDR look, with its highly detailed sky, lifted shadows, and toned highlights, has an eerily strange feel to it. Even though it simulates our vision, it feels "unreal" because it lacks the deep shadows or blown out highlights we are so used to see in photography. Again, just as with tilt-shift effects, the attempts to emulate human vision in photography have not been very successful, which supports the notion that photoreal digital content should look like a photo (that said, HDR images have an essential role as a CG lighting tool which is unrelated to HDR as a photography genre. This role is discussed in Chapter 11).

In this render, artist Julian Sadokha uses overexposure to emulate photography. Created in 3D Studio Max, rendered with Corona.
©Julian Sadokha.

REALITY AND PHOTOREALISM

The Uncanny Valley

The term uncanny valley was originally coined in the 1970s in relation to humanoid robots, but was later adopted by the media in discussions about CG characters in movies. The "valley" denotes a dip in positive emotional reaction to a human-like character, particularly when the appearance and behavior of that character feels almost (but not quite) real. We seem to react very positively to CG characters when they are distant enough from real humans (for example, the main characters in *Toy Story*). The uncanny valley, that eerie, spooky sensation, is our reaction to characters that look and behave very much like real humans, yet something, just "something", doesn't quite feel human in them. Movies like *Final Fantasy: The Spirits Within* (2001) or Robert Zemeckis' 2004 *The Polar Express* drew considerable criticism regarding this subject. Both represented a milestone in motion capture techniques, and the CG humans in those movies displayed a higher level of realism than anything seen before. But precisely because of that, they drew negative reactions. In his review of *Final Fantasy*, Peter Travers noted "a coldness in the eyes, a mechanical quality in the movements",[1] while Marc Savlov of the *Austin Chronicle* wrote that "Watching the humans in *The Polar Express* is like watching people through a smeary car windscreen – the realism is there, but there's something a tad skewed and surreal about the whole affair".[2] The term uncanny valley has been used numerous times since to describe similar reactions to CG characters, even as hyper-real CG characters continued to evolve and improve.

This is not an animation book, neither does it focus specifically on CG characters. But I think that the uncanny valley can be observed from a much wider perspective, one that applies to any element, animated or static, as well as to entire environments. Although inanimate objects do not draw the same emotional response from the viewer as human characters, a milder version of that uncanny sensation does happen whenever we view digital visuals that are almost photoreal, but still lack that "something" to look truly believable. For example, when watching a movie where the visual effects are impressive, yet still feel "off", or when viewing an architectural render that is impressively realistic, except that something, just "something" in it feels too sterile perhaps? Or too perfect? When we watch CG or matte-painted environments that are deliberately not photoreal, we are essentially in the same comfort zone as traditional 2D animation, at a safe distance from the uncanny zone. It is not surprising that successful CG animated features (like most Pixar movies, for example) intentionally keep their environments (detailed and beautifully lit as

The Polar Express (left) and *Final Fantasy: The Spirits Within* (right) generated much debate on the subject of the uncanny valley.

© Castle Rock Entertainment, Warner Bros. © Chris Lee productions, Columbia Pictures.

CORE CONCEPTS

they are) within a non-photoreal region. But any attempt at creating photoreal imagery, whether it is for VFX, games, or visualizations, carries with it the inherent risk of the uncanny valley – that little "something" that kills the illusion of realism. That something is often quite elusive. As a VFX supervisor I find myself frequently chasing that intangible cause as I review a shot and try to figure out why exactly it does not feel quite real. The key here is to be aware of a wide range of factors that can affect photorealism. This book examines these factors and provides guidance that can help bridge the uncanny valley.

The Detail Conundrum

Nothing embodies the challenge of creating believable imagery more than the huge gap between the real world's level of detail and the constraints of computer graphics. Imagine one of those "infinite" camera moves that starts on a single blade of grass and gradually pulls back to reveal the clearing, the forest, the hill, and finally the entire mountain range. In the real world, every single element that makes up the environment continues to exist regardless of whether it is distinguishable in the frame or not. But from a practical point of view, only some of the detail is necessary at every stage of the camera move. When the camera frames a single blade of grass, we probably only need to create the neighboring plants, and maybe a rock or two in the back. There is certainly no reason to create the forest, cliffs, or the entire hill. Conversely, when our camera is pulled back all the way and frames the entire mountain range, it does not make any sense to create every blade of grass, every rock, and every tree. Although we are looking at trillions of grass blades and leaves and millions of trees and rocks, we cannot, from that distance, see any of them individually.

We can thus place an imaginary threshold (let's call it "the bare necessity line") that defines the amount of crucial detail at various distances from the subject. This variable level of detail is approached differently in VFX, visualization, and games. In visual effects, the position and movement of the camera is usually already known, which makes it easier to define where the bare necessity line lies, and create exactly the amount of detail that's needed for a specific camera in a specific shot. However, when elements or environments are created as an asset that is intended to be used in multiple shots (and be viewed from different distances), enough detail must be created to cover all scenarios. That is normally the case in games, where the camera is roaming freely, and real-time performance is paramount. The bare necessity line in games is almost always handled through a system of **dynamic level of detail** (LOD). In such a system, elements have multiple versions with varied amount of detail, and the game engine automatically switches between the versions depending on the distance from the camera.

It seems then, that the detail conundrum can be solved quite successfully with some careful consideration of camera distance and framing, or an effective LOD system. But this is only a partial solution. In the context of photoreal digital imagery, the true challenge is not creating the right amount of detail for a certain camera, it is accounting for the detail that is left out. Let me explain: in the real world, all detail is always there, every little bit of it. While the grass, rocks, and leaves in our camera pullback example may not be visible to the camera when viewed from half a mile away, they still contribute in a million tiny different ways to the perceivable look of that hill. The incredible visual complexity of the world around us is the accumulation of all the massive amount of detail at any scale level. When we look at a brick wall from a hundred feet away, we cannot possibly see the detail on every single brick. But the

The closeup detail (right) cannot be distinguished when zoomed out (left). But it is still there – giving this shingled roof the elusive richness of real-world textures.

cumulative result of all these minuscule features forms a larger assembly that affects the overall appearance of the brick wall and gives it that intangible photoreal richness that is so difficult to replicate digitally.

Emulating that richness without committing to generating every tiny feature on every scale level is a continuous challenge. Moreover, it is a challenge that runs through all of the different crafts: modeling, texturing, shading, lighting, matte painting, and compositing. At every step of the way, the necessity of adding enough detail is balanced against the limitations of hardware, schedule, and budget. And at every step of the way, there are methods, shortcuts, and tricks to keep that balance at a good place while avoiding an artificially digital look. The concept of detail is thus at the core of photorealism and runs as a thread through the entire length of this book.

The Role of Imperfections

Nature is chaotic and infinitely varied. There are rarely any straight lines, no two leaves look exactly the same, no two rocks are identical, every tree is unique, and every cloud is a different shape. Surfaces are twisted, broken, muddy, covered with moss, covered with dirt, stained with humidity or decay. Man-made objects are of course much more structured and organized: straight lines, perfect angles, polished surfaces, uniform colors. But even precisely manufactured objects are not perfect: weather, dust, gravity, human interaction, and a whole range of factors allow at least some of nature's chaos to invade our creations. Computer graphics is a virtual medium born out of pure mathematics and is inherently perfect. In the world of CG, nothing is easier than creating a perfectly accurate sphere with a perfectly shiny, spotless surface. And of course, nothing feels more fake. Photorealism therefore requires a persistent "battle" against the default flawlessness of CG. This is done at any level – from breaking symmetry in modeling through adding grime and dirt to textures and all the way to introducing lens aberrations, flares, and grain at the compositing stage.

Case Study: Detail and Imperfections in Man-Made Objects

Dashboard Piece by Raphael Rau.
© Raphael Rau.

I chose this render by Raphael Rau because it exemplifies the artist's attention to the kind of delicate, almost imperceptible detail that makes CG emulations of man-made objects truly photoreal. This dashboard piece is a very simple object – a glass cover, four screws, four gauges, and a generic dashboard surface – yet this simplicity is deceiving: CG scenes such as this can easily fail the photorealism test, exactly because they contain very little visual complexity. Raphael's image succeeds because of careful attention to a few essential aspects of modeling, lighting, texturing, and lens emulation (each of these aspects will be discussed in depth in the chapters noted below):

- A depth of field that matches this type of close-up shot but is not overly done. It successfully emulates real-world photography, as if the photographer tried to maximize sharpness despite the close focal point (DOF discussions in Chapters 10 and 18).
- Just enough bumps on the dashboard cover to provide a sense of faux-leather texture, without feeling overly noisy or "bumpy" (Chapter 13, texturing).
- A simple, realistic daylight lighting, suggesting stronger light coming through the car window from the top left (real-world and CG lighting discussed in Chapters 6 and 11).
- Subtle but very effective dust accumulation around and underneath the bolted cover, and equally effective hints of scratches and dust hits on the glass where the light is reflected (texturing, Chapter 13).

- Tiny bevels at the corners and edges of the metal pieces (even on the little screws), which enhance photorealism by suggesting rim highlights (specular reflections discussed in Chapter 5, modeling for lighting in Chapter 14).

Such attention to detail ensures that even the simplest 3D render would look believable and photographic.

The Reality of the Unreal

While architectural and product visualizations are generally rooted within the confines of reality, VFX and games often depict imaginary worlds: alien planets, futuristic cities, fantastic creatures, or environments that do not abide by earthly laws. What role does photorealism serve in the context of fantasy and science fiction? Is it still an important factor, considering that the visuals often depict things we have never seen or experienced? Photorealism is achieved by studying and mimicking the world around us – light, surfaces, atmosphere … but what if these behave very differently in the imaginary environment we want to portray? Can we still maintain believability while creating otherworldly environments? How can we make the unreal look real?

With all the digital tools we have at our disposal, we can certainly break every rule. We can create a world where physical laws are upside down, a world that is so different from anything we've ever seen, that it makes no sense visually. But it is hard to draw the viewer into such a world. If you examine prominent sci-fi and fantasy movies, you'll notice that the most visually believable ones do not break all the rules, but instead maintain certain earthly aspects. Take, for example, *Avatar*'s iconic Hallelujah Mountains: while their most striking aspect (giant forested cliffs floating in mid-air) is certainly unreal, specific features like the jungle vegetation, rock surfaces, lighting, clouds, and atmospheric depth all feel familiar and recognizable. This careful balance between real and unreal, combined with meticulous attention to detail, places an otherwise impossible environment deep within the sphere of believability. Handled differently, the concept of floating mountains could have easily succumbed to overly fantastic visuals or poorly done VFX, causing the viewers to distance themselves from the environment. This kind of thoughtful balance between unreal and photoreal elements contributes to the success of many other sci-fi/fantasy visuals, for example: the folding Paris streets in *Inception*, the motionless floating alien spaceship in *Arrival*, the lobster-roach aliens in *District 9*, or the environments in games like *Horizon Zero Dawn* and *Crysis*.

Inception's folding Paris streets (top left) and *District 9*'s alien spaceship (top right) are great examples of a successful visual balance between fantasy and familiar realism.

© Warner Bros. © TriStar Pictures, Sony Pictures.

Image Quality and Photorealism

We live in a world where visual quality is highly venerated. Camera manufacturers tout their products' megapixels, phones are judged by their screen quality and resolution, and ultra-HD TV's are the new norm. While some of this "bigger is better" hype is more marketing than substance (more megapixels will not necessarily give you better photographs), one cannot ignore the impressive technological advances in digital imaging and display, and the striking improvements in quality over

Gorilla by Massimo Righi. Maya, Zbrush, Mudbox, Xgen, rendered with Arnold. © Massimo Righi.

the last decade. It is important to note, however, that photorealism has little to do with the quality of digital capture and display. The essence of photorealism has not really changed since the first photographs of the 19th century. A grainy, black and white, low-quality 300×200 pixels photo can still look more photoreal than a shiny 8K render. Resolution, number of pixels, bit depth, dynamic range – all these features are critical for creating, capturing, and displaying high-quality, high-definition imagery, but they do not necessarily augment the photoreal quality of the digital content.

This is a notion that I often find hard to convey to students. Much attention is devoted nowadays to technical specs, yet the essential qualities required for achieving photorealism are not necessarily tied to such specs. Those qualities include the subtle interaction of light and surface, the richness of textures, the sense of depth, the characteristics of optical lenses, and many other aspects that are discussed here. While factors like bit depth and high dynamic range do play an important role in the actual process of creating photoreal imagery, successful visual recreation of reality is independent of specs like resolution and color depth, and the results should look as convincing at the lowest quality as they would at the highest.

2D and 3D Workflows

In contemporary digital content creation, the distinction between 2D and 3D is often blurry. Visual effects in particular are driven by a pragmatic "use whatever method works best" approach. 3D and 2D workflows are combined in matte painting and compositing (in fact, 2D compositing applications like Nuke or After Effects offer quite an extensive array of 3D tools). Architectural visualizations also often require a combination of 3D and 2D, and while games are inherently 3D, matte painting and compositing techniques are increasingly used to augment their cinematic quality.

From the photorealism perspective, 2D and 3D seem, initially, like very different workflows. Ask a 3D generalist and a matte painter to create an image of a castle on a hill, for example. The first will model and texture the structure and terrain in 3D, and then illuminate the entire scene to produce the final render. The matte painter will gather pieces of images from various sources, and meticulously combine them into a coherent environment using coloring, masking, and painting. Photorealism is achieved in 3D through the complex mathematical process of simulating the interaction of light and surfaces, and in 2D by manipulating real photographic material.

Yet 2D and 3D workflows also converge at multiple points (for example, depth of field and motion blur can be part of the 3D render, or applied separately in 2D through depth and vector passes) and complement each other (2D techniques are used extensively for texture map creation, while 3D lighting and surface properties are often re-adjusted in compositing). So, while the separation of 3D and 2D in this book is indeed somewhat artificial, it allows the reader to examine photorealism from two perspectives: that of the CG artist in Part 3 and that of the compositor/matte painter in Part 4.

Notes

1 Peter Travers, "Final Fantasy", *Rolling Stone*, July 06, 2001.
2 Marc Savlov, "The Polar Express", *The Austin Chronicle*, November 12, 2004.

Daniel Bayona's matte painting of the reconstruction of St. Peter's Basilica is a great example of combining 3D and 2D workflows. He used 3D Studio Max and Corona renderer to create a spectacular amount of 3D detail, and then painted on top of the render in Photoshop to add finer features, break up specular highlights, and generate what he calls "divine randomness".

© Daniel Bayona.

Chapter 2

Photorealism in Digital Media

The principles of photorealism are rooted in the physical interaction of light and matter, and thus apply equally to the various fields of visual digital media. However, each field represents different aesthetics, expectations, challenges, and methodologies. In this chapter we will look at the role of photorealism and how it is approached in three main categories: visual effects, games, and visualization.

Visual Effects

I doubt that there is a VFX artist out there who likes to be told that their work "doesn't look real" or "looks too CG". Creating believable "real" visual elements is at the heart of VFX work because those elements are combined with live-action footage. When visual effects do not share the same photoreal qualities of the footage, they damage the believability of the film and the flow of its storytelling. Even when a specific shot is completely done in CG and involves no integration with live action, it still sits in the cut among other live action shots and thus must maintain a comparable photoreal quality.

The importance of photorealism and integration in VFX dictates certain approaches that put greater emphasis on plausibility than on aesthetics or style. A pretty sky may end up looking rather ugly when overexposed and blown-out, for example, but this is often necessary to integrate the sky with the footage. A beautifully detailed matte painting may end up completely out of focus if the camera is focused on the foreground in a practical shot. Such compromises on beauty for the sake of realism are arguably more common in VFX than in games or visualization. Yet even within the world of VFX, approaches vary. In advertisement, for example, there's greater emphasis on presenting the product or concept at its best over preserving photorealism, and some movies or TV shows may intentionally opt for a non-photoreal look as a stylistic choice. Yet overall, such artistic deviations are more an exception than the norm, and VFX artists generally strive for the highest level of photorealism.

Since VFX production happens mostly in post, after the film has been already shot and cut (or at least roughly cut), the work is usually performed for specific camera angles, moves, and framings. This allows the VFX team to focus the resources only on areas that are visible to the lens and ignore everything that is outside the frame. Matte paintings are rarely done out of context of a specific shot or sequence, as is the case with most 2D compositing shots. Some assets serve

Changing the season, fixing the road, and adding a ceiling in *The Greatest Showman*. Even such seemingly simple VFX tasks require great attention to detail and integration, and a thorough photoreal approach.
© Twentieth Century Fox. Visual effects by Brainstorm Digital.

multiple shots (like game environments and characters) and must look good from multiple angles, but the final lighting and compositing tweaks only take place when the asset is integrated with the footage. That last 10% of the work has a critical role in establishing the level of photorealism and believability in VFX.

Although the use of realtime game and VR technologies in VFX is constantly increasing, the core VFX work is still a non-real-time (**offline rendering**) process. This allows for incredibly high CG complexity and rendering quality. Those massive VFX scenes we see in high-budget films require equally massive simulation and rendering times, not to mention large teams of artists performing a variety of tasks, from modeling and texturing to lighting, rotoscoping, and compositing. Yet such big resources are not necessarily a guarantee for photoreal results. Visual effects for films and TV are not done in limbo – there are strict (and not always realistic) schedule and budget constraints, while various factors such as the aesthetic taste of the VFX supervisor, the director's vision, or the studio's agenda can also affect the output. It would be naïve to assume that every film with a big VFX budget is the embodiment of photorealism, or that small-budget movies or TV programs cannot reach comparable levels of realism. Examples of stunningly photoreal VFX can be found throughout the entire budget range, and while it certainly helps to have larger resources, what really matters at the end is the artists' understanding of light and color and their keen eye for detail. The concepts, principles, and techniques in this book should serve any VFX artist, whether they are working on a tentpole blockbuster or a student project.

Games

One can go back 30 years and still find some incredibly convincing visual effects (*Jurassic Park*, for example). But when it comes to games, the 1990s feel like the Stone Age. Compare the 1991 adventure game *Indiana Jones and the Last Crusade*, to a contemporary equivalent such as *Uncharted 4* (2016): the difference between the two-dimensional pixelated graphics of the first and the rich, cinematic visuals of the second is so immense that it is hard to believe these two games are only 25 years apart. Indeed, no other aspect of visual digital content has seen such a remarkable progress as realtime video games graphics. In the four decades since the *Atari* console, hardware and software developments have completely transformed the visual experience of video games. As technology grew ever more powerful, the once unachievable dream of creating immersive, photoreal games became feasible. And game engines continue to evolve faster than ever: at the time of writing this book, Epic announced Unreal 5, a revolutionary update that includes realtime global illumination and unlimited poly count.

Game artists today are often expected to design, model, texture, and light environments, props, and characters that are as detailed and believable as their counterparts in cinematic visual effects. To be clear, photorealism is certainly not a prerequisite in games. There are many popular game genres that proudly and happily remain within the realm of stylized or cartoonish graphics (for example, most *Nintendo* games or the majority of indie games). But there is certainly a growing number of titles that strive to offer gamers the most realistic experience possible, and their level of photorealism reaches higher grounds every year.

Unlike VFX, games graphics are rarely combined with live action footage, and are predominantly computer generated. This alleviates the challenges of integration that characterize VFX and allows for more stylistic freedom. But the road to photorealism in video games requires overcoming some tough obstacles: first, most 3D game environments cannot be designed for a specific camera framing or movement. All playable environments must accommodate a freely moving camera and look believable from every angle. Common VFX methodologies like 2D or 2.5D projections can only be used outside the playable area (distant backgrounds or skies, for example). Environments in open-world games, in particular, must be very large, and maintain quality and level of detail throughout their extent. In addition, everything needs to perform smoothly in real-time through the game engine. This requires constant attention to polygon count and texture sizes, a robust LOD system, and adherence to hardware and software rules and restrictions.

These key challenges show why VFX is still ahead of video games in terms of photorealism. Working for specific cameras and without the restrictions of real-time rendering (and adherence to a specific engine) gives VFX a distinct advantage. But as is evident by new games and all the latest developments, things are changing very fast. The restrictions are diminishing while hardware capabilities increase, and game engines now offer truly cinematic features like depth of field, realistic lens flares, or discreet color grading. It will not take much longer before the gap between VFX and games is bridged. Already, game engines and realtime technologies are used on movie sets and in VFX, and games look more and more like movies. To that end, all of the principles of photorealism and photoreal CG techniques discussed here, as well as many key 2D aspects, apply to contemporary games creation as much as they apply to VFX.

A frame from *Apocalypse*, a realtime environment by Pasquale Scionti. Rendered in Unreal Engine 4.25, built with 3ds Max, SpeedTree, Quixel Megascans, and Substance Painter.
© Pasquale Scionti.

Visualization

The visualization field is vast and varied. Not every type of visualization requires a photoreal look, and in some cases such a look may be unnecessary, or even counterproductive. In medical, scientific, or forensic visualizations, for example, precise graphical representation of concepts, procedures, and events often takes precedence over photorealism. A scientist examining a visualization of a certain type of protein is interested in the molecular structure and is quite content with simple colored shaders. A forensic visualization needs to precisely depict an event, so effort is invested in animation and timing rather than photoreal lighting or peripheral detail. But photorealism is an essential ingredient whenever the goal of a visualization is to present the subject in the most faithful and true-to-life way possible. This is often the case in architectural and product visualizations.

Architectural Visualization

The need to visually present a yet-unbuilt building existed of course long before computer graphics. The art of architectural illustrations goes all the way back to ancient Greece and reached the highest level of sophistication through the industrial revolution and into the 20th century. Unlike technical working drawings (floor and elevation plans, sections, schedules) which are intended for contractors, illustrations strive to convey the aesthetics and visual impact of the architecture rather than its technical details. Artists creating such illustrations need to master not only the technical aspects of this craft, but also the artistic skills required to present the subject in a dynamic and enticing way. Indeed, many such illustrations are considered true works of art, and go well beyond their practical purpose.

Paper Mill Loft Interior.
© Suburbia Studio.

The art of architectural illustrations changed drastically when 3D computer graphics entered stage. As the process of conceiving, planning, and drafting moved almost entirely to CAD software, architects discovered the potential of 3D models, detailed textures, and realistic lighting. CG renders became the standard in architectural visualizations because they effectively combine the traditional mediums of illustration and miniature models by allowing viewing and rendering from any position and angle. Virtual CG architecture can be used for walk-throughs or fly-overs, and offers the invaluable flexibility of changing interior lighting and time of day, or swapping textures and colors for quick design prototyping.

In VFX and games, the image is the final product. But visualization is only a waypoint to the final product – it is the means and not the goal. In architectural visualization, the imagery is rendered long before the final product has materialized. This leads to a certain inevitable tension between photorealism and abstraction: developers and clients want to see photoreal renders, to get the most accurate representation of the yet-to-be-built building or interior. Architects prefer more abstract renders – after all, what if the final product fails the image that predicted it in some way? Photorealism could in fact be a liability. There is yet a different tension that lies at the boundary between art and commerce: in a craft so steeped with tradition as architecture, it is only natural that CG rendering stirred resistance at its onset and

ArchViz Interior by Pasquale Scionti. 3D Studio Max and Substance Painter. Rendered with V-Ray.
© Pasquale Scionti.

is still a subject of some controversy. Opponents of the medium point to its computerized precision and lack of human touch, its soulless objectivity (as opposed to the subjective flow of an artist's drawing), or (as is sometimes the case) the drab and unexciting appearance of computer-generated images.

Indeed, the world of architectural visualizations has its share of generic and uninspiring renders. But when done well, such renders become a truly powerful medium for presenting architecture as an immersive and moving experience. This is where photorealism comes into play. Unlike traditional illustrations, where a few strong lines are often more effective than fine detail, CG architectural renders do not fare well when they lack convincing photoreal quality and detail. It is not surprising that many of the early forays into physically based rendering (radiosity, photon mapping, IES lights) were adopted first by ArchViz artists.

The extent of photorealism in a specific architectural project depends on the intended purpose of the visualization and the style of the architect and the artist. For example, many ArchViz artists go to great lengths in creating the most detailed textures and lighting, but completely disregard optical lens properties like depth of field, producing images that are unrealistically sharp across the entire depth. This is often done intentionally to allow viewing the entire structure sharp and clear, even at the price of some loss of photorealism. Another example: consider the ubiquitous use of libraries of generic 2D humans. From my own perspective as a VFX supervisor, I am sometimes perplexed by the apparent dissonance that rises from populating a meticulously built and rendered environment with hard-edged 2D cutouts that clearly don't match the lighting (and sometimes not even the perspective). In a movie, such a dissonance would certainly be shrill, but in the world and language of architecture, the added human cutouts are viewed more as an embellishment rather than co-equal elements. As such, their apparent lack of realism does not necessarily hamper the impact of the main subject. Here is yet another example: in both VFX and games, great care is taken to add the right amount of dirt, grime, and imperfections to avoid a synthetic, CG look. But dirt and imperfections are not necessarily the architect's highest priorities. The common aesthetic and stylistic approach to ArchViz naturally emphasizes a clean, fresh look, and what may feel overly sterile from VFX and games points of view is the norm in ArchViz. To compensate for the lack of grime and imperfections, artists add highly detailed auxiliary elements such as furniture, upholstery, carpets, curtains, wall decorations, or potted plants.

Contemporary architectural visualizations range from basic renders and quasi-illustrated presentations to elaborate clips that feel more like Hollywood-produced movies. These go beyond the standard CG rendering aspects of ArchViz and usually involve animation and compositing techniques that are more characteristic of visual effects. In addition, game engines like *Unreal* and VR technologies are increasingly being used to present architectural projects within an interactive, real-time environment. Such visualizations share the same challenges and limitations as games and VR, especially when attempting to maintain a high level of photorealism.

Product Visualization

People are often astonished when told that roughly 75% of IKEA's catalogue is completely CG. Why would IKEA choose the CG path? After all, they are not attempting to show a building that does not yet exist. They already have all those pieces of furniture in their warehouse, so wouldn't it be

SLV–SA Keyboard by Raphael Rau. Created in Cinema 4D, rendered with Octane.
© Raphael Rau.

easier to just photograph them? The reality is that the costs associated with arranging, lighting, and photographing product sets like IKEA's can be much higher than creating them in CG. Add to that the advantages of working in a virtual environment – the ease of changing the lighting, colors, and textures, or moving the camera or objects around – and the CG option becomes very lucrative. Yet the success of such visualizations is completely dependent on photorealism. The product must look exactly as it does in real life, and the tiniest crack in believability shatters the illusion of photographic reality.

Not all product visualizations rely on photorealism, but photoreal renders are now a vital part of product design and marketing in virtually every industry, from cars and furniture to phones and jewelry. They serve a wide range of media: printed and online catalogues, animated clips and interactive content, and immersive VR and AR presentations. In comparison to ArchViz, scale is generally smaller (not many products are as large as buildings or bridges), and renders contain fewer objects. On the other hand, the close-up presentation of smaller products necessitates a high level of accuracy. A cell phone may not have much exterior detail – a few buttons and sockets maybe, but this detail must be rendered with extreme precision to be convincing up close. So, while product visualizations may not require much of the kind of auxiliary detail (trees, plants, people) that is necessary to make ArchViz renders come to life, they present greater challenges in texturing and shading. Lighting can greatly affect the impact when focusing on a single small object, and lighting techniques in product visualizations often mimic studio photography.

Case Study: Exterior Architectural Renders

The House Above an Old Road.
© Julian Sadokha, Suburbia Studios.

In my search for photoreal architectural renders to feature in this book, I noticed that it is much easier to find believable interior renders than outdoor ones. It is understandable, considering that interiors contain mostly man-made objects, and their realism does not depend so much on highly detailed natural environments, which are arguably harder to generate. But there are other reasons too: in photography, the sky is often blown out as the photographer exposes for the architecture, yet ArchViz artists and clients often strive to produce more aesthetically pleasing renders by preserving detail in the sky and avoiding overexposing it. Likewise, overblown areas on white walls and other elements are often toned down to keep the architectural detail clear (in general, interior renders are not as bright and present fewer issues of this sort). Lastly, the tendency to keep surfaces clean becomes more of a hindrance to photorealism in outdoor scenes, where dirt, grime, and wear are naturally more prominent than indoor.

The House Above an Old Road is a project by Suburbia Studio, an architectural visualization company led by Julian Sadokha. I think it is a good example for a photoreal exterior rendering that hits the right notes. There is much attention here to natural detail like the bark textures on the pine trees or the pebbled ground, as well as the grass and shrubs. The artist does not shy away from bright sky exposure, and in fact, I think that the plain, white sky actually contributes to the believability of the scene because it feels naturally photographic. Likewise, the reflections in the windows and some brighter parts of the structure are also slightly overexposed. By not trying too hard to preserve all the detail in the highlights, the artist is emulating real footage. Finally, grime and wear detail like the water flow marks on the outer wall (lower left image) add a level of richness while still keeping the overall look modern and sleek.

Chapter 3
Color

Nearly every aspect of photorealism relies on color. Color defines not just lighting, but also surface properties, reflections, distance, depth, atmosphere, environment, and even camera and lens characteristics. Sometimes a simple color tweak is all that is needed to make things "look real". A little lift to the blacks, a slight reduction of red in the midtones, and suddenly everything falls into place. I cannot stress enough how beneficial it is for digital artists to master color, both in the inner, perceptual sense and in the ability to use digital tools to control it. But color is a vast subject. Navigating it can be daunting, the terminology is often confusing, and practices vary widely. Various software applications use different (and sometimes conflicting) names for color operations, and it is not always clear which tool should be used for a specific task. There are many books that cover color science, or the emotional and aesthetic attributes of color, and there are many ways to approach color theory and practices. In this chapter I chose to focus specifically on those aspects of color that I think are essential in the context of achieving photorealism. In particular, the way we perceive, observe, and interpret color, and how to think and work in additive color. I will simplify color terminology to the bare essentials, and then focus on the most relevant color operations.

Most humans can detect around ten million individual colors. We may not be champions of the animal kingdom (many reptiles, insects, and birds can see more colors), but we still possess a highly developed color vision that allows us to separate what we see into very fine detail. Unlike comic and clip art, objects in the real world do not have a black outline that defines and separates them. Yet we can still effortlessly tell one object from another, or an object from the background, solely by color detection. Even if we take the hues out (for example, in a black and white photo), we can still make out the finest detail by sensing minute difference in grey shades. Our ability to visualize and interpret our surroundings based only on subtle color differences is truly astonishing – especially since we do it instinctively, without giving it a second thought, at every single moment of our life.

Yet there is a marked difference between our instinctive perception of color and how we think and talk about it. As toddlers, we learn to identify an object's dominant color: "What color is the ball? Red!". "What color is the truck? Green!". "What color is the cloud? White!" As we mature, we may talk about "That lavender tablecloth", or "this indigo shirt", or "a charcoal gray car", but despite our extended color vocabulary, we still by and large do the same as our toddler selves: we focus only on the dominant color of an object, and ignore the secondary colors. In our minds and in our discourse, we "paint back" what we see in uniform flat colors, like the simple illustrations in a children's book. Granted, this simplification is crucial to our everyday life. It is rather impractical to

All the trees in this photo are green, but we can still make up the distinct shape of almost every tree just by detecting minute differences in brightness and hue.

What color is the car? Black, we would normally say. But it's black only in a hypothetical sterile environment. In this particular photo, as captured by the camera, the colors of the car's black paint range from red and green to light blue and near-white.

ask the car salesman about "this charcoal-grey car with orange-white highlights and slightly bluish shadowed areas and somewhat desaturated green and red reflections". But this is exactly how we must observe and describe color if we seek to recreate reality digitally. We need to rid ourselves of that lifelong conditioning of simplifying color and instead train ourselves to see colors objectively, in all their complexity. And we can surely do it – after all, we can see over ten million colors! Now, there is nothing new or groundbreaking in what I say – artists have been observing color this way for millennia. But I think that we, digital artists, are prone to becoming a little lazy in this respect. A painter has nothing but color to recreate reality on the canvas. We have all those tools at our disposal – we model highly detailed 3D objects and texture them and throw different lights in the scene and use physically plausible shaders and realistic simulations – and in the process, we sometimes tend to forget that, at the end, it all comes down to color. So, looking at the complexity of color in the world around us, is there a way to organize it so that we can make better sense of it?

The Six-Layer Approach

Let us revisit our charcoal-grey car and assume we photographed it on a sunny day. If we concentrate on a single surface, say, the dark-grey painted body, we can observe a multitude of different colors: small imperfections like smudges and scratches shift the color to a lighter grey or reveal the underlying base paint layer. Areas that are directly lit by the sun appear as a brighter, warmer tone, while areas that are occluded from sunlight are darker with a slight bluish tint. Where the sky and sun are reflected, the highlights are almost fully white, and where light can hardly reach, the color shifts toward black. The environment surrounding the car is reflected in its glossy body, adding splashes of various colors, from the greens of the trees to the colors of nearby cars and structures. If we photograph the car from a distance, a subtle bluish haze is added to the mix, and finally, our camera's white balance and exposure settings shift the colors even further.

As is evident from this example, color represents not only the surface properties of a material or an object, but also the light that's hitting it, the environment that surrounds it, its distance from the camera, the atmospheric conditions, and even the camera itself. It is hard to process and analyze all these factors without a methodology, so allow me to suggest one here. I call it "the six-layer approach", and it is by no means scientific, nor is it set in stone. It is my own, basic method for splitting up a multi-factor process into manageable chunks, which I find very handy for organizing color interpretation into a simple hierarchy:

Layer 1 is the "base color" – essentially, the color of the surface if lit by a completely uniform, perfectly white light, in a complete void, with absolutely nothing to reflect, and is shot by a fully unbiased camera. These conditions are, of course, not achievable in the real world, on earth, or even in outer space. Ironically, this is just about the easiest condition to achieve in CG (add an object to an empty scene, assign a uniform color texture, add a uniform ambient light, and voila!). Under these imaginary conditions, a red ball, for example, will look like a perfectly uniform, flat red disc.

Layer 2 adds the surface detail and imperfections that vary the base color (subtly or drastically). The rule here is that these changes in color can be visible in our hypothetical void (i.e. they are not caused by any specific lighting, reflections, or atmosphere). The red ball still looks like a flat red disc, albeit now not uniformly red.

Lighting is added in **Layer 3**, including any light sources in the scene, as well as the surrounding environment (which contributes by bouncing some light back on the surface). The red disc now takes the shape of a ball, and the colors shift depending on the intensity, direction, and hues of the light source/s (and to a lesser extent, the reflected light from the environment). The environment also affects the occlusion of light, which changes the color wherever less light can reach. For example, the ground causes a noticeable darkening around the lower part of the red ball.

Layer 4 is the reflection layer. Depending on the material, the reflections may be anything from isolated highlights where the brightest parts of the environment are reflected, to a fully detailed mirror view of the surrounding environment. This layer can therefore add a considerable amount of color variation to the surface.

Layer 5 is the atmosphere layer. The specific effect on the surface color (if any) depends on the distance of the surface from the camera, as well as the atmosphere itself (dry air has much less visible effect than fog, for example).

Layer 6 is the camera layer. Factors like lens flares, white balance, or the exposure can subtly or drastically shift the colors of a given scene.

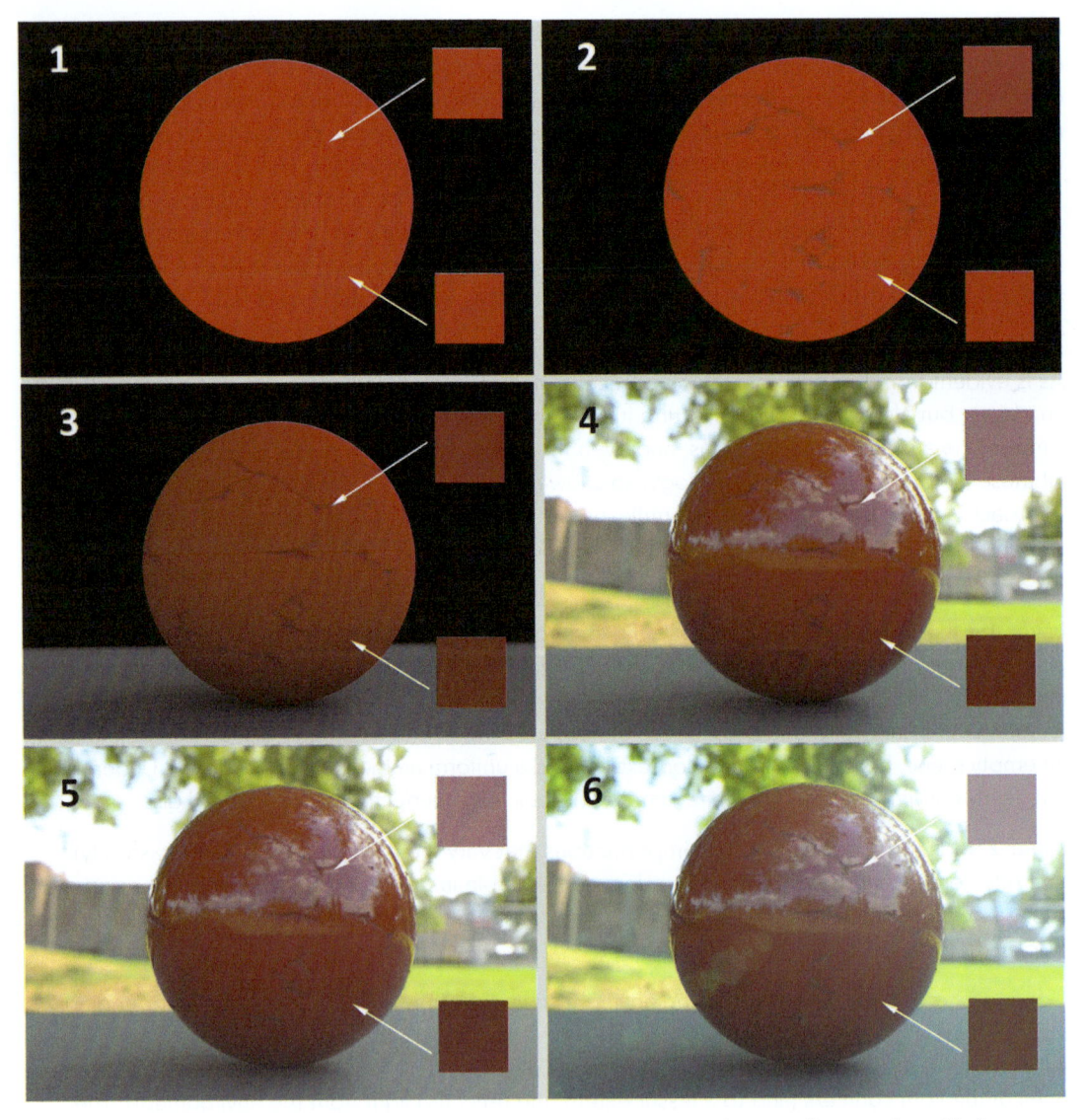

Since it's not possible to strip a photograph down through color layers, I used CG to illustrate the red ball example: 1: base color layer, 2: texture color detail, 3: lighting, 4: reflection, 5: atmospheric haze (very subtle here since we're close), 6: lens flares and camera color interpretation.

CORE CONCEPTS

This layered approach comes in handy when analyzing a photograph or a shot. By stepping backwards through the layers, we can "reverse-engineer" an image all the way back to the stripped-down basic colors of its components. By doing so, we can extract a great deal of information about the lighting, atmosphere, and environment in the image. This kind of "color detective" work is an essential step when integrating elements into existing footage or emulating a certain lighting scenario in CG, and it can only be done successfully through a methodic interpretation of color. Incidentally, these six layers reflect the process of creating a CG scene and finishing it in comp: modeling (layer 1), texturing (layer 2), lighting (layer 3), shading (layer 4), adding depth/atmosphere effects (layer 5) and adding lens/camera characteristics and effects (layer 6).

Thinking Additive

Subtractive Color

Back in kindergarten, when we created our first artwork with finger paints or gouache, we discovered that the more colors we mix, the more likely we are to end up with a dark-brown mush. When we mix paint materials, we are in fact mixing reflected (not emitted) light. Each paint material contains pigments that define which light frequencies are absorbed and which frequencies are reflected. Green paint absorbs most of the red and blue light, while red paint absorbs green and blue light. When you mix red and green together you get a darker brown, because the combined pigments now absorb more of the light spectrum and reflect less. Subtractive color mixing is strongly governed by absorption – painters usually avoid starting out with primary colors (red, green, and blue) and instead use secondary colors (yellow, magenta, and cyan) because they reflect more frequencies than they absorb. Mixing two secondary colors reduces the reflected light to a single pure primary and increases light absorption (for example, cyan and yellow produce green). Since subtractive color mixes get progressively darker, painters rely on the use of white pigment (which reflects most wavelengths and absorbs little) to lighten

When mixing paint materials, two secondary colors produce a primary color, and mixing three secondary colors produces black.

up or desaturate the mix. Similarly, most ink printers use cyan, magenta, and yellow as their base colors (usually with added black ink, the combination known as CMYK).

Additive Color

Unlike paints and inks, display devices like computer monitors, televisions, tablets, phones, and digital projectors actively emit light. Since digital art is created with light emitting devices, color is achieved and controlled as direct light – absorption and reflection play no role. Color mixing in computer graphics is akin to mixing light of various frequencies: with additive color, the result of mixing wavelengths will always be brighter, and the more colors are added, the more the mix approaches pure white. Unlike subtractive color, the additive color workflow is based only on the three color primaries (red, green, and blue), because every possible hue, intensity, or saturation value is achievable by additively mixing just those three primaries. The use of red, geen, and blue (RGB) primaries is also tightly connected to the mechanism of display devices: CRT monitors use three phosphor dots, red, green, and blue (called triads), for every pixel, and the specific color of the pixel is achieved by causing the triads to glow at varying intensities. Similarly, in LCD displays, red, green, and blue filters control the light as it passes through the liquid crystal. Moreover, our own color vision is achieved through three types of cone cells, each sensitive to either red, green, or blue light.

Understanding color through RGB values is therefore vital for the digital artist. If you are able to perceive any color as a specific combination of red, green, and blue or perform different color operations solely by varying the relationship between the three primaries, you are controlling color through its most fundamental elements. Achieving photoreal imagery often involves small, measured tweaks rather than broad stroke changes, and accuracy and control are paramount. Brightness, contrast, or saturation sliders are handy tools, but not always the best for precise fine-tuning or for reaching a very specific result. To get to the essence of color correction, digital artists need to learn how to control hue, saturation, and brightness by balancing red, green, and blue light.

When mixing light, adding two primary colors produce a secondary color, and all three primaries produce white.

Hue, Saturation, and Brightness in RGB

Since we are able to distinguish between roughly ten million different colors, it is not feasible to assign a name for each possible color. There are hundreds of color names in English. For example, "ginger", "carrot", "tiger", "apricot", "clay", "sandstone", and "marmalade" are all names for different hues of orange. Designers or home decorators may be familiar with the subtleties of such naming conventions, but these names, lovely as they are, are far from a precise description of color. One person's "apricot" may be quite different from another's. There have been several attempts to come up with a standardized, accurate color catalogue. A good example is the Pantone color coding, where roughly 1000 different colors are specified based on measured mixing of 13 pigments and black. The Pantone color chart is widely used in print and manufacturing because it allows for very accurate color matching, but it is obviously not very useful for digital color work – it defines a rather limited number of colors and is based on subtractive mixing of pigments, not additive mixing of light.

In the early 20th century, Professor Albert Munsell came up with a color system based on hue, value (lightness, or brightness), and chroma (color purity, or saturation). He imagined this system as a three-dimensional cylindrical space in which the color values move independently on three axes: hue is changed by rotating around the perimeter of the cylinder, saturation by moving from the rim toward the center of the cylinder, and brightness is increased or decreased by moving up and down the cylinder's height. Munsell's goal was to find an accurate way to define specific colors, so he divided each dimension into small numbered steps. Munsell designed his color model long before computers existed, but his design foreshadowed the digital age, and is indeed the basis for the **HSV (Hue, Saturation, and Value)** color system. Many artists prefer to perform color corrections using HSV tools, as this is a somewhat more intuitive approach. But full mastery of color can be gained by working directly with RGB light mixing. To understand the correlation between HSV and RGB values, we will use three sliders for red, green, and blue, each going from zero (no intensity) to one (full intensity).

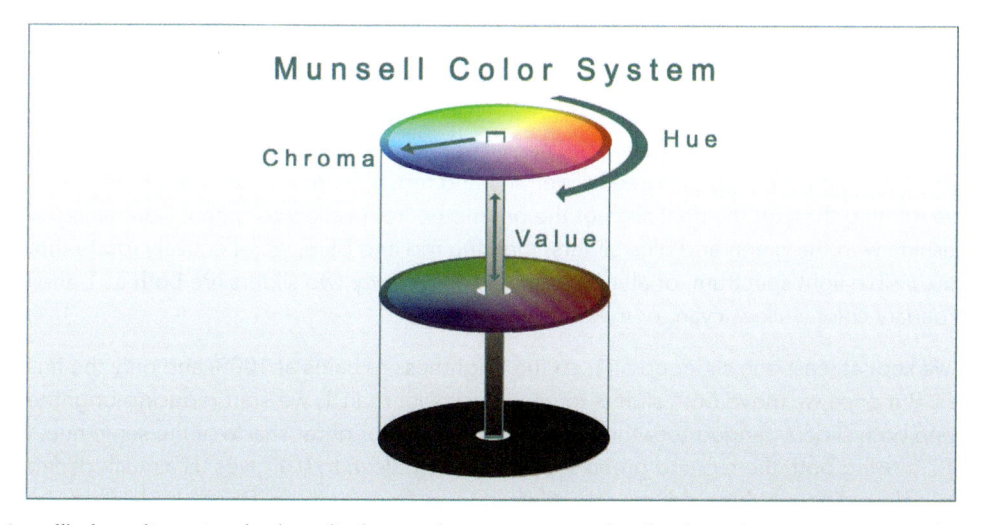

In Munsell's three-dimensional color cylinder, up–down represents value (brightness), rotation represents hue, and chroma (saturation) is changed by moving from the perimeter to the center.

COLOR

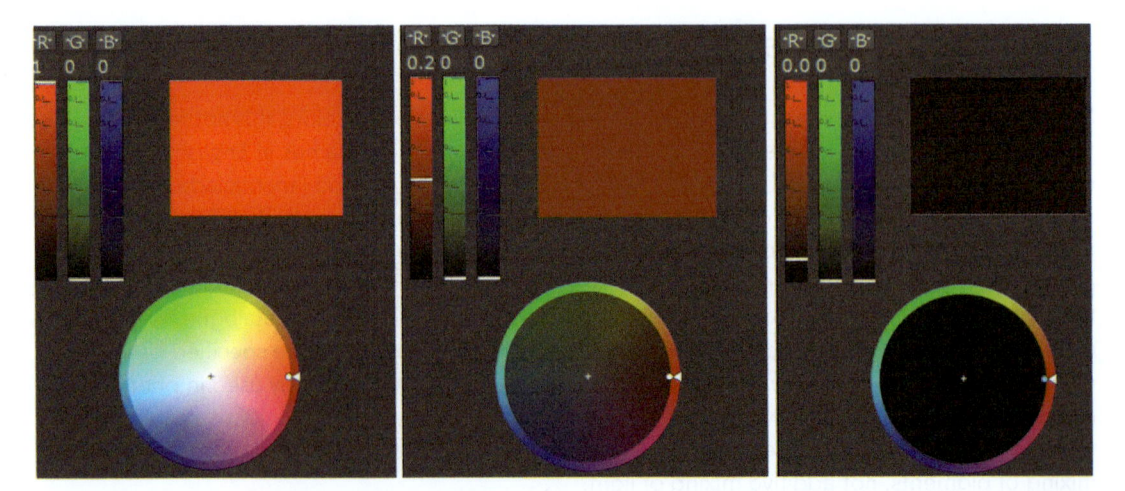

As the red slider is brought down, only the brightness (value) changes. The hue and saturation remain exactly the same on the color wheel, as we move along the third axis of the cylinder. This represents three shades of the same pure red hue.

Brightness represents the intensity of light, not its frequency. In RGB light context, if we start up with all three sliders at zero (pure black, or absolute absence of light), and then raise just the red slider, we are effectively increasing the intensity of the red light while keeping both the hue and saturation fixed. When the red slider is all the way up at one, we reached the brightest possible shade of red (while increasing the value above one is possible, the perceived color is not affected). As we lower the slider back down, red becomes progressively darker as the intensity of the light decreases. Notice that the position on the color wheel is fixed throughout – there is no change to either hue or saturation, because we are moving only on the third, imaginary "up down" axis of our 3D color cylinder (an axis which cannot be shown on a 2D color wheel). This is important to note, because it is a common mistake to refer to different intensities as "different hues". Using the word "shade" instead helps make the distinction between different hues and different intensities of the same hue ("a darker shade of red" vs. "a more greenish red hue").

Hue can only be changed by introducing another primary to the mix. If the red slider is all the way up at 1, and we start raising the green slider, we are shifting the hue from pure red to orange and then to yellow. Notice that the color wheel indicator starts rotating along the perimeter of the wheel (hence the term "hue rotation"). The rotation from red to yellow is exactly one sixth of the perimeter. If we now keep the green slider at 1 and move the red slider down from 1 to 0, we continue rotating through the next sixth of the perimeter, from yellow to green. Continuing in the same fashion with the green and blue sliders, then the red and blue, we effectively rotate through the entire visible light spectrum, or all possible hues. When any two sliders are both at 1, the result is a secondary color (yellow, cyan, or magenta).

So far, we kept at least one slider up at 1, so the brightness remains at 100% and only the hue changes. But once we move both sliders to positions lower than 1, we start reducing brightness. If we keep both sliders ganged together, we get a darker or brighter shade of the same hue. For example, moving both the red and green sliders from 1 (yellow) to 0.4 gives us a much darker shade of yellow. Though this color may be referred to as "mustard" or "Dijon" in designers' jargon, it is still pure yellow, only darker (in other words, it is still pure yellow light, just less intense). But we can, of course vary the positions of both sliders independently, which shifts hue

CORE CONCEPTS

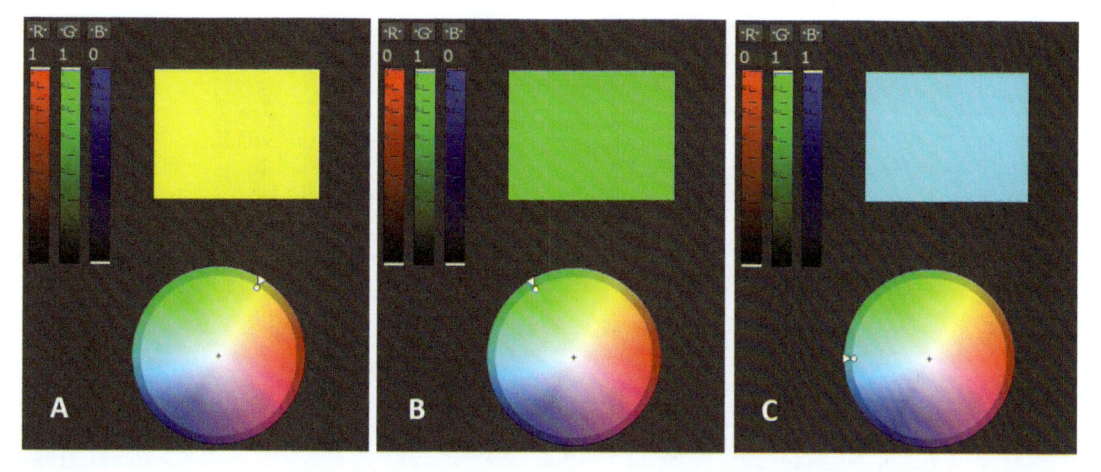

Hue rotation: using three combinations of primaries we rotate one third of the wheel, from yellow (A) through green (B) to cyan (C).

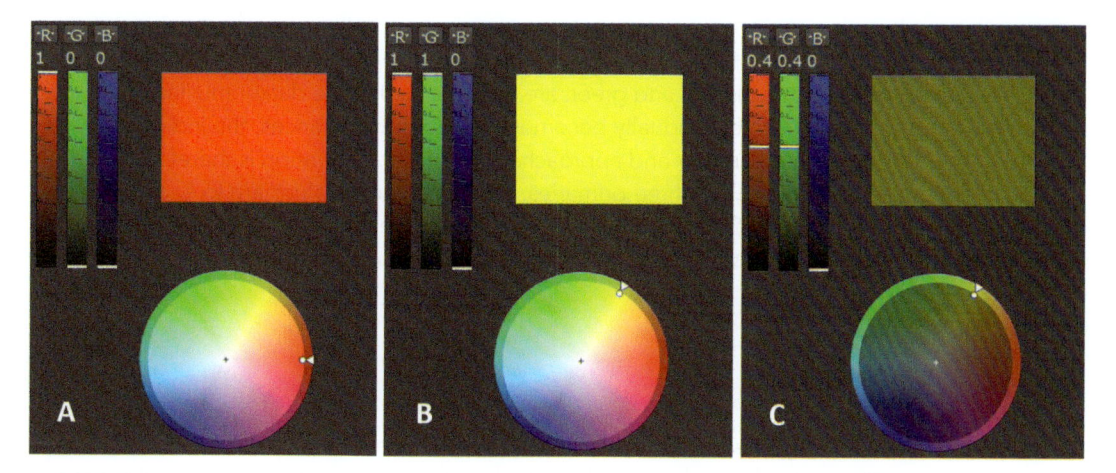

Red (A) and green fully at 1 produce pure bright yellow (B). With both at 0.4, the result is a darker shade of yellow (C). Notice that the marker is still at the edge of the wheel – the mustard color is still pure, fully saturated yellow.

and brightness simultaneously. By using just two sliders (two primaries), and covering only one third of the color wheel, we can still achieve a staggering number of possible colors. Notice that up until now, the saturation remained 100% (the point on the wheel sticks to the outer perimeter). This is important to emphasize, because saturation is often confused with brightness. Darker shades, in general, feel more subdued and less vibrant than brighter shades, so we tend to think of them as less saturated. That mustard color, for example, is commonly considered less saturated than pure yellow, but technically it is still pure yellow. We should not confuse brightness (intensity) with saturation (purity of color, or how close it is to neutral grey).

To reduce **saturation**, we must introduce the third primary into the mix. If, for example, red and green are at 1 (pure yellow) and we start raising the blue slider, the color gradually gets closer to

COLOR

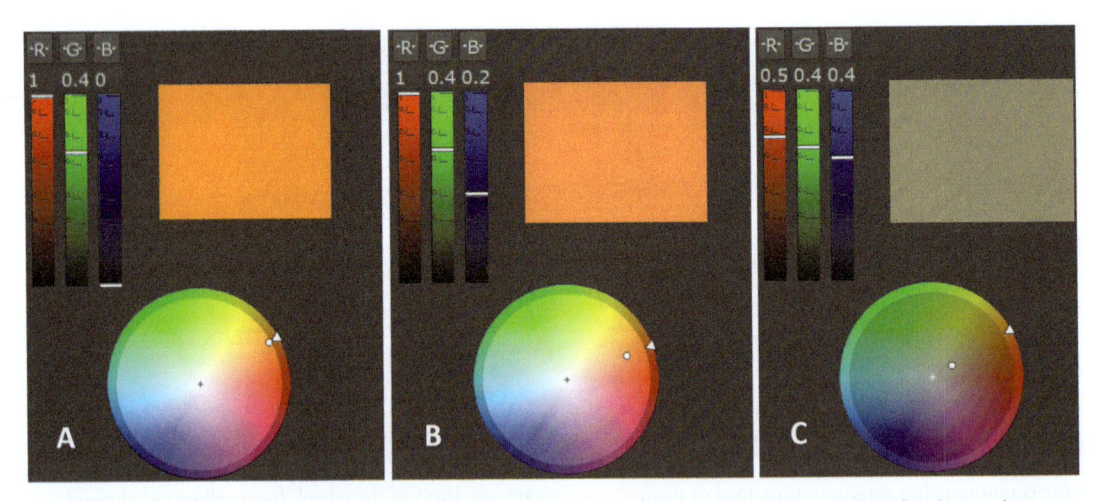

Pure orange (A) becomes less saturated when blue is added to the mix (B). Notice how the marker leaves the perimeter of the wheel and starts moving toward the center. When all three primaries are brought closer together, the saturation is further reduced and the color approaches pure gray.

white as its purity decreases. If the red and green are both set to 0.4 (the darker mustard color), and we start raising blue, the color gradually becomes grey. In both instances, the indicator on the color wheel leaves the outer perimeter and approaches the center. Saturation is therefore affected by the distance in value between the three primaries: the closer those values are to each other, the more desaturated the color. One or two primaries always generates pure hues, and only a combination of all three primaries can reduce the color purity, or saturation.

Color operations

Color operations terminology is a source of much confusion. There is no unified color vocabulary, and names and functions of color tools vary substantially between different software applications. Take a quick look at the basic color tools in three different applications: Photoshop, Maya, and Nuke. Photoshop offers Brightness/Contrast, Levels, Curves, Exposure, Vibrance, Hue/Saturation, and Color Balance. Maya's texture map color controls include Exposure, Default Color, Color Gain, and Color Offset. Lastly, Nuke's grade node includes Blackpoint, Whitepoint, Lift, Gain, Multiply, Offset, and Gamma. This is a rather confusing list. Not only are similar operations named differently in different applications, some applications even offer multiple controls for the exact same color operation (for example, brightness, exposure, gain, and multiply are basically all the same operation). These redundancies and overlaps certainly don't make color handling any easier for the digital artist.

To simplify things, we can narrow down most color tools to just five basic operations: **Gain**, **gamma**, **lift**, **offset** and **saturation**. All these operations essentially control the brightness (intensity) of RGB light. However, they control brightness differently, which makes each operation suitable for a specific goal. It is helpful to look at the simple math behind each operation, and even more useful to understand the visual outcome of each operation and its functional place in the digital color toolset. You may have noticed that I did not include contrast as one of the five color operations above. The reason is simple: each of these operations can be defined by an absolute value and applied to a single pixel. Contrast, on the other hand, is the relationship between dark and bright colors within an image. A "contrast value" is a relative term and cannot be assigned to a single pixel. Contrast can in fact be changed using a combination of two of the operations discussed here, as I will show later on.

Gain (exposure)

The most basic color operation is a simple multiplier. Raise the gain to 2, and every pixel value is doubled. Set it to 0.5 and the value is halved. A value of zero (absolute black) always remains zero. Gain raises or lowers brightness in a linear fashion throughout the entire range. Since it is a multiplier, it affects brighter tones much more than darker ones. For example, if you set the gain to 3, a black pixel with a value of 0.001 becomes 0.003 (just slightly less black), while a medium grey pixel with a value of 0.33 goes all the way to 0.99 (near-white). This is an important characteristic of the gain operation because it results in a relative preservation of contrast and tonal balance. Our eyes are much more susceptible to brightness changes in the low end, and much less sensitive to changes at the high end. This makes gain the best operation for increasing overall brightness, as it conforms to our vision – when gain is increased, the image does not simply wash out. Gain is also the most suitable operation for shifting the hue by changing the relative brightness of each of the RGB channels.

In some applications the gain operation is called brightness – a rather inaccurate name since all color operations manipulate brightness. Other applications offer gain as **exposure**, which is a correct terminology. Exposure is also a multiplier, but it uses stops as units. Stops are powers of two: raising the exposure by three stops is the same as setting the gain at 8, and lowering the exposure by four stops is the same as setting the gaining down to one-sixteenth (0.0625). Photographers and cinematographers may prefer to operate the gain in stops rather than multipliers, though the result is essentially the same.

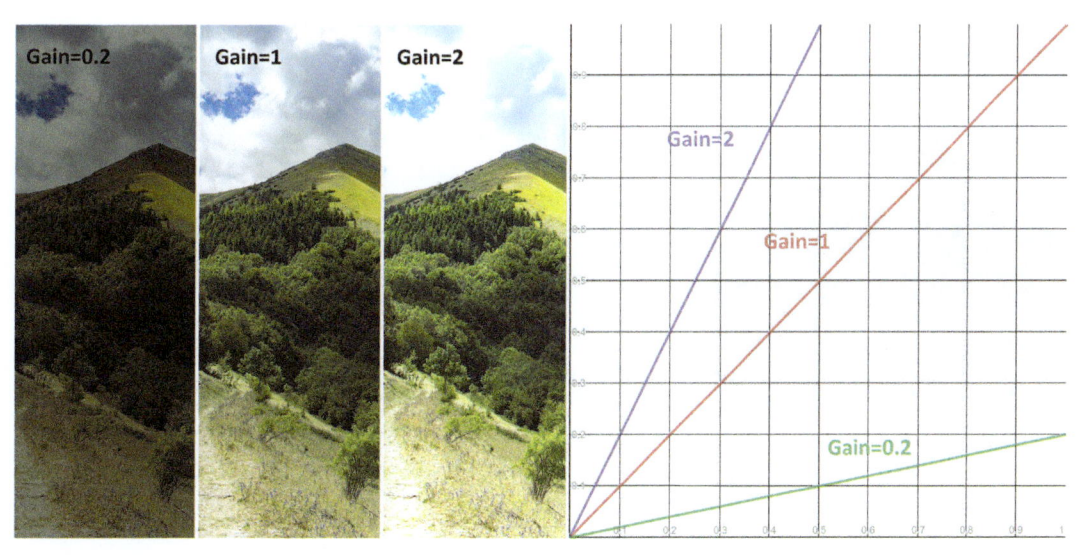

Because the gain curve pivots at the zero point, it affects brighter tones much more than dark ones. This makes it ideal for overall brightness control because we are much more sensitive to changes in the darks.

Offset

Offset is an additive operation. An offset of 0.2 raises all the values across the color range by 0.2. Like gain, offset is a linear operation. However, the differences are obvious: offset affects every color value equally, shifting blacks and highlights by the same exact amount, and it also affects zero. Due to our biased perception of brightness, offset does not appear to brighten the color range equally: as the offset slider is raised, the blacks are lifted first, dragging the midtones and highlights along, until the entire image goes white. Clearly, offset does not work as well as gain for controlling overall brightness or hue, but it is useful as a tool for manually controlling saturation (as I will explain later).

Lift

The math behind the lift operation is slightly more complex than gain or offset: output = input*(1 – lift) + lift. Throw some numbers into this equation, and you will notice that the lower the input value, the bigger the change. For example, if lift is set to 0.2, a dark grey shade of 0.01 jumps to 0.208, while a near-white grey of 0.95 barely nudges to 0.96. Plotting this operation as a curve shows a sort of a mirror image of the gain curve: instead of pivoting on the zero point, the lift curve pivots at 1. Lift is therefore the best choice for tweaking the low end of the spectrum with minimal impact to the high end. Accurate blacks are crucial for integration and photorealism, so this operation has an important role in color correcting.

Gamma

Unlike the previous three operations, gamma produces a non-linear curve: the pixel value is raised to the power of the inversed gamma value (output = input$^{1/gamma}$). For example, with a gamma of

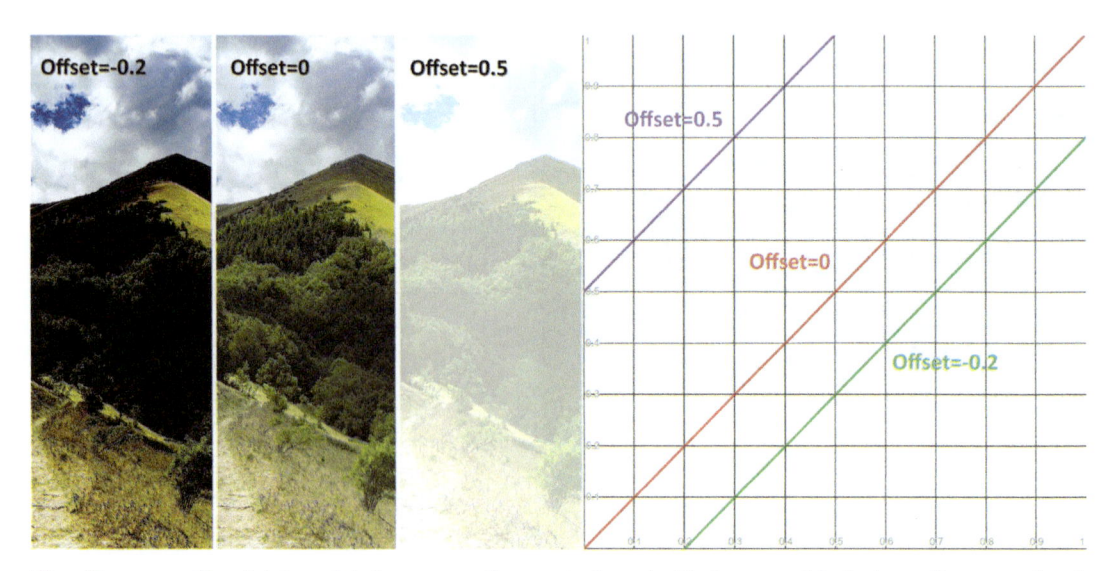

The offset curve affects bright and dark tones equally – notice how the blacks appear lifted when offset is raised and crushed when offset is lowered. Notice also that the bright parts like the clouds are blown out when offset is raised.

CORE CONCEPTS

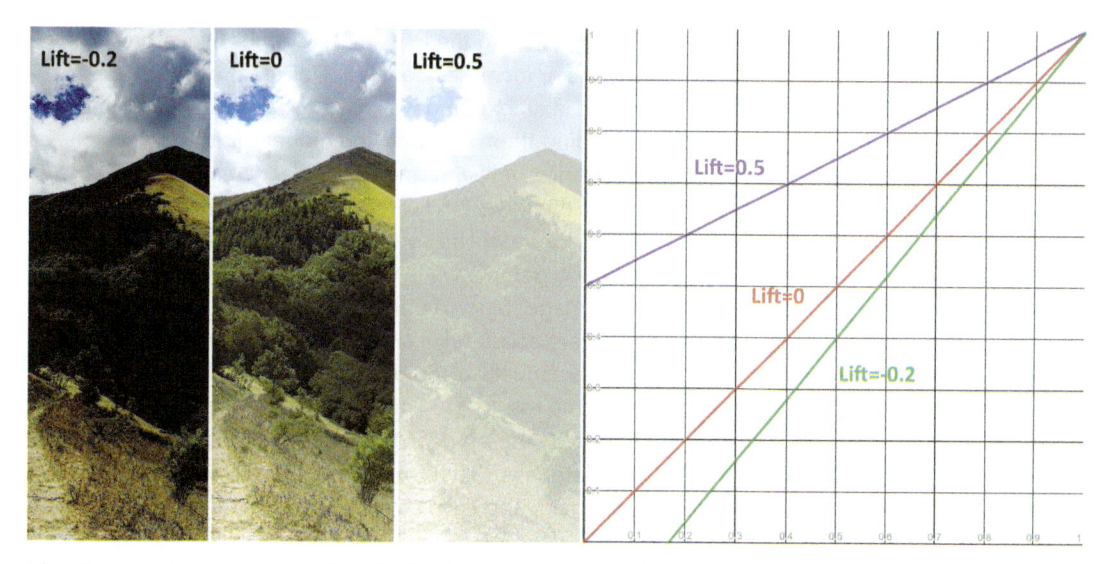

The lift curve pivots at 1, so it affects the blacks much more than the whites. Notice that, unlike offset, lift does not blow out the clouds when raised.

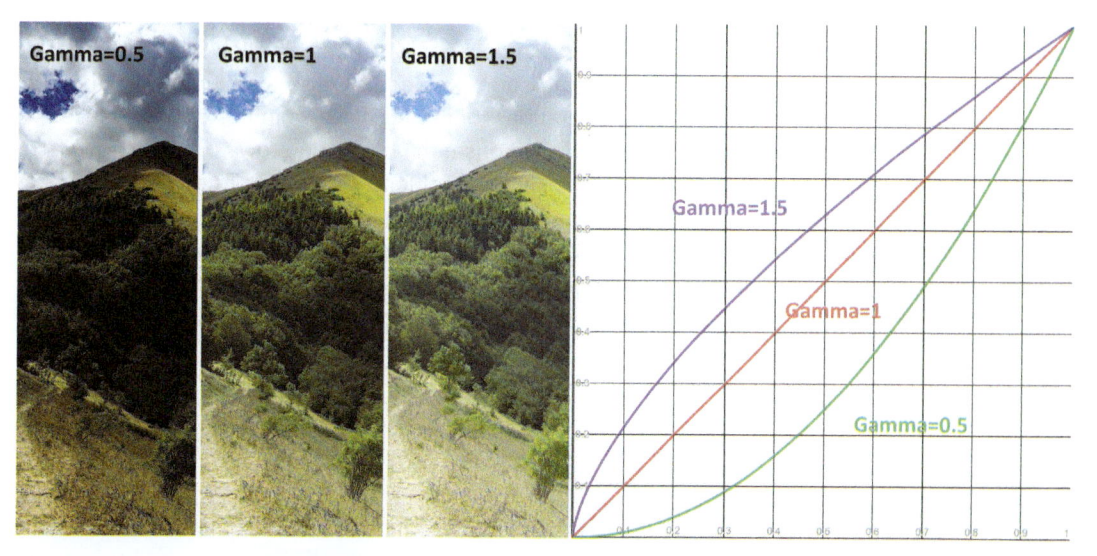

The gamma curve pivots on both the zero and one points, and affects mostly the low and low-mid range, which makes gamma ideal for controlling contrast.

2.2, a pixel with a value of 0.1 becomes 0.35 (the inverse of 2.2 is 1/2.2, or 0.454, so 0.1 to the power of 0.454 is 0.35), and a value of 0.9 becomes 0.95 (0.9 to the power of 0.454). It may seem that this operation is similar to lift, where lower values are affected more than higher values, but the gamma curve is quite different: a logarithmic curve that has a "belly" around the low-to-mid end, then settles toward the top end. The curve also shows that, unlike gain (which is anchored at zero) or lift (which is anchored at 1), gamma is anchored at both ends. If you feed either 0 or 1 as the input value into the equation, they will remain the same.

COLOR

The unique effect of gamma is that by raising or lowering the low and mid tones (while preserving the black and white points), it effectively reduces or increases contrast. Unlike lift or offset, when gamma is increased, it does not flash the blacks in an extreme way, but rather gently raises their brightness along with the lower midtones, bringing them closer to the higher midtones and highlights. Doing so, gamma reduces the difference between bright and dark areas, and thus reduces contrast. Lowering the gamma darkens the lower end without crushing the blacks, and preserves the higher end, effectively increasing contrast. The overall change in brightness can be counteracted with gain. For example, lowering gamma while raising gain increases contrast while preserving the general luminance of the image. Since gamma can be applied separately to each RGB channel, contrast can be controlled very accurately using the combination of gamma and gain. As previously mentioned, contrast is essentially a subjective term, and different contrast tools can vary greatly in their built-in math and the results they produce. Some contrast operations boost the highlights too much, while others muddy the blacks. In general, the perceived effect of contrast is highly dependent on the visual material and its context, and so is much better controlled using a combination of gamma and gain, and if necessary, also lift or offset.

Saturation

In the previous section I explained that all the shades of primary and secondary colors are 100% saturated, and saturation can only be reduced by mixing all three primaries and decreasing the relative difference between their values. Take for example a fully saturated yellow with the values red=1, green=0.9, and blue=0. To reduce the saturation, we need to raise the blue toward the red and green. Gain or gamma are not suitable operations for raising the blue in this case, because they do not affect zero values, but offset does. As we offset the blue value toward the red and green, we reduce the saturation, but we introduce a new problem – the desaturated yellow is now substantially brighter than the original, because we added a lot of blue light to the mix. To properly increase or reduce saturation, we need to maintain the original luminosity, as well as maintain the relative relationship between the primaries. It is very tricky to do so manually – and

In this example, the goal is to increase the orange hue of the afternoon light and the blue of the sky (original photo at left). However, increasing the overall saturation (middle image) does not help, as it mainly increases green, the dominant color in the photo. A better approach is to use specific hue corrections (right).

CORE CONCEPTS

this is where saturation tools come quite handy, because they take care of this tricky balancing act for us.

Saturation should be used thoughtfully. As I mentioned before, we tend to view bright shades as more saturated than darker ones. A very bright orange, for example, may appear as overly saturated. But (and this depends on the context) desaturation may not be the best remedy. A simple gain reduction around the dominant color may be much more effective, as it affects only the intensity and not the hue. Often, it is not the overall saturation that needs to be increased or reduced, but rather one or two hues that are overly dominant, missing, or just don't sit well within the whole.

Bit Depth and Dynamic Range

When you count in binary (only zeros and ones), digits accumulate fast. The number 4 in binary is 100, and 40 is 101000. An 8-bit color system can handle up to eight digits, so the highest number possible is 11111111 (or 255 in decimal). Including the zero, this allows for 256 possible shades for each of the three primaries, and a total of 16,777,216 (256×256×256) possible color permutations. Considering that we can detect up to about ten million colors, 16 million seems more than sufficient for representing color accurately. Indeed, a photograph saved as an 8-bit image preserves all the visible color detail. JPG is by far the most widely used 8-bit image format, and it holds more than adequate color detail for display and print. Now, a 16-bit color image has 65,536 shades per primary, for a total of over 280 trillion (!) different colors. This number seems like a massive overkill, especially since there is no visible difference between a 16-bit and an 8-bit version of an image. But the difference is hidden within: 8- and 16-bit images may look identical, but they react quite differently to color manipulation. Once you start pushing and pulling the colors, an 8-bit image soon shows signs of distress, especially in areas of fine color gradation. Banding, stepped transitions, and artifacts are all possible results of manipulated 8-bit images; 256 steps per primary are simply not enough to withstand substantial color correction. Therefore, 16-bit imagery is superior to 8-bit not because "it looks better", but because it is significantly more flexible.

Previously in this chapter we looked at RGB colors ranging from zero to one, where RGB 1,1,1 represents pure white. While this is perfectly fine for most digital display devices and for print, it is not enough to truly represent the range of light intensity in a given environment. Modern digital cameras can capture a wide dynamic range, and require a digital format that can preserve such a range; 8-bit formats like JPG clamp all color information below zero and above one, but 16- and 32-bit color formats allow for a much extended range, especially with the help of floating point math (in a nutshell, floating point is a way of covering a very wide range of values by shifting the position of the decimal point between the digits). Extended dynamic range is invaluable for color manipulation because it maintains hidden information in the blacks and the whites – information that may not be visible at the photo's original exposure but is revealed once that exposure is modified. For example, reducing an overexposed sky's brightness in a JPG image will not show more detail, because all the values above 1 are clamped, and whatever detail was there has been lost. The low range in 8-bit formats suffers a similar clamped fate. But 16-bit formats preserve hidden detail in the highlights or shadows, and thus provide an incomparably superior starting point for color editing and manipulation. The high dynamic range stored in 16- and 32-bit formats is also useful for image-based lighting (see Chapter 11), because photographed light sources preserve their true luminance.

The 16-bit and 8-bit images (top) look exactly the same. However, when the gain is pulled down, the "hidden" detail is revealed in the 16-bit image, but cannot be resurrected with the clamped values of the 8-bit image (bottom).

The Low End

Blacks – in plural, not singular! In school we learn that "black is not a color, it's a shade", and that is very true. Although blacks are commonly referred to as "shadows" in photography and color grading jargon, this is a rather inaccurate term (not every shadow is black and not every black is a shadow). Blacks are simply the darkest shades of any hue. Hence the plural, as there is in fact an infinite number of blacks. Moreover, there is no precise definition of "blackness". There is no threshold that delineates when exactly a very dark blue becomes black, for example. Even for a single hue, there could be many levels of intensity around the range we would generally consider as black, even though such subtle differences may be nearly imperceptible. Black in digital art is therefore a relative term. One can argue that the only "singular", pure black is RGB 0, 0, 0. This is a theoretical color, since it means an absolute lack of light (or a material that absorbs 100% of incident light). But to the digital artist, this argument is rather irrelevant. Photorealism is as much about photographs as it is about nature, and areas of zero-black, or even negative values are common in photography and cinematography because of exposure settings, color correction, or the sensor's characteristics.

Blacks play a crucial role in integration and photorealism. Even minute tweaks in this low range can have a profound effect on the image, and how it conveys distance and depth. As mentioned

CORE CONCEPTS

By lifting the low end, the "black" in the background (left) is revealed to be many colors (right). Compositors must be aware of the true values of blacks because a mismatch can be easily exposed when the final content is color-corrected.

previously, our eyes are much more sensitive to brightness changes in the low end than in the mid and high ranges. Some of the subjects explored in this book, like aerial perspective, lens flares, or light scattering, are most noticeable in the blacks. A mismatch of blacks between different elements can kill the believability of a composite or a matte painting, and inconsistent black levels in a texture map can ruin an otherwise photoreal render. There is a bit of a paradox here: we take, almost subconsciously, crucial cues of distance and depth from blacks, and we can easily sense that "something is wrong" when black levels are not consistent. Yet we normally pay little attention to blacks in everyday life – naturally, it's the midtones that attract our eye, because hues in this range are most vibrant and easy to discern. Untrained people may have a hard time distinguishing between different hues in the blacks, but digital artists need to develop a keen sensitivity to the lowest range and an ability to identify the RGB makeup of the darkest of colors. Hardware plays a role here too. Most computer monitors (even those considered above average), fail at the very low end. For color-crucial crafts like texturing, lighting, matte painting, and compositing, a good monitor with accurate black representation is a must.

Blacks are usually controlled with lift or offset (Levels in Photoshop), or by range-specific tools such as Nuke's color correct node or Photoshop's curves. Naturally, changes are subtle and numerical variations are small. Since it is hard to "see" in the blacks, even with a good monitor, it is helpful to temporarily raise the display gamma a bit. Some applications provide built-in viewer gamma and gain control. If no such controls exist, you can always add a temporary gamma color correction.

The High End

Whites, in plural, too: while most display devices peak at or near RGB 1,1,1, actual values may be higher (much higher, in fact) when working with full dynamic range. So, although white areas in an image may appear identical when viewed on a monitor, their numerical values can in fact be very different. A multitude of colors live in that "white zone", invisible when pushed above one, but visible at lower exposures. Noting the actual values at the top range of the spectrum is therefore important for rendering and integration, because it ensures coherent colors even at lower brightness settings or under extensive color manipulation.

Just as with blacks, what we perceive as "white" is often multiple colors. And just like with blacks, successful integration of elements relies on careful matching of white values.

Though the term "highlights" is generally used in art to describe the brightest parts of a painting or a photograph, it is often associated with specular reflections, and is not the best term for whites. The brightest parts in an image are usually light sources, as well as light-scattering elements like lampshades or the sky. Specular reflection on shiny surfaces preserves much of that brightness, so even if none of the light sources are visible in the frame, their reflections constitute the brightest whites in an image. Keeping whites consistent in digital imagery is as important for integration as matching the blacks, but the process can be somewhat more confusing with HDR material, because the true luminosity of white is often only revealed by inspecting the values. For example, a matte white plastic surface may be much less bright than a shiny black car paint, where that paint reflects high-intensity areas such as the sun or the sky. It is therefore important to sample the precise numerical values of whites in an image and match those contextually when integrating 2D or 3D elements.

PART 2

THE REAL WORLD

A late-afternoon view of Todi, a lovely town in Umbria. Or, in the language of this book: Sunlight photons scattering through air, humidity and dust in the atmosphere, bouncing off stone, wood and leaf surfaces, refracting in the lens, and finally hitting the sensor.

Chapter 4

Light Essentials

Is light particles or waves? It travels in a straight path and is reflected at a predictable angle – a particle behavior. But specific light phenomena like diffraction can only be explained through wave interference patterns. The waves/particles question was already a subject of debate back in the 17th century, when Huygens' wave theory was pitted against Newton's Corpuscular theory (which argued that light is particles). Newton's approach was widely accepted, and the wave theory went out of favor until the early 19th century, when fresh ideas from Augustin-Jean Fresnel and Thomas Young revived it. The understanding of electromagnetic waves continued to evolve throughout the 19th century and solidified the light wave theory. As a result, the particle approach was nearly neglected. Then came Albert Einstein, who, along with other revolutionary physicists like Max Planck and Niels Bohr, established the theories of quantum physics. The centuries-old debate was no longer relevant, as these theories proved that light can in fact be both particles and waves.

The wave–particle duality of light is certainly a baffling concept, as it seems to contradict basic notions of classical physics (Bohr called it the "duality paradox"). But since this book is not about quantum physics, the question to be asked is: does the concept of particle/wave duality bring any benefit to the digital artist? I believe it does! Looking at light from either a wave or a particle perspective (and sometimes both), makes it easier to understand different aspects of light behavior. For example, color is best approached from a wave perspective, while the difference between specular and diffuse reflections is easier to understand from a particles perspective. Later in this book, when we explore CG rendering techniques, you will notice that some relate directly to either one of those perspectives. For example, thin film diffraction calculates light as waves, while photon mapping calculates light as particles. Digital artists, therefore, can embrace the concept of light duality to advance their understanding of light behavior and optics, even without delving into quantum physics. Here is a quick description of light from each perspective:

Light as Waves

Visible light comprises a rather small portion of the entire electromagnetic spectrum. Waves on this spectrum are defined by their frequency (measured in hertz units) and their wavelength (measured in metric units). At the very bottom of this spectrum lie extreme low frequency radio waves (around 10 hertz), which can be as long as 100,000 kilometers. At the top end, Gamma ray frequencies lie around 300 exahertz (300 × HZ^{18}), with wavelengths as small as one trillionth of a meter (1 picometer). In between (moving from long to short waveforms) are medium and high frequency radio waves, microwaves, infrared, visible light, ultraviolet, and X-rays. The visible light portion of the spectrum starts with red (frequency around 400 terahertz) and ends with violet (frequency around 780 terahertz). There is no specific quality that differentiates visible light from other electromagnetic waves, except for the fact that this is the portion of the spectrum that the human eye can detect. Moreover, the visible light range is not consistent for other living beings. Some animals can see only a limited part of it, others can detect frequencies below or above it (some types of snakes, for example, can sense infra-red, while many insects and birds can see ultraviolet). The range of colors along the visible spectrum (red, orange, yellow, green, cyan, blue, and violet) is considered pure (fully saturated), because it represents a single light frequency. As I showed in Chapter 3, pure colors can be achieved by mixing just two of the three primary colors (red, green, or blue). However, most light sources tend to radiate a mix of different frequencies, so most of the light we see is somewhat desaturated (sunlight, which encompasses nearly all visible light frequencies, is white, or fully desaturated when unfiltered by the atmosphere).

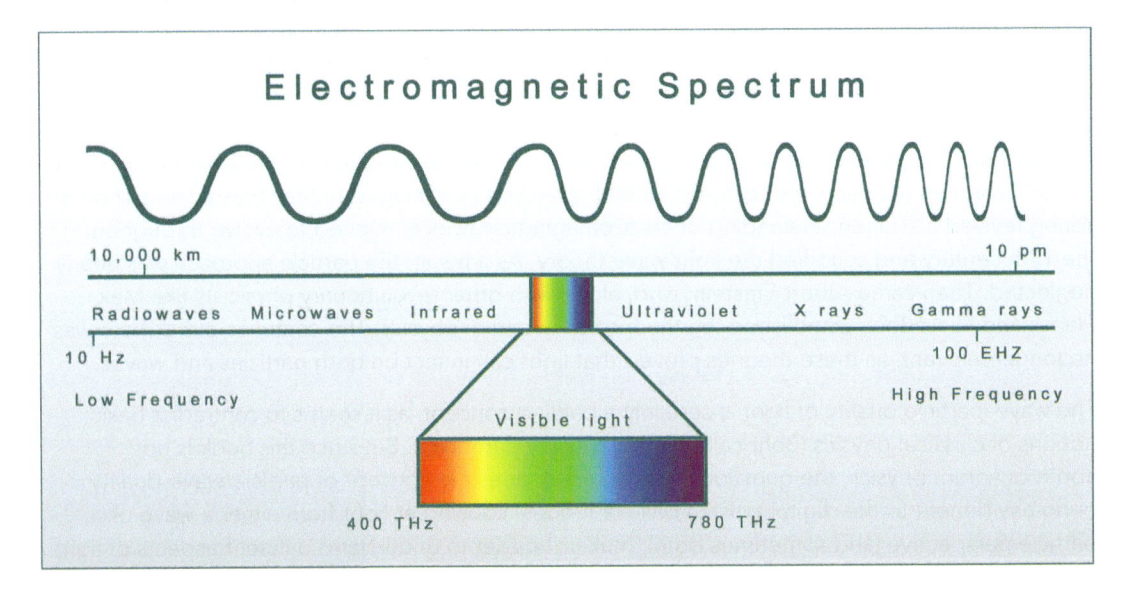

Electromagnetic Spectrum

10,000 km — 10 pm

Radiowaves | Microwaves | Infrared | Ultraviolet | X rays | Gamma rays

10 Hz — 100 EHZ

Low Frequency — High Frequency

Visible light

400 THz — 780 THz

Light as Particles

Like all electromagnetic waves, the energy of visible light depends on its frequency. The smaller the frequency, the higher the energy. In quantum mechanics, this energy is said to be quantized (quanta = "how much" in Latin) into defined "energy packets" called photons. Blue light photons (higher frequency) have more energy than red light photons; however, all photons travel at the same speed, regardless of their frequency (in vacuum, the speed of light is roughly 300,000 km, or 186,000 miles, per second). We are surrounded by light photons travelling in all directions as they are emitted and then scattered/reflected by surfaces. But most of this activity is completely invisible to us because our eyes can only detect light when photons hit the retina directly. This means that we can only see light if we look directly at its source (the object that is emitting radiation in the visible spectrum), or if we look at a surface that reflects photons back toward our eyes. In other words, we cannot observe photons "from the side" like watching traffic on the highway. Photons must be on a straight collision path with our eyes (or cameras for that matter) for the light to be registered by the brain (or the camera's sensor). Therefore, we cannot see "light rays". Those shafts of light on a concert stage, or the beams of sunlight entering a room through cracks in the shades, are visible only because light is reflected off particles like dust and water droplets and redirected toward our eyes. Without some presence of a reflecting/scattering volume, even laser beams are invisible (indeed, and despite the sci-fi convention, you cannot see laser beams in space).

Light Decay

The intensity of light falls off with distance at a **quadratic rate**. The **inverse-square law** states that light intensity is inversely proportional to the square of the distance from the light source. For example, if we consider the intensity of light at a distance of a foot from the source as one, then that intensity will drop to a quarter at 2 feet (one divided by the square of 2), and to a mere sixteenth at 4 feet (one divided by the square of 4). Light decay has nothing to do with the energy or speed of the light, as both are not affected by distance (we can see stars that are hundreds of light years away). Light decay is only related to how thinly the photons are spread out. At any given moment, a certain number of photons are emitted from a light source. These are tightly bunched together close to the emitter, but as they travel out in all directions, the distance between them becomes progressively larger. Thus, the farther away an object is from the light source, the fewer photons are likely to hit it. When we look at a star in the sky, we look directly at the source, where the photons are closest together. Traffic lights, to use another example, are too weak to even illuminate the sidewalk just a few feet below them, yet can still be easily visible from hundreds of feet away, because we see the densely packed photons at the source.

The quadratic decay of light means that there is a substantial increase in luminance in the vicinity of a light source. If you moved a light meter around a living room that is only illuminated by

Quadratic Light Decay

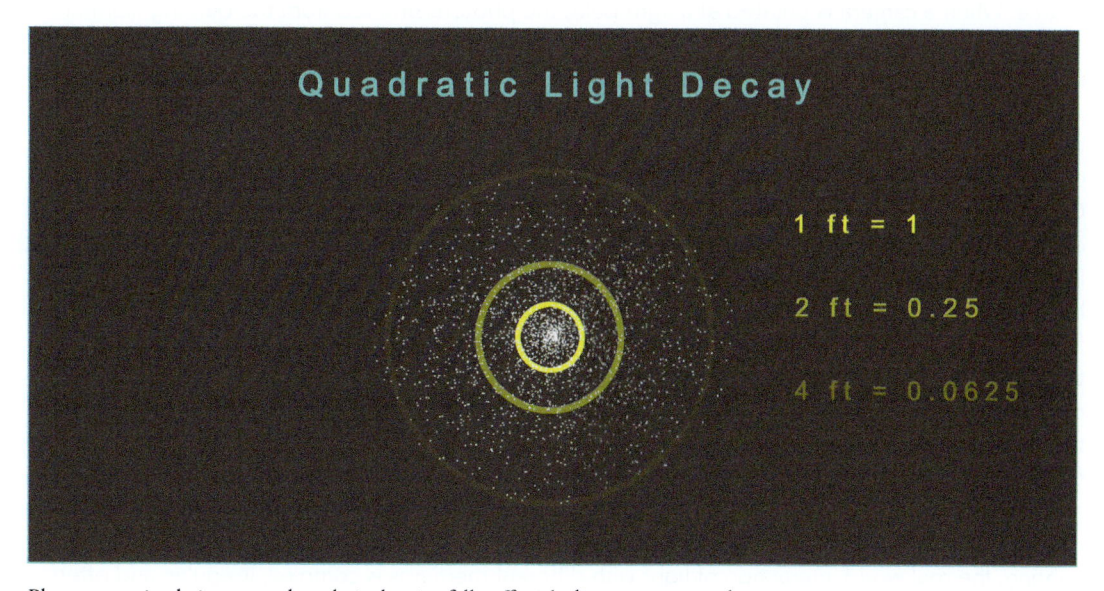

1 ft = 1

2 ft = 0.25

4 ft = 0.0625

Photons retain their energy, but their density falls off with distance at a quadratic pace.

Pulling down the exposure shows the huge spike in luminance in the vicinity of the light sources.

artificial lights, you would notice the luminance values spiking sharply when the meter is close to a lamp. If you would do the same during daytime, the values will spike even higher when you aim the meter at a window (the window is of course not a light source, but it is an opening to the considerably brighter environment outside). This is important, particularly in the context of specular reflections. Typically, light sources are much more dominant in specular reflections than the rest of the environment, due to that pronounced spike in luminosity (more on this in Chapter 5).

Direct and Indirect Illumination

The only way our eyes (or the camera) can pick up direct light is by looking straight at the light source. When a camera is pointed at a light bulb, the photons emitted from the burning filament reach the sensor on a direct path. We can therefore say that the sensor is recording **direct illumination**. Everything else that is visible in the frame is the result of **indirect illumination** – photons that bounce off one or more surfaces before reaching the sensor. Simply put, most of the light that the camera captures is indirect (bounced light). This notion is, however, somewhat confusing for digital artists, because direct and indirect illumination is defined differently in CG jargon, where the distinction is based on the light-receiving surface, not the camera: if a certain surface is illuminated directly by a light source, it is said to be receiving direct light. If it is illuminated by light that is bouncing off surrounding surfaces, it is said to be receiving indirect light. This separation makes more sense from a rendering perspective: direct light is substantially faster to calculate and less noisy than indirect light (it is coming from a small, defined area rather than from multiple surfaces and directions). But in real-world terms, even the separation between direct and indirect light is somewhat artificial. One can argue, for example, that a camera aimed at the sun is not recording purely direct light – by the time sunlight reaches the sensor it has passed through many miles of air, water droplets, and dust, and has already been scattered, absorbed, and refracted to a certain extent. Categorizing light as direct or indirect is helpful when analyzing photographs and understanding light behavior, but it is important to remember that, unlike in CG lighting, the real-world interaction of light with different mediums is complex, irregular, and often difficult to categorize neatly.

Direct / Indirect Illumination

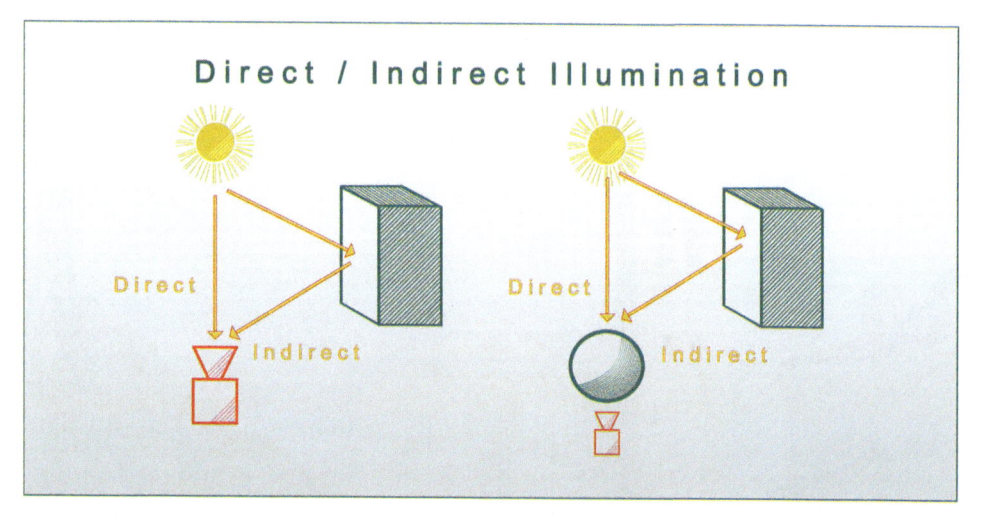

Left: In real-world/photographic terms, the camera is capturing direct illumination only if it is aimed at a light source – everything else is reflected/scattered light. Right: in CG, the distinction is made per surface: is it receiving direct or reflected light?

What Is "Ambient Light"?

It is more of a notion than a physical definition. In other words, there really is no such thing as "ambient light". This may sound like an odd statement, considering how much we use this term in digital (as well as traditional) art. Let me explain: first, we need to acknowledge that the term ambient light has more than one meaning, depending on the context: when photographers talk about ambient light, they usually refer to the existing, available light in the scene (as opposed to additional lighting supplemented by the photographer). For an interior designer, the term ambient light distinguishes between the basic, general lighting layer in a room and more specific lighting layers such as task lighting and accent lighting. These usages of the term ambient light are quite different from (and not related to) the particular meaning I am referring to here: the common use of the term "ambient light" in visual art (and specifically in digital art) to describe the sort of complementary, soft, uniform light in the scene that does not seem to be coming from a distinct source or direction and is not casting distinct shadows.

This categorization can be misleading, because it infers that such a light exists as a discrete entity that is separate from other "direct" lights in the scene, or that some light is "directional" and some is "non-directional". In the real world, there is of course no separate "ambient light emitter", and all light is directional (every photon moves from point A to point B). All illumination starts out as directional light emitted from a distinct source, but some of this illumination becomes multi-directional, as it bounces off surfaces or is scattered by solid, liquid, or gaseous volumes. In CG lighting, for example, it is common to pair a directional "sunlight" with a separate spherical "sky light" to simulate natural daylight (see Chapter 11). This is an effective shortcut in CG, but it does not truly represent reality. The sky, of course, is not a light emitter, and the soft, multi-directional light that emanates from it originates exclusively from the sun and is tightly connected to it. The type of soft light in a room illuminated by a window on a cloudy day is commonly referred to as "ambient light", but all of it is coming from one source: the sun. It is thus more accurate to use terms such as **diffused light** or **scattered light**.

LIGHT ESSENTIALS

Direct sunlight is visibly hitting parts of the church. But the rest of the scene is also illuminated by sunlight that has been scattered by the atmosphere. All the light in this photo, therefore, originates from a single source, and there is no separate ambient light component.

Does this distinction really matter? It does, especially nowadays, when CG rendering is getting closer and closer to a true simulation of real-world light behavior and relies heavily on accurate global illumination. When lighting a CG scene or integrating elements with footage, it is better to avoid looking at any portion of the light as "ambient", and instead see it in context of the environment's light source/s and the subsequent interaction events (such as reflection or scattering) that cause it to become diffused and soft.

Chapter 5

Light Interaction

As light travels through vacuum, nothing about it changes: the photons move at a constant speed and in a straight path, and carry the same energy (frequency). They may continue, unaffected, for an infinite distance and time – indeed, we can see through telescopes celestial bodies that are millions of light years away. But this perpetual motion is interrupted when light photons encounter an obstacle. That obstacle can be anything from a lone molecule in a thinly spaced gaseous volume, to a wall of densely packed electrons in a solid metallic surface (for the sake of simplicity, I will use the term "volume" here to collectively refer to solids, liquids, and gases). When a photon interacts with the molecules in a volume, three main outcomes are possible:

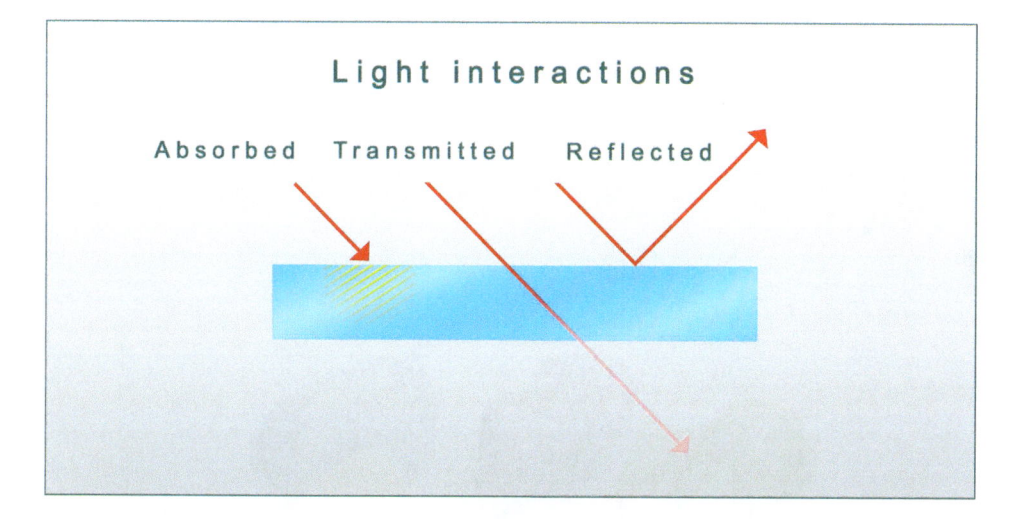

- **Absorption**: the photon's energy is converted into another type of energy (heat) which is no longer in the visible light spectrum.
- **Reflection and scattering**: the photons are reemitted from the volume's molecules, at predictable angles or in random directions.
- **Transmission (transparency)**: the photons are transmitted through the volume and exit at the other end.

These basic interaction events are at the core of every aspect discussed in this part of the book, from the appearance of the sky or the visual characteristics of different materials to fog or lens flares. The following brief description of each of the three main interaction types should serve as a base for further understanding light interaction.

Absorption

Absorption has nothing to do with how soft, thick, or "spongy" a material is. Like all light interactions, it happens at the molecular level. A surface can be highly absorbent to certain light frequencies and still be hard as steel or thinner than paper. Think of different car paints – each paint's color is determined by the light frequencies it absorbs, yet white, blue, or black car paints all have the same material consistency. The term absorption is thus somewhat misleading – photons are not "swallowed" by the volume, rather, their interaction with the electrons in the material's atoms transforms their energy.

Here is a simplified way to describe the physical process: imagine that the electrons are attached to the atom's nucleus by springs, and constantly vibrate at a certain frequency. That frequency (known as the "natural frequency") is different and specific for each type of atom. Now, each photon also carries a certain frequency, and when that frequency matches the electrons' natural frequency, the electrons vibrate in resonance. This high excitation of the electrons is passed from atom to atom and transforms the photon's energy to heat. If, on the other hand, the photon's frequency does not match the electrons' natural frequency, a brief period of electron excitation re-emits the photon (the photon is reflected/scattered). Absorption therefore affects the color of a surface by way of negation: the perceived color of a certain surface is the incident light color minus any absorbed frequencies. Absorption does not only affect the reflected light's frequency balance (i.e. its hue), it also affects its intensity. Black surfaces are much darker than white surfaces because most of the light energy is absorbed and very little is reflected. A similar loss of energy

These toy pieces are all made from the same plastic material, but different paint pigments on each surface absorb different wavelengths.

happens when light is transmitted through a semi-transparent material. Tinted glass absorbs some of the light, which results in darker transparency, as only a portion of the original light energy is transmitted.

Reflection and Scattering

Any surface that is not emitting light is visible only because it is reflecting light. Every photograph and every frame of a movie is essentially a capture of (mostly) reflected light, and every CG render is first and foremost a representation of reflected light. Reflection is therefore the most important aspect of the three main light interactions, and understanding reflection is key for any digital artist who strives to create photoreal imagery.

First, let us clarify the definition of reflection. In common discourse, we use the word reflection to describe the mirror-like appearance of the environment on smooth, shiny surfaces, like reflections in a lake, in a window, or on the surface of a chrome ball. But dull, rough, matte surfaces like wood, rubber, fabric, or paper reflect light too. The difference between what we commonly call "reflective" and "non-reflective" (or "matte") depends on whether the photons are reflected at a unified, predictable angle, or bounce off in random directions. An "orderly", predictable reflection is called a **specular reflection**, while a random, chaotic reflection is called a **diffuse reflection**. While most CG workflows separate the two types of reflections (diffuse controls the color of the surfaces, and specular controls its shininess), in reality they are not so neatly divided, and there is no precise boundary or distinct separation between specular and diffuse reflections (one could say that a diffuse reflection is just a "messed-up specular reflection"). Still, it is important to examine each of the two reflection types separately to get a better understanding of the differences and how they affect the characteristics of various materials.

Specular Reflection

Squash players can anticipate the ball's trajectory even before it bounces off the wall, because they know that the bounce angle will be the same as the incoming angle. A ball that travels straight toward the wall will bounce straight back, while a ball that travels at an angle will bounce off at the same angle but mirrored along the wall's facing direction. The law of reflection states that: "the angle of reflection is equal to the angle of incidence". If you draw a line that represents the facing direction of a flat surface (the **surface normal**), than a photon hitting the surface at a certain angle relative to the surface normal will reflect at exactly the same angle in the opposite direction. Now replace the squash wall with a mirror, and the single squash ball with billions of photons: in a perfect specular reflection, every single photon bounces off the mirror at exactly the same angle. This means that every detail in the reflected image is preserved – no blurring, no displacement, no distortion or degradation.

Mirrors are an excellent example for specular reflectivity because they are manufactured to produce the clearest reflection possible. A mirror must allow light to follow the law of reflection with minimal deviations. This requires a material that is consistently smooth even on a microscopic level. Any irregularities in the material must be smaller than the wavelength of the incident light, to ensure that photons are uniformly reflected at a predictable angle and do not scatter. The amount and scale of a material's micro-roughness is the principal deciding factor between specular

Specular Reflection

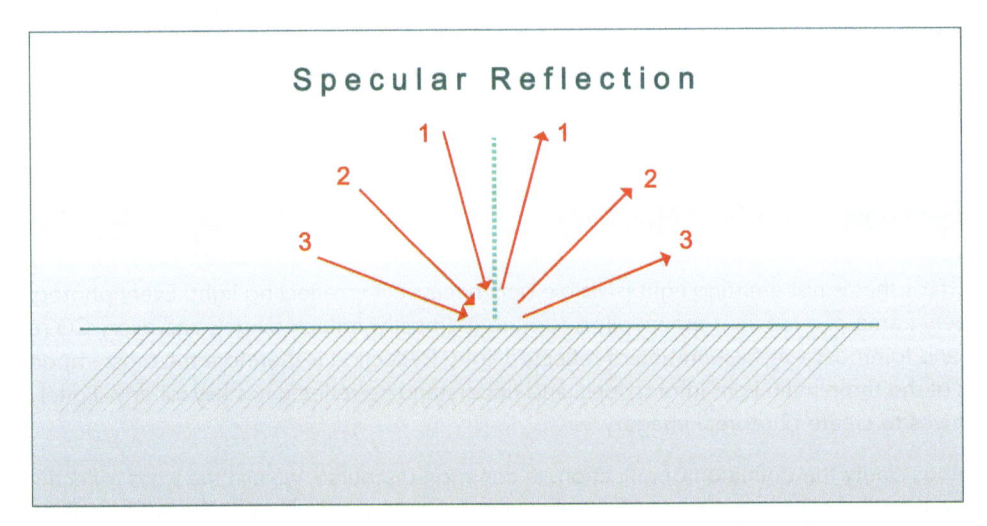

The angle of reflection is equal to the angle of incidence, mirrored along the normal (cyan line).

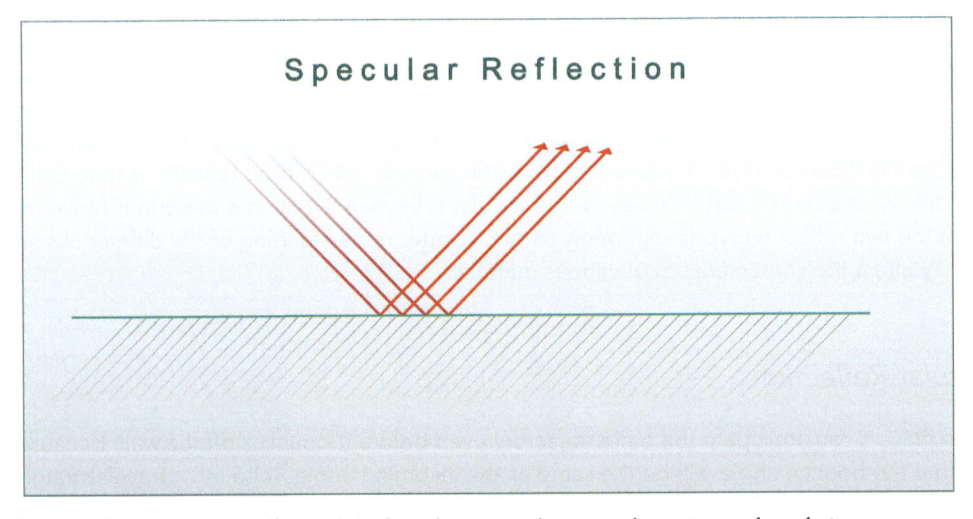

Specular Reflection

A perfect specular reflection transforms the reflected image without any distortion or degradation.

and diffuse reflections. Glass is a non-crystalline material and has no grain boundaries, which makes it an ideal material for mirrors (especially when coated with silver or aluminum to boost its reflectivity). But on top of its microscopic smoothness, the mirror glass must also be perfectly polished and even. A curved mirror is still highly specular, but it produces a distorted reflection. This does not happen because the photons are being scattered in different directions – they still bounce at a predictable angle, but the facing normals of the mirror change along its curvature, which affects the angle of the reflected photons and distorts the reflected image.

Most specular surfaces do not reflect as perfectly as mirrors. Imperfect or partial specular reflections blur the reflected image to some degree, and when that happens, the brightest areas in the reflection are naturally the last ones to remain distinct. Since light sources are substantially brighter than their surroundings, their appearance in a soft specular reflection can greatly affect its visibility and intensity. Where a light source (including the sky or even a window) is reflected, the

Specular On Curvature

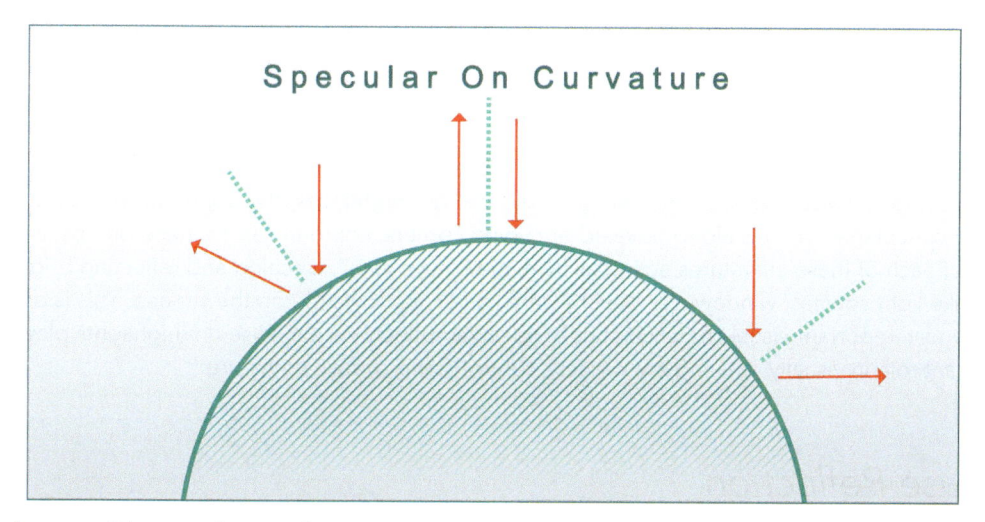

The direction of the normals varies along a curved surface, which changes the angle of reflection and distorts the image – just like a fish-eye lens.

specular reflection is substantially brighter and more noticeable. This dominance of light sources or very bright areas of the environment in specular reflections is commonly called **highlights**. If we want to catch a highlight on a flat surface, we need to aim that surface directly toward the light source. But what happens when the surface is curved?

Replace a flat mirror with a chrome ball. The spherical surface acts very much like a fish-eye lens – it covers a much wider angle, reflecting a much larger portion of the surrounding environment.

These spoons display different specular characteristics. Notice the mirror-like, detailed reflections on the metal spoons. The top spoon's surface is just slightly rougher, showing a softer reflected image. In contrast, the reflection on the non-metallic green spoon is much more subdued, showing mainly the brightest parts. Notice the rim highlight along the side. Finally, the wooden spoon may have some specularity, but the roughness is so strong that reflections are practically invisible.

LIGHT INTERACTION

Such a curved surface has a much higher chance of reflecting a light source than a flat surface. If you photograph a reflective cube and a reflective sphere on a sunny day, you will need to carefully rotate the cube to catch the direct reflection of the sun. The sphere, on the other hand, stands a 50% chance of reflecting the sun – if the sun is anywhere in the hemisphere behind the camera, it will be visible in the specular reflection. This is the reason why specular reflections are much more noticeable on curved surfaces. What we generally call **rim highlights**, the appearance of bright, distinct specular reflections along beveled or curved corners, contours, and surface bumps, is the result of each of these curvatures acting as a "mini-fish-eye lens", catching and reflecting bright areas like light sources, windows, or the sky within a very narrow area on the surface. This is one of the most important visual characteristics of specular reflections, because rim highlights play an important role in visually defining the object's contours and surface curvature.

Diffuse Reflection

The micro-structure of highly specular materials has very few irregularities at the scale of the light wavelengths – it is flat and smooth, just like a squash wall. Now imagine playing squash against a rocky cliff full of outcrops and cavities: it would be virtually impossible to anticipate the trajectory of the bouncing ball. Many materials are composed of microscopic "pieces" (called **grain**) bound together. These pieces can be crystals (polycrystalline materials like rock and ceramics) or fibers (materials like wood, paper, and fabric). The irregularity of grain and grain boundaries causes the photons to scatter in random directions as they hit the surface. Light is reflected, but the arbitrary direction of the photons means that detail of the reflected image is not preserved. Perfectly diffused reflection appears as a uniform color rather than an image of the environment, as the outcome of photons reflecting in random directions is an average of the light intensities, not unlike applying a very heavy blur to a photo. That color represents those frequencies that have not been absorbed, so the balance between absorption and diffuse reflection is what gives a surface its color (hence the term **"diffuse color"**).

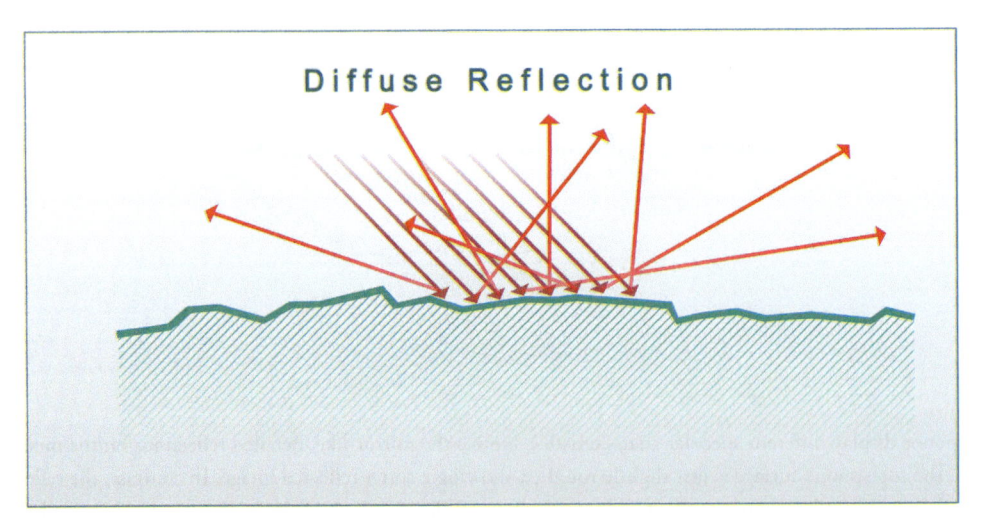

Micro-roughness causes reflected light to bounce in random directions. The reflected image becomes completely diffused.

Scattering

Diffuse reflection is in fact a form of scattering, a much broader term that is used in physics to describe a wide range of interactions and disturbances between particles, atoms, and molecules. While many scattering phenomena are not related to visible light, there are some specific types of light scattering that greatly affect the visual world. The term scattering is often used to describe light being diffusely reflected by particles or gas molecules. Typical light scattering occurs when light hits dust, smoke, or water particles, and in Chapter 6 we will look at Rayleigh and Mie scattering and their important contribution to daylight and the appearance of the atmosphere.

Subsurface Scattering

Going back to the example of playing squash against a cliff full of outcrops and cavities, the ball may sometimes enter one of the cavities, bounce inside a few times and then exit at a different location from where it first hit the cliff. In most non-metallic materials, diffuse reflection also involves at least some penetration of photons below the surface. This internal scattering, and the slight displacement of photons off their original course contributes to the characteristic "soft" feel of many diffuse surfaces. When the photon penetration is deeper and more pronounced (as in marble), materials take on a sort of milky appearance, as the surface features become slightly blurred and less defined. When the penetration is even deeper and the scattering radius larger (as in wax or human skin) the material appears to be almost translucent, although light is not really transmitted through it (see next section).

Subsurface scattering is in fact a CG term, and it is usually an additional shader parameter that is separate from diffuse reflection (see Chapter 12). Although this makes sense on a practical level (subsurface scattering is computationally intensive, and many diffuse materials can be emulated well enough without it), it is important to note here that subsurface scattering is not exclusive to only a few special materials, neither is it a separate process from diffuse reflection. In fact, it is an integral part of the diffuse characteristic of almost all dielectric (non-metallic) materials.

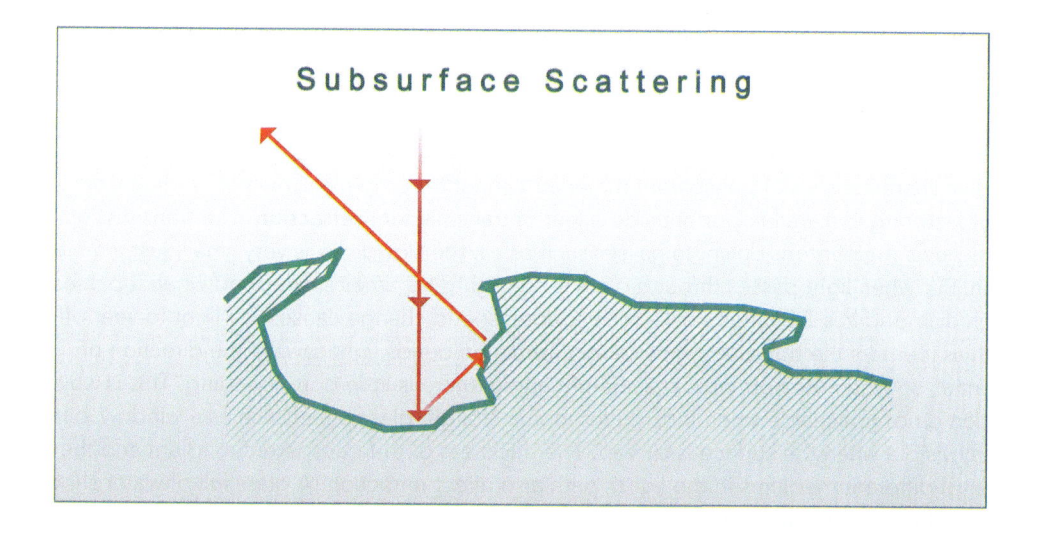

Each of these objects shows some amount of subsurface scattering, giving them a subtle "soft" look: various leaves (A), a marble bowl and polished marbles (B), a wax candle and lacquered clay candle holder (C), a plastic soap dispenser (D).

Transmission and Refraction

Whenever light is not completely absorbed or reflected by a volume, the photons are transmitted through the volume and exit on the opposite side. We perceive a surface as transparent when reflected light from objects behind the surface (or direct light from a source) is transmitted through it and reaches our eyes, allowing us to "see through" that surface. Just like specular reflections, clear transmission happens in materials that have a uniform microscopic structure with little or no grain to scatter the light and cloud the transparency. Clear liquids like pure water are a good example. Glass is not a typical solid either (In fact, it is considered "super-cooled liquid"). When the structure of the material is less uniform, the transmitted light is scattered within the volume, and the transmitted image becomes blurry. Such materials are often called **translucent**, but one can say that the difference between translucency and transparency is similar to the difference between diffuse and specular reflections – translucency is a "messed up transparency", as light is transmitted and scattered at the same time.

The visual characteristics of transparent materials cannot be properly simulated in digital art without factoring in the all-important side effect of transmission: **refraction**. The transmission process slows the photons down. In gasses such as air, the slowdown is very small, just a mere fraction. But when light passes through glass it is roughly 1.5 times slower, and when it passes through diamond it is 2.5 times slower. The sudden speed change causes the light to veer off its path as it enters the transmitting medium. Refraction bends light toward the direction of the normal, so when the normal is at a straight angle, there is little or no bending. This is why refraction is not noticeable when looking through a straight glass panel such as a window, but is clearly visible when the surface is curved. The thickness of the transparent medium and the number of different mediums in the light's path also affect refraction. A glass full of water shows stronger refraction than an empty one.

Refraction

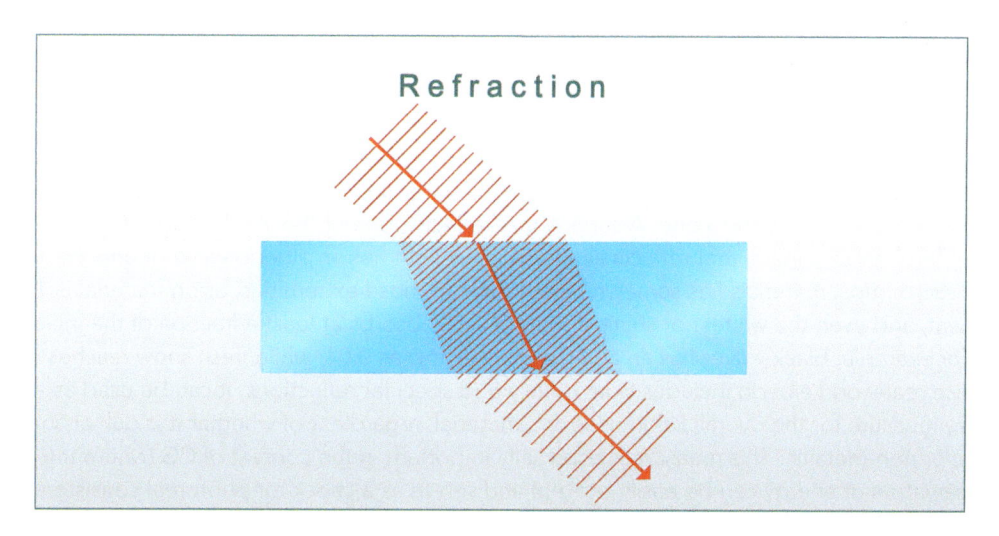

The ratio between the speed of light in vacuum and the speed of light within a certain volume is called the **refractive index** (also **index of refraction**, or **IOR**). The higher the ratio, the stronger the deviation, and subsequently, the distortion of the transmitted image. The IOR of water is 1.33, and most liquids like alcohol or oil have an IOR between 1.33 and 1.5; the human cornea has an IOR of around 1.38; plate (window) glass has an IOR of 1.5, and most transparent plastics hover around this value; some gemstones and minerals have values higher than 2, with diamond at 2.42 and silicone at 3.45. However, as you can tell, the IOR of most transparent materials lies within a rather limited range of 1.33 to 2.5. So, in most cases, incorrect IOR is not as detrimental to photorealism as some may think, especially since we are not inherently sensitive to this aspect (most people will not notice anything wrong in a render of a wine glass that has an IOR of 2.5). That said, refraction index plays other roles in physically based rendering, such as determining the amount of Fresnel effect (see Chapters 9 and 12), so adherence to correct IOR in CG rendering is still advisable.

An empty wine glass shows only minimal refraction, but when filled with water, the much thicker volume and the transmission through two different materials increase the effect of refraction substantially.

LIGHT INTERACTION

Albedo

According to the **law of conservation of energy**, a surface cannot reflect more light than it receives. The combined luminance of both the diffuse and specular reflections can never exceed the luminance of the incident light. Albedo is a simple measurement of a surface's reflective luminosity on a scale of zero to one. A surface that reflects none of the incident light has an albedo value of zero, and a surface that reflects all the incident light has an albedo value of one. Naturally, the albedo of most materials lies somewhere in between those extremities, as no material is 100% absorbent, and even the whitest or shiniest material still absorbs at least a fraction of the incident light. For example, black velvet has an albedo value as low as 0.01, while fresh snow reaches 0.9. Since real-world albedo includes both diffuse and specular reflections, it can be used as an effective measure for the overall brightness of a material, regardless of whether it is dull or shiny, metallic or non-metallic. This measure is especially important in the context of CG (where the law of conservation of energy can be easily broken) and serves as a check for photoreal consistency. In CG, separating the diffuse and specular albedos can help gauge the balance within a specific material, and how it is affected by absorption and transmission. For example, the diffuse albedo of clear glass is very low (nearly black), even though there is almost no absorption. Instead, most of the light is either transmitted or reflected.

It is, of course, not possible to extract an albedo image from a real photograph, but a CG render engine can easily do that. The image on the right is a diffuse albedo pass of the full render (left). Notice that metallic (fully specular) and transparent surfaces are black (zero diffuse albedo).

Case Study: Side by Side Comparison

© Pasquale Scionti.

Pasquale Scionti is an architectural visualization artist with an impressive talent for producing photoreal interior renders (several examples of his artwork are featured in this book). In this particular work, Pasquale offers us a rare opportunity to compare, side by side, his CG render and the photograph that he used as reference. This is unique, because Pasqual's render (top image) is strikingly similar to its real-world inspiration (bottom image). When I first saw these images, I thought that the bottom image was simply an improved version of the render. The fact that I did not immediately realize that one is a CG render and the other a photo speaks volumes about the quality of this artist's work. Conversely, the fact that I preferred the photograph over its CG emulation shows how elusive the goal of photorealism is, even when we get as close as Pasquale did here.

What makes this render so successful, and where can it still be improved? The area of the sofa and the wall behind it, in my opinion, is outstandingly photoreal, and cannot be distinguished from the photo. The leather texture, the blanket and pillows, the plants, the carpet – the entire left half of the image is incredibly well done. Where the CG may be lacking compared to the photo is mostly in the window area: the trees outside, though nothing more than blurry yellowish smudges in the photo, add the kind of depth and detail that is missing from the render. A subtle bloom effect is a good addition around areas of bright light (see Chapter 10), but here it seems a tad too strong, almost sucking the color out of the objects on and around the window sill. Adding some out of focus exterior detail, reducing the light bloom and bringing back some color and definition around the window could lift this fantastic render even higher. But, to be perfectly honest, would I even point out these specific factors without being able to compare the render to a photograph? Most likely not. Photorealism is tricky – it is easier to achieve when we reference real-world footage, yet this process also exposes the tiniest facets that can otherwise go completely unnoticed.

Chapter 6

Daylight

Earth is illuminated by a single source of light: a G2 V type yellow dwarf star, roughly 93 million miles (150 million km) away. But the light generated from this lone star would have felt very different without the other, inseparable component of daylight: earth's atmosphere. Even Though it does not produce any light of its own, this thin layer of gases acts as a multi-purpose diffuser/reflector/filter that affects the constant, unchangeable sunlight in a myriad of ways and generates the richly varied qualities of daytime light. Understanding the complex interaction between sunlight and the atmosphere is the key to simulating realistic outdoor daytime lighting and plausible environments.

The Sun

The sun is a sphere of hot plasma roughly 860,000 miles in diameter. Light radiates from it in all directions, in the same way light radiates from a light bulb. However, what makes the sun such a unique light source on earth is the fact that it is so far away. It is impossible to illustrate the actual distance between earth and the sun on a single page, but this great online true-scale illustration by Josh Worth, "*If the Moon Were Only 1 Pixel*" (http://joshworth.com/dev/pixelspace/pixelspace_solarsystem.html), provides a frighteningly true sense of how incredibly far the sun is. That distance, as well as the miniscule size of earth relative to that distance, means that we are receiving only an extremely narrow slice of sunlight rays. If you draw many lines emanating from a circle (the sun) and then place the earth at the correct relative scale and distance, you'd see that the earth sits on a single line, with the nearest lines virtually parallel (here is another useful animation: https://javalab.org/en/parallel_rays_of_sun_en/). So, is sunlight on earth parallel? Not exactly: even when factoring our distance from it, the fact that the sun is such an enormous light source means that some of the rays that reach us do so at slightly converging (or diverging) angles. But the difference is miniscule, no more than half a degree, and while mathematically sunlight rays on earth are not absolutely parallel, for all practical (and visual) purposes they are. Direct sunlight hits every object in our view at the same angle, and its shadows are always parallel. This is distinctly different from any other light source we experience on earth, natural or man-made. The inverse square rule applies to sunlight as it applies to any light. Indeed, Mercury's sun-facing side receives substantially more radiation than, say, Mars, and even on our planet, there's a significant difference between the equator and the poles (which are farther away from the sun). But for all visual purposes, sunlight has no perceivable distance-related decay. On a clear, dry day, there is no perceivable difference in sunlight intensity between an object right next to the camera and one five miles away (the atmosphere, of course does have an effect over distance, as will be discussed later in this chapter).

To experience raw, unfiltered sunlight, we need to go up above the atmosphere. Nowadays we are used to seeing space photography, so it's easy to forget that up until October 24, 1946 (when the first grainy photograph from space was taken by a camera mounted on a German V2 rocket), people had no way of experiencing such visual oddities as bright sunlight in a pitch-black sky, the stark contrast between light and shadow in space, or the eerily sharp and depthless horizon on the moon. But thanks to more than 70 years of space photography, we have substantial visual reference to what raw sunlight looks like. First, the color: the sun emits radiation across much of the electromagnetic spectrum, including X-rays, ultraviolet, infrared, and the full range of visible light. So, without atmospheric filtering, sunlight is white – not yellowish or orange as we experience it on earth.

In the absence of any scattered sunlight, fully occluded areas are very dark. Shadows are only illuminated by reflected light from nearby surfaces. If no such bounce light exists, shadows are truly black. For example, in many of the iconic Apollo moonwalk photographs, the astronaut's shadow on the lunar ground is pitch black, yet the fully occluded areas of his spacesuit are still relatively bright. This is because the spacesuit is illuminated by light bouncing off the ground, yet there is nothing above the lunar surface to bounce light back onto the shadows on the ground. Imagine daylight on earth without atmosphere: sunlight is white, harsh, and consistent day-in day-out. There is extreme contrast between lit and occluded areas, and shadows are always sharp and

Two photographs from the Apollo 11 mission. Notice the bright unfiltered light, harsh, pitch-black shadows, and complete lack of atmospheric depth. The shadowed parts on the spacesuit are much less dark than the shadows on the ground because of reflected light from the ground.

© NASA.

well defined. Sunsets are a rather dull affair, a simple transition from full illumination to complete darkness as the sun unceremoniously disappears behind the horizon. The sky is always pitch black and the horizon always clear and well-defined, without the familiar visual cues for distance and depth. But thanks to our atmosphere, this harsh white light is transformed into the constantly shifting visual magic we call daytime light.

The Atmosphere

The layer of gases that envelopes earth is comprised mostly of nitrogen and oxygen, about 1% of argon, and small traces of other gases like carbon dioxide, helium, and methane. It also contains some water vapor, with amounts varying from mere traces in dry areas to about 5% in humid tropical areas. Most of the atmosphere's mass (about three quarters) is concentrated in the first 6.8 miles (11 kilometers) above earth's surface, and the rest gradually thins out over a distance of several hundred miles (thus there is no precise definition of the atmosphere's height). Closer to the surface, additional elements like dust, pollen, and other particles (mainly from human pollution) may also be present in the atmosphere.

Like other gases, air molecules are spaced far apart. However, the thickness of the atmosphere layer means that collision events between air molecules and photons are much more likely to happen. With the additional influence of other elements in the atmosphere such as water and

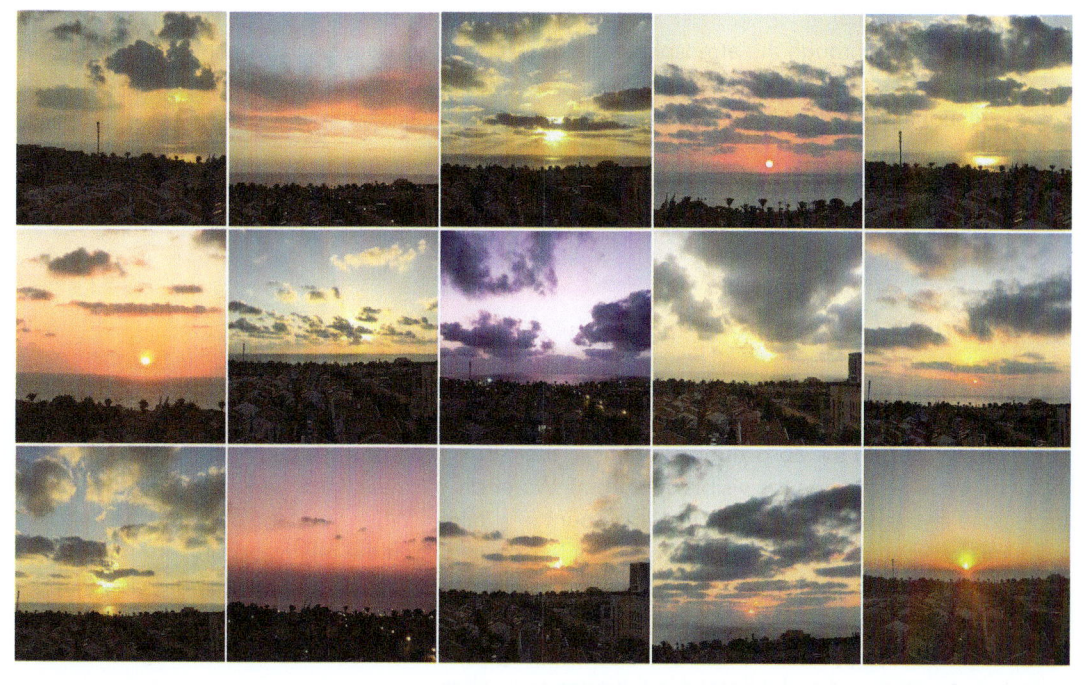

Every evening for several years, my father would take a photo of the sunset from the balcony with his phone. This small selection shows how differences in the balance of atmospheric elements can produce a stunning variety of moods and colors at one single location.

© Ouri Dinour.

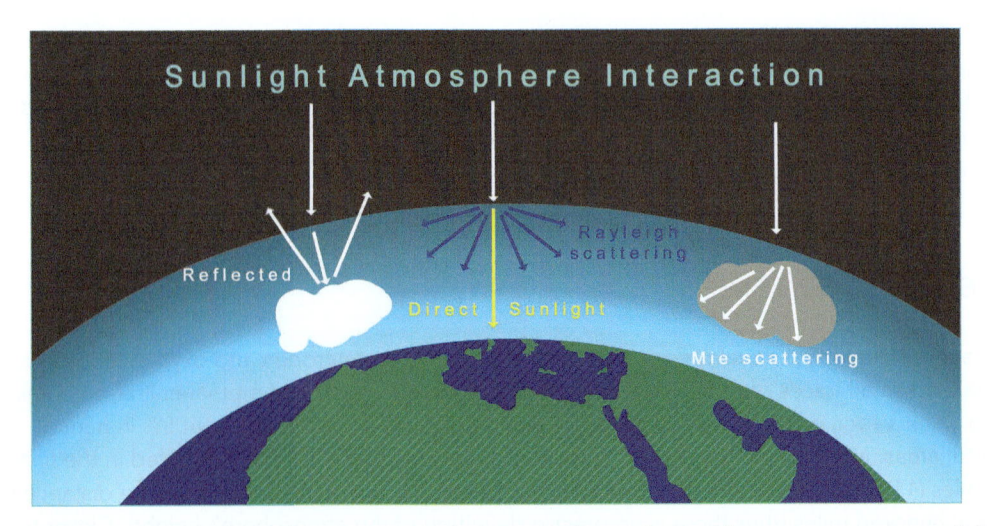

The three main outcomes of sunlight interaction with the atmosphere: reflection/absorption, scattering, and direct sunlight.

dust, the atmosphere becomes a considerable obstacle that substantially alters sunlight. When a sunlight photon enters the atmosphere, three main outcomes are possible:

- It can be absorbed or reflected by atmospheric elements (in which case it never reaches earth's surface).
- It can pass through the atmosphere and reach earth's surface as direct sunlight.
- It can be scattered by air molecules or larger particles and reach earth's surface as multi-directional scattered light.

Daylight is a combination of all three outcomes, and to better understand their collective effect, we will examine each of them separately.

Reflection and Absorption

Just a little less than half of the sun's radiation that reaches earth never makes it through to the ground. About a quarter is reflected into space, and another fifth or so is absorbed by the atmosphere (most of the absorption happens in the ozone layer and affects mostly ultraviolet radiation, which is outside the visible spectrum). Water droplets in clouds are highly reflective, and thick cloud layers can reflect a substantial amount of sunlight. When you take off on a plane under a cloudy sky, you may experience the strong difference between the relatively dark, attenuated light on the ground, and the bright light above the clouds, which is augmented by the cloud layer, which acts as a formidable light reflector. Seen from above, even the most massive storm clouds are white, but they appear particularly dark from the ground because most of the sunlight has already been scattered and reflected in their upper reaches.

While the amount and density of clouds in the sky significantly affects the attenuation of sunlight on the ground, other types of particles contribute as well. Absorption and reflection by dust, smoke, or pollution further reduces sunlight brightness. Like all atmospheric light interaction,

Clouds act as a formidable reflector, bouncing sunlight back into space and substantially attenuating daylight on the ground.

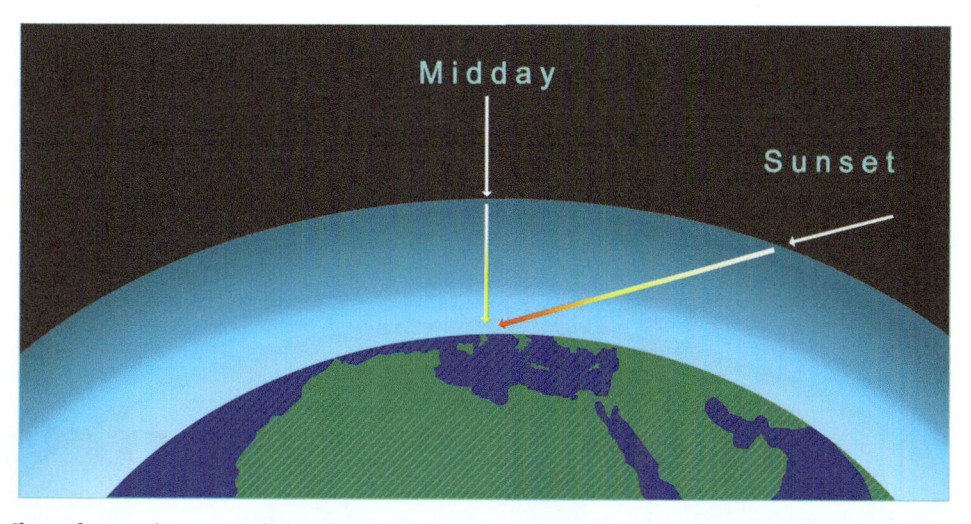

The effects of atmosphere on sunlight substantially increase during sunrise and sunset, as sunlight travels longer through the atmosphere.

the amount of attenuation strongly depends on the position of the sun in the sky. When the sun is at the zenith, sunlight travels through the least amount of atmosphere before reaching the ground, but when the sun is low on the horizon, its light needs to travel a considerably longer path through the atmosphere (and atmospheric elements like clouds or dust) before it reaches our eyes. Sunlight attenuation is thus substantially stronger during sunrise and sunset, so much so that when the sun is low enough, we can stare at it directly without any harm to the eyes.

Atmospheric Scattering

Scattering happens when a light photon collides with a molecule or a particle and is redirected while retaining most of its energy. Scattered light is widely propagated through the atmosphere with little attenuation, and hits the ground from multiple directions, from the zenith down to the horizon. Scattering effectively converts the sky into a giant diffuser (or softbox) which transforms direct sunlight into multi-directional diffused light. This effect is called **diffuse sky radiation**, or sometime just **skylight**. The latter term is both accurate and inaccurate – the light is indeed coming from the sky, but the sky is not a light source, it merely propagates the light of the sun. Two principal types of scattering, **Rayleigh scattering** and **Mie scattering**, happen in the atmosphere, and the balance between them, as well as the balance between direct and scattered sunlight, all contribute to the infinitely varied color and character of daytime light and the appearance of the sky.

Rayleigh Scattering

The most transformative effect of the atmosphere on sunlight, Rayleigh scattering occurs when sunlight photons hit air molecules (mostly nitrogen and oxygen) which are smaller than the light's wavelengths. Rayleigh scattering affects shorter wavelengths more than longer ones, so blue and violet light is scattered considerably more than red and yellow light. This gives the clear sky its distinct blue color (and diffused sky radiation a bluish tint). It also strips some violet and blue from the white sunlight, causing direct light to tint toward yellow. At sunrise and sunset, when the sun is low on the horizon and its light passes through substantially more atmosphere before reaching the surface, the increased scattering removes even more of the short wavelengths, tinting sunlight color further toward orange and red.

Rayleigh scattering caused by air molecules accounts for the blue color of the sky, but Mie scattering, caused by low-altitude water droplets and dust particles shifts the horizon color toward white.

Mie Scattering

Mie scattering happens when photons hit particles that are larger than the radiation wavelength. These particles are commonly water droplets (in humid air and clouds) or dust, but they can also be smoke and pollution particles. As with Rayleigh scattering, sunlight photons are redirected in all directions, but Mie scattering is not wavelength-dependent, and since all frequencies are scattered equally, sunlight color remains unchanged in the process. The perceived color of Mie scattering depends on how sunlight color is shifted by Rayleigh scattering. When the sun is it at the zenith and sunlight is closest to white, clouds are white too (or grey, where attenuation happens). As the sun moves toward the horizon, Rayleigh scattering shifts sunlight color toward orange and red, which in turn affects the color of Mie scattering. During sunrise and sunset, clouds, humidity, dust and pollution take an orange/red tint, especially around the sun.

Since water and dust particles lie mostly in the lowest layers of the atmosphere, Mie scattering is considerably more visible at the horizon than at the zenith. In general, the horizon appears brighter and more desaturated, but the color shift and the rate of gradation from zenith to horizon can change drastically depending on the time of day and the atmospheric conditions – from pale blue or white or grey at midday, to yellow/orange/red during sunset and sunrise. It is important to note that the air in the atmosphere remains blue during sunset and sunrise. It is the additional atmospheric elements (clouds, humidity, dust, and pollution) that turn red and create the familiar effect of "flaming sky" (indeed, some of the most spectacular sunsets occur when there is a strong presence of particles in the atmosphere).

When sunlight travels through more atmosphere, a larger amount of blue and violet light is scattered, and it takes a reddish hue. Mie scattering propagates that red light at lower altitudes where larger particles lie, but the blue color of Rayleigh scattering still dominates the higher altitudes.

Left: Volumetric scattering in water, showing the parallel nature of sunlight. Right: God rays are parallel too, and only seem to converge because of the effect of perspective over distance.

Volumetric Light

The term volumetric light comes from the CG world and is used for a wide range of scenarios where light beams are distinctly visible due to molecular or particle scattering. These scenarios include atmospheric phenomena like **crepuscular rays** (aka sun beams or god rays), shafts of sunlight entering a room, or spotlight beams on a stage. The two ingredients that are needed for such light beams to appear are a dense enough accumulation of particles like humidity, fog, smoke, or dust, and some kind of obstacle that creates distinct separation between light and shadow. In the case of sunlight rays in a room, the obstacle could be narrow slits in the blinds, an opaque/transparent pattern in the curtains, or a crack in a wooden wall. For crepuscular rays, it is usually a cloud formation with relatively small and well-defined gaps. In all these cases, it is the sharp contrast between light and shadow that makes scattered light appear as distinct rays rather than a general diffused glow. The direction of volumetric rays usually spreads out from the light source (though stage spotlights limit the spread to a narrow, focused area). The two exceptions are laser beams (essentially, an extremely focused light) and sunlight. God rays are in fact parallel, and only appear to be fanning out from a single point because of perspective (just like railroad tracks appear to be converging in the distance).

Aerial Perspective

The moon landing conspiracy theories must have been at least somewhat motivated by the Apollo moon photographs. After all, everything in those images, from nearby rocks to far-away mountains appears to be at the same distance from the camera. The complete lack of atmospheric perspective does make the lunar photos look as if they were shot in a studio with a black screen as a background. The accumulative influence of the atmosphere on the way objects appear at a distance is strongly ingrained in our spatial perception, and it constitutes a fundamental aspect in visual art, traditional or digital. **Aerial perspective** is the commonly used term for the atmospheric depth, but contrary to what the name implies, air is not the only factor in atmospheric depth.

The atmosphere is not just above and around us – it engulfs us. All the atmospheric light interactions described so far (absorption, reflection, attenuation, Rayleigh and Mie scattering) affect not only sunlight entering the atmosphere, but also the reflected light within the environment. Any object we photograph is visible because of light reflecting from its surface, and this reflected light needs to travel through a certain amount of atmosphere to reach the sensor. The farther the reflected light photons travel through the atmosphere, the more likely they are to be affected by it. On a clear, dry day, light reflected from an object 50 feet (15 meters) away does not pass through enough atmosphere to be affected in any perceivable way, and the air between the camera and the object appears to be completely transparent. However, light reflected from an object 5 miles (8 km) away passes through 500 times more atmospheric volume, which strongly influences the look of the object: its features become less pronounced, contrast and saturation are reduced, and the blacks are lifted.

Aerial perspective is affected by the same atmospheric elements that shape daylight: air, water droplets, dust, smoke, and pollutants. We commonly use the term "haze" to describe the effect of any one of these elements, but technically, haze only refers to the effect of dust and pollution, not air or humidity. A common phrase like "the bluish hills on a hazy summer afternoon" is not quite accurate – the bluishness of the hills is mostly due to air molecules (Rayleigh scattering), not haze (Mie scattering). Let's examine each atmospheric depth component separately:

Air

Rayleigh scattering is the dominant factor in the way air visually affects distant objects. Light reflected from the object is partially scattered by air molecules, and the farther away the object is, the more scattering happens. In terms of color values, the object does not get brighter nor darker. Rather, the blacks are lifted toward the midtones, which reduces contrast and "flattens" the object, making it harder to see distinct features. On a clear, dry day with minimal presence of clouds, fog, or aerosols, distant objects take on the classic bluish tint (aka "blue haze"). It is important to remember that brightness is not squashed by clean air. A bright specular reflection on a lake or a metallic surface can be as bright even when viewed from miles away. It is the low end that is the most heavily affected with distance, starting with the darkest blacks and gradually onto the lower midtones.

Rayleigh scattering of the light reflected from the hills increases with distance. For each layer in depth, contrast is reduced, blacks are lifted, and RGB values unify around desaturated blue. Notice that brightness is not reduced with distance.

Water Droplets

Humidity in the atmosphere has a similar effect to air, but Mie scattering does not tint the light, so distant objects on an overcast or foggy day retain their hues while the blacks are lifted toward neutral gray. In most environments (except in the driest deserts or high-altitude settings), there is usually some humidity hanging in the lower atmosphere. This causes some desaturation at the horizon, which shifts the deep blue hues of distant objects toward a more desaturated cyan or white (colors of distant objects may change to orange or red during sunset and sunrise). While the effect of air is always subtle, dense accumulation of water droplets in clouds and fog can dramatically change the scale of aerial perspective. Reflected light that passes through heavy fog, for example, is strongly scattered, reducing visibility from several miles to mere feet.

Rayleigh and Mie scattering create a mixed aerial perspective in this photo (left). When the photo is artificially "de-hazed", bands of white fog are revealed along the valleys and lower altitudes.

A combination of pollution aerosols and water droplets lies over Bogota, Colombia. Notice the difference in black levels between the foreground trees and the city.

Haze

Haze is formed by dry particles of dust, smoke, and pollutants. Like fog, heavy haze can dramatically reduce the scale of aerial perspective, but it also has a greater light attenuation effect. Haze not only lifts the blacks and decreases contrast – it can also reduce brightness, as light is not only scattered through the particles but is also heavily absorbed. Haze colors vary depending on the type of particles. Dust usually appears as brownish-orange haze while smoke and pollution cause grey or bluish haze. Lighter amounts of particles in the lower atmosphere often form a yellow-grey band at the horizon, and attenuate sunlight even further when the sun is low.

Case Study: Natural Environment in Clarisse IFX

© Aron Kamolz.

DAYLIGHT

Aron Kamolz is a freelance architect and self-taught 3D artist from Germany, who focuses on creating digital plants, assets, and landscapes. I asked Aron to discuss one of his natural environment renders, a river scene which he assembled and rendered in Clarisse IFX. Here is his description:

"I grew up in a rural area with a dense forest near our house, and as a child, I was interested in painting landscapes and trees. My interest in CG started in school where some of my friends played with an early version of *3DS Max*, but my real interest started later, during my architecture studies: I had to plan a site with lots of vegetation and stumbled upon Vue *Infinite*. I was amazed by the beautiful landscape renders you could achieve with it. I used it for my study-project, and after that I was very eager to learn more about Vue and CG in general. While I started working as a freelance architect, I also took my first steps as a CG artist in ArchViz, plant creation, and landscape renders for book covers and advertising, which eventually led me to work for *SideFX*, testing their new terrain tools in Houdini 16.

This image was inspired by a bike tour near my hometown. There are lots of little streams in this area, surrounded by dense trees. I recently discovered Clarisse IFX, in my opinion, a very powerful tool for building large and complex scenes, and I used it to create this particular render.
Creating the base landscape for this scene was quite simple, since I knew that much of it will be covered with dense trees. The terrain was generated in World Machine using a basic landscape setup. I then painted the river mask and extruded the riverbanks, then mixed in a little Perlin noise for additional detail and variation. I also used World Machine for the riverbed, which I exported as a height field map into Clarisse where I used it as a displacement map on a plane.

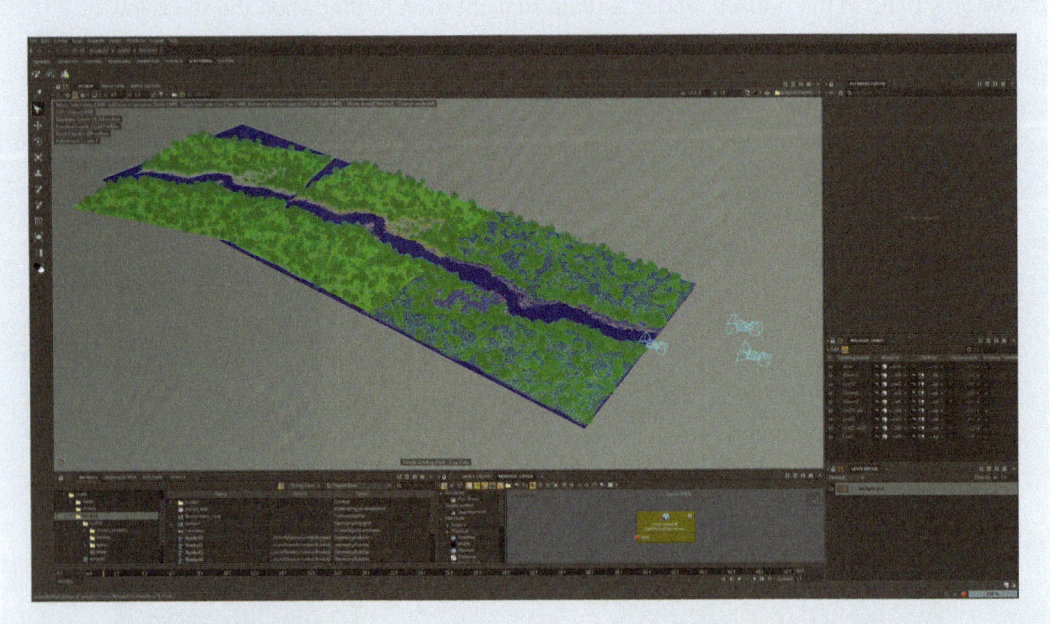

Laying out the scene in Clarisse.
© Aron Kamolz.

The vegetation was created with e-on software's Plant Factory and distributed in the scene using Clarisse's scattering system. I created a point cloud which was used to scatter the objects and added a more natural distribution using fractal functions to control the point cloud density, as well as a gradient to control the height and slope. Altogether I used four different scatter setups: one for the stones in the riverbed and on the riverbanks, a second one for the grass, the third for the bushes, and finally a fourth setup for the trees.

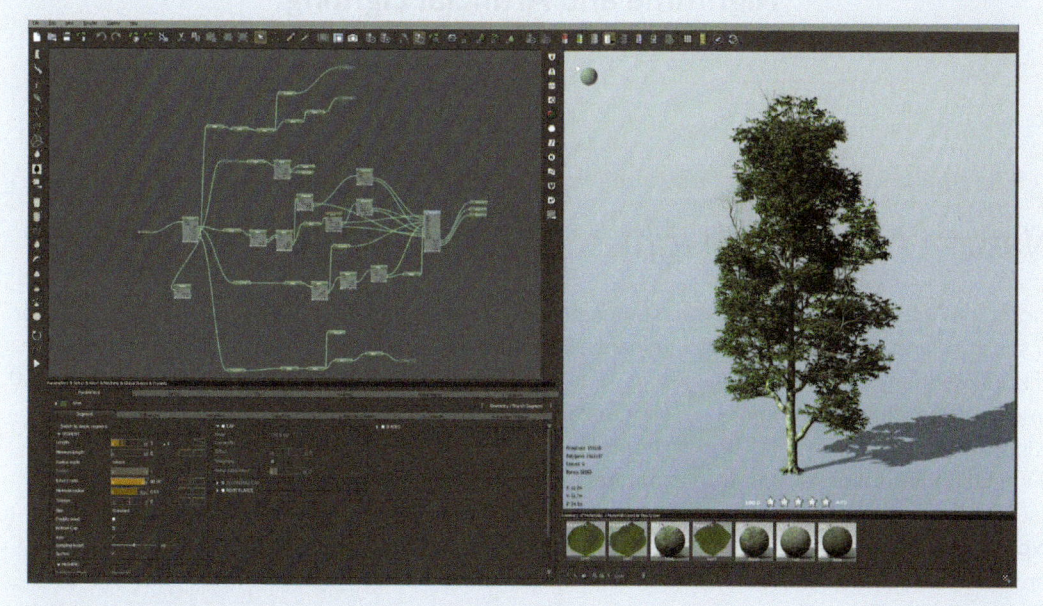

Creating one of the trees for the scene in e-on's Plant Factory.
© Aron Kamolz.

For the lighting, I used Clarisse's physical model. For the sun I chose a distant physical light with high exposure. For the sky light I use a physical environment light with a spherical HDR image. I usually stick to this type of setup and rarely use additional light sources to brighten up a scene. Another important aspect for realistic rendering of nature scenes is the materials. Since I use a physical renderer, the materials had to be physically correct. I like to use Quixel Megascans for texturing my plants. It is also very important to take care of the translucency of the leaves and how they transport the light, as this adds much to the believability of natural environment renders."

Chapter 7

Nighttime and Artificial Lighting

Natural Nighttime Light

Nighttime light comes from only two sources: the moon and the stars. The moon is just a reflector of sunlight, and even when full, its luminance is but a tiny fraction of the sun's (based on the scale of apparent magnitude, which is used to measure the brightness of stars, the sun is about 400,000 times brighter than the moon). The luminance of the stars is much lower than the moon's, and since the sky is rarely clear of clouds, humidity or pollution, starlight contribution to nighttime illumination is negligible. Put simply, natural nighttime illumination is just too dark to produce visually meaningful photography without the help of a long exposure and/or high ISO. Long exposures can produce some beautiful nighttime sky photos, but as far as subjects on the ground, the results are usually flat, desaturated, and overall, rather uninspiring.

It is therefore not surprising that almost all nighttime movie scenes take advantage of man-made lights, either by using light sources that are integral to the scene (street lamps, lit windows and doorways, car headlights, a flashlight, an actor's lit cigarette), or by using movie lights to create an illusion of natural night light (the ubiquitous "Hollywood moonlight"). A similar approach is taken in architectural visualizations or video games – nighttime renders and environments are illuminated by artificial lights, whether the purpose is to show the beauty of a building or create drama. This section is therefore brief. By and large, nighttime photorealism largely falls within the subject of artificial lighting, which will be discussed next.

The Purkinje Effect

One question about natural nighttime light deserves special attention here: What color is moonlight? The above-mentioned "Hollywood moonlight" is usually distinctly blue – is this a photoreal depiction or movie fantasy? The moon is merely reflecting sunlight, which is white, so one would expect moonlight to be white, not blue. The truth is somewhere in the middle. Light reflected from the moon is slightly warmer than pure sunlight (the moon reflects long wavelengths more strongly than short wavelengths). However, our eyes tend to shift colors toward blue in low-light situations, a phenomenon known as the **Purkinje effect**. Therefore, moonlight does not appear warm to us, but rather neutral or slightly bluish. The blue color of artificial moonlight in movies is thus not completely incorrect, though cinematographers often like to exaggerate it for visual drama.

Artificial Lighting

The incredible diversity of man-made lighting is a combination of many lamp types and an endless assortment of lamp shades, diffusers, reflectors, filters, and lenses. Different **light fixtures** (also called **luminaires**) can produce an almost infinite range of light intensity, color, shape, and focus, and these variations affect the feel, mood, and atmosphere of artificially illuminated environments in countless ways. Approaches to real-world lighting design are as varied as the different fields they serve (architectural and interior lighting, stage lighting, film and TV lighting) and each of these fields embodies different goals, aesthetics, and techniques. While the art and craft of real-world lighting is well beyond the scope of this book, there are some key aspects that are relevant to digital artists, particularly in the context of emulating man-made lighting in CG and achieving seamless integration in 2D.

Color Temperature

Kelvin Color Temperature

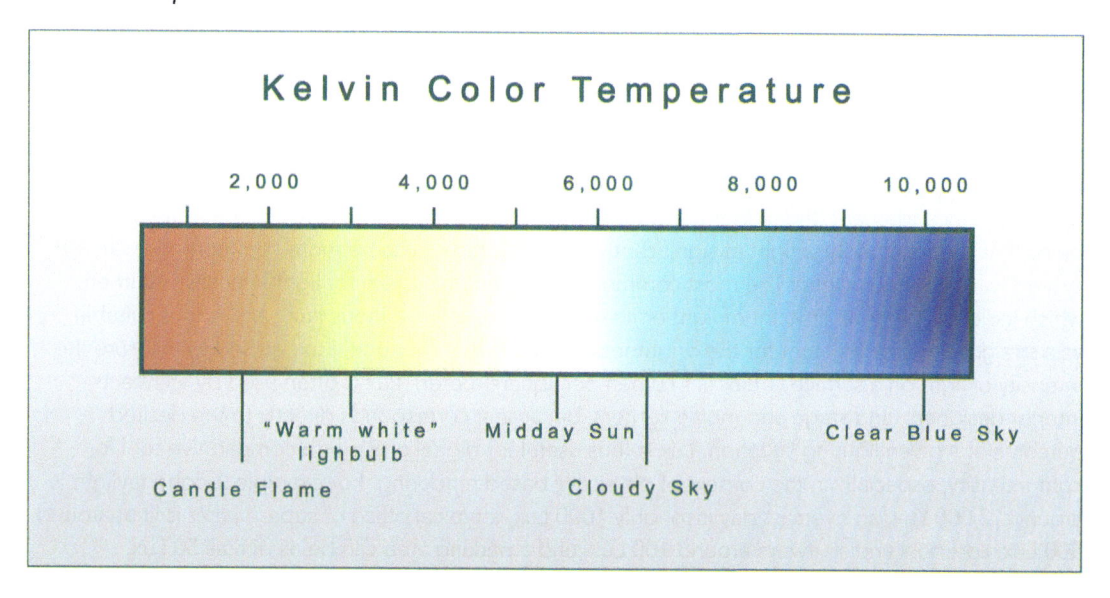

2,000   4,000   6,000   8,000   10,000

"Warm white" lighbulb — Midday Sun — Clear Blue Sky
Candle Flame — Cloudy Sky

The color of emitted light is measured in **Kelvin** (K) units. The saturated orange color of sodium vapor lamps is around 1700K, while a typical CRT monitor produces a blueish light at around 7000K. The common range for household lamps lies roughly between 2400K (standard incandescent bulbs) and 6000K (cool white fluorescent lamps). The Kelvin scale may be somewhat confusing for artists, since low-temperature values indicate what we consider "warm" colors, and high-temperature indicates "cool" colors. Moreover, a high-temperature blue light is not necessarily physically hotter, because many lamp types do not produce light through a burning filament. For example, Fluorescent lights produce much less heat than incandescent lights, yet their Kelvin temperature is higher. It is important to note that Kelvin temperature does not indicate saturation. Highly saturated light is rarely used (except for special effects or stage lighting) because it produces poor color definition, and most bulbs, either warm or cool, generate a rather desaturated light color.

Light Intensity

Lumen vs. Lux

Luminous Flux (Lumen)

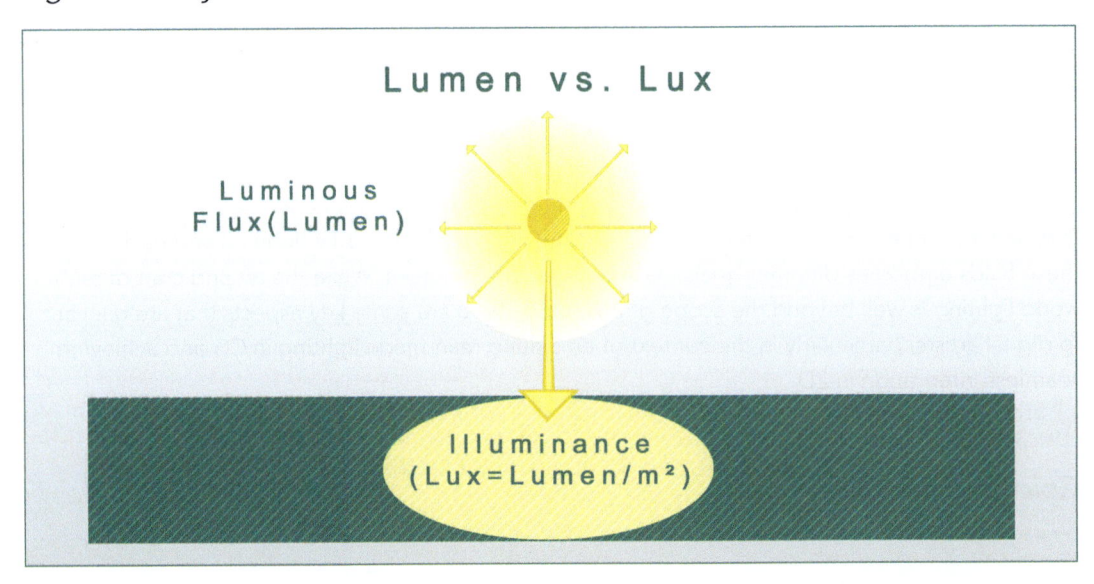

Illuminance (Lux = Lumen/m²)

There are several ways to measure light intensity, but no single universally accepted measurement unit. In the past, household light bulbs were commonly differentiated by their wattage. Watt is a power consumption unit, not a light intensity measure, but it still worked well enough when most light bulbs were incandescent (the higher the wattage, the brighter the light). However, as new types of bulbs that produce brighter light at significantly lower Wattage became more common, the wattage system was no longer useful. The most common measurement system for light intensity is **Lumen**, which indicates the total amount of light emitted from a source (luminous flux), and is thus suitable as a straight-forward indicator for the brightness of a bulb. Another unit, **Lux**, is used to measure the intensity of light on a surface (1 Lux = 1 Lumen per square meter). Lux is often used by architects, interior designers, and stage and movie lighters, because it corresponds directly to the desired outcome at a given lighting situation. Lux is thus useful for digital artists as a comparative tool for light intensity, especially in the context of physically based rendering. For example, bright daylight is around 12,000 Lux, an overcast day is roughly 1000 Lux, a typical office or supermarket is lit at around 500 Lux, corridors and stairways around 100 Lux, and a parking area can be as dim as 50 Lux.

Common Lamp Types

– Good old **Incandescent lamps** have been our lighting workhorses since the 19th century, and despite their relative inefficiency are still the most common household lamps. They use a burning filament in a vacuum as the light-producing element. Incandescent lights are typically in the warm color range (2000–3000 K).

– **Halogen lamps** use a Tungsten filament inside a small transparent envelope filled with a halogen gas (Iodine or Bromine). Halogen lamps have similar characteristics to incandescent, but can operate at much higher temperatures, and thus produce much brighter light. They are used both at home and for many professional photography, film, and stage lights.

– **Fluorescent lamps** do not use a burning filament, and instead produce light by electrically exciting mercury vapor within a tube, which in turn causes the tube's phosphor coating to glow.

They are substantially more efficient than incandescent and halogen lamps (and gradually replacing them). Originally, fluorescent lamps where large, elongated tubes that produced a rather cold bluish light (around 5000 K), and were used mainly for impersonal spaces like hospitals, supermarkets, factories, and offices. But nowadays, **compact fluorescent lamps** produce a much wider range of color temperature and are small enough to effectively replace incandescent lamps in most fixtures.

– **Neon lights** preceded fluorescent lamps by about 25 years. They use electricity to ionize one or more gases in a tube, which causes them to emit colored light. The specific color depends on the gas used: neon for orange, hydrogen for red, helium for yellow, etc. The energy output is relatively weak and not very suitable for illuminating spaces, but neon tubes have been used for decades for colorful signs and decorations. Despite their historical and artistic appeal, neon lights are ceding their place to the much more flexible LEDs.

– **Sodium-vapor lamps** are extremely efficient but produce a rather ugly orange light and poor color definition, so are primarily used to light streets, roads, parking areas, and industrial spaces.

– **LED lights** (Light Emitting Diodes) have been around since the early 1970s, but their limited color production and low intensity restricted their use to (mostly) little red signal lights in electronic appliances. However, development of blue and white LEDs and a substantial increase in output power completely transformed LEDs into today's most versatile light type. LEDs can be combined to create RGB lighting units that can produce a wide range of light color and intensity, and today's usage of LEDs runs the gamut from small flashlights through efficient household lighting to giant LED advertisement screens and revolutionary LED lighting domes (see epilogue).

Light Modifiers

Just as the atmosphere transforms sunlight, light modifiers such as lamp shades, diffusers, reflectors, filters, and lenses transform the light of man-made emitters in a myriad of ways. While bare fluorescent tubes are a familiar sight in industrial spaces, homes are rarely lit by naked bulbs, which are uncomfortable to stare at and throw a harsh, unpleasant light. Lamp shades have been

The same lamp, with and without its plastic shade. Notice the difference in luminance, contrast, hue, shadows, and light diffusion.

NIGHTTIME AND ARTIFICIAL LIGHTING

used to diffuse and soften electric light from the very start, and today they exist in infinite shapes and are made from a wide variety of materials such as plastic, glass, linen, burlap, metal, and paper. Opaque shades are coupled with reflectors to direct and intensify the light, while lenses are used to create focused beams in some home lighting fixtures and many stage lights. Soft boxes and other types of diffusers are used in professional photography and cinematography to create larger, softer light emitters.

From the perspective of digital art and photorealism, lamp modifiers are in fact more important than the actual bulbs, because it is those modifiers that define the final visual characteristic of the light fixture. A given lamp generates a specific light intensity and color temperature, but the eventual shape, pattern, color, intensity and softness of the fixture depends on the light modifiers. For example, an incandescent bulb inside a square-shaped diffuser generates a square-shaped soft light, even though the bulb is spherical. When emulating man-made lighting, therefore, it is important to look at the characteristics of the entire fixtures and its final output.

Chapter 8

Shadows

Shadows are the glue that holds elements together in a CG environment, 2D matte painting, or composite. The photoreal coherence of an image easily falls apart when shadows are missing, mismatched, or incorrect. Shadows play an important artistic role in visual art, and of course in photography and cinematography, but do not always receive enough attention in CG lighting or 2D compositing, as they are often seen as a mere by-product of light. Understanding shadows is crucial for achieving photorealism. What happens when two or more shadows overlap? What affects the softness of a shadow? Could there be shadows within shadows? To address such questions, we need to move away from common categorizations of different shadow "types" and instead adopt a more holistic approach.

To most people, the word shadow brings to mind the clearly defined dark area that an object casts on the ground on a sunny day, such as our own shadow on the sidewalk, or the shadow of a tree on the lawn. Such shadows are commonly referred to as "cast shadows". But what about shadows on an overcast day? Photographers like to call overcast days "shadow-less days". But there are plenty of visible shadows around on such a day. You may not see your own shadow on the sidewalk when the sky is overcast, but look under any parked car, and you will notice a very distinct, dark shadow. One can also spot similar shadows inside bushes, in the canopy of trees, at the bottom of rocks, in between bricks in the wall or cracks in the pavement – generally inside any cavity, large or small, and in every nook and cranny. These shadows are often called "ambient" or "occlusion" shadows, but are they really any different from "cast shadows"? On a clear day, our own shadow on the sidewalk represents the area where most of the sunlight is blocked by our body. On a fully overcast day, the shadow under the car represents the area where most of the diffuse sky radiation is blocked. In both cases, shadows form in areas where less light can reach, because the light source is partially occluded. We can thus state that **shadows are simply the relative lack of light**. It does not matter if the occluded light comes directly from a source or from a diffused version of it. The separation between "cast shadows" and "ambient shadows" is rather artificial – there is no clear line of separation, and in most lighting situations (especially man-made lighting) there can be a variety of shadows in the same environment that range from sharp to diffused, dark to light.

Taking this notion even further, the term "cast shadows" forces the assumption that one object casts a shadow onto another. But shadows appear wherever some of the light cannot fully reach, and this can happen between two separate objects or within the same object. The shadow inside our nostrils is not cast by a separate object, just like the shadow inside a half-opened bag or in a rock crevice. In fact, one can argue that, from the "light's perspective", everything – the ground, the trees, the

The word shadow brings to mind the defined dark area that an object casts on the ground on a sunny day (left). But "shadowless", overcast days also produce shadows, albeit not as sharp and well-defined (left, top and bottom).

cars, the people – everything is just one single giant "object". And within that object, any area that is partially or fully occluded from one or more light sources is shadowed. Rather than thinking of an environment as a collection of objects that cast shadows on each other, we can approach the scene as a unified entity where the intensity, color, and softness of shadows is determined by the characteristics of the light sources and their interactions with the various surfaces.

Shadow Softness

Imagine standing behind a wall, in its shadow. If you cannot see the light source at all, you are standing in the umbra, the darkest part of the shadow where all the light from that source is occluded. As you slowly move sideways toward the edge of the wall, part of the light source becomes visible – you are now in the penumbra, the lighter part of the shadow where only some of the source's light is occluded. There is a clear correlation between the size of the light source and the transition between umbra and penumbra. If the source is an infinitely small point, the light source is either fully occluded or fully revealed. There is no transition between the two stages, so there is no penumbra, and the shadow is 100% sharp. But point lights exist only in the virtual world of CG, and every real-world emitter has a size and a shape, so all real-world shadows have at least a minimal amount of softness. With larger light sources, the changeover from full occlusion to full reveal is more gradual, and there is a noticeably softer transition between umbra and penumbra.

This, however, does not explain why shadows also fall off with distance. In fact, the scale of a light source is only one of several factors that affect the softness and falloff of the shadow. The illustration below shows how each factor affects the size of the penumbra and its falloff direction:

THE REAL WORLD

Factors Affecting Shadow Softness

A: scale of light source

B: angle of Light

C: distance of occluding surface

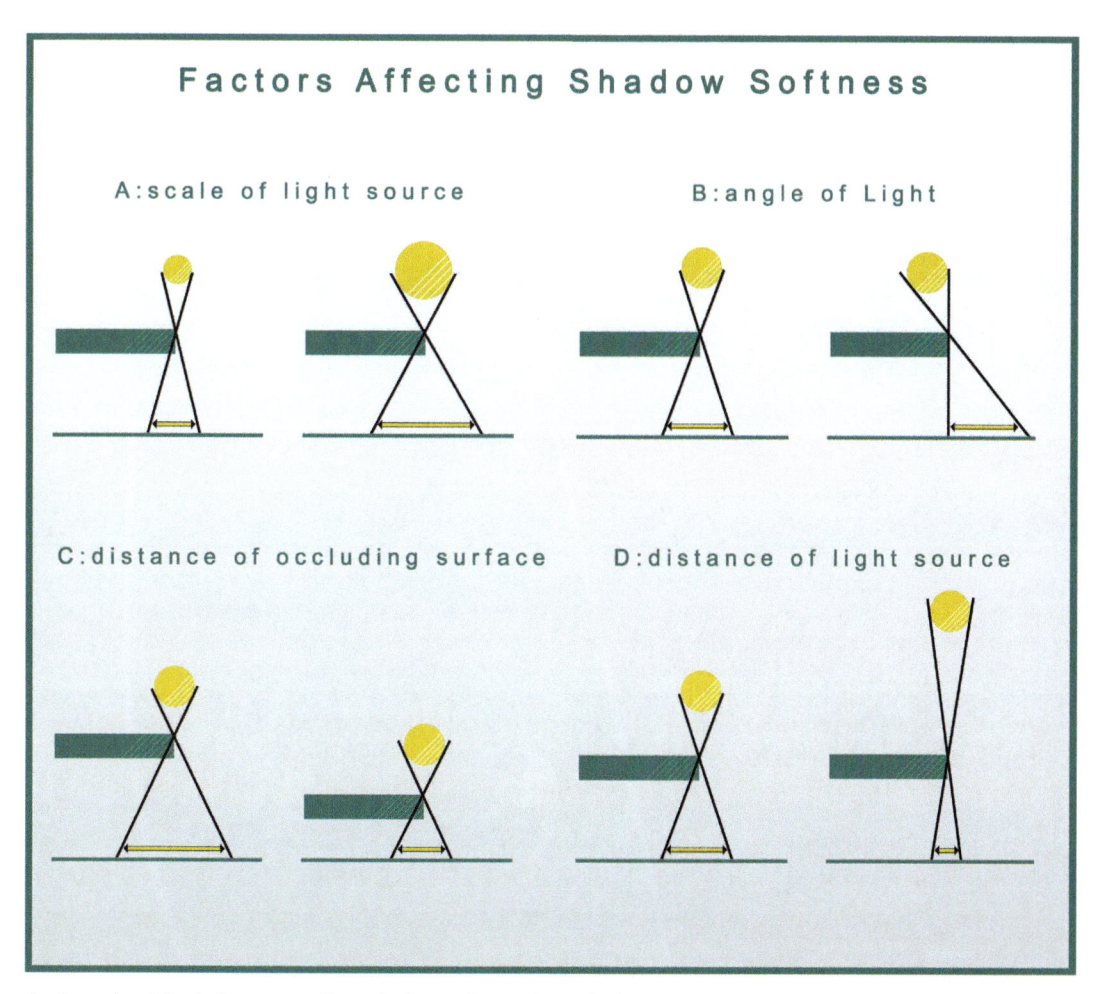

D: distance of light source

A: the scale of the light source affects shadow softness (larger light = larger penumbra), B: the angle of the light source relative to the occluded and shadowed surfaces affects the direction of the penumbra (when the angle is straight, the penumbra surrounds the shadow equally, but as the angle becomes shallower, the penumbra stretches in the opposite direction to the light), C: the distance between the occluding surface and the shadowed surface directly affects shadow softness (larger distance = larger penumbra), D: the distance between the light source and the occluding surface inversely affects shadow softness (larger distance = smaller penumbra).

Factors B and C explain why the shadow of a tree on the ground, for example, is strongest and sharpest at the base of the tree and why this softness is accentuated at sunset. The base of the tree is closest to the ground while the tree top is farthest away (factor C), and at sunset the angle of the light stretches the penumbra in the opposite direction of the light (factor B).

However, factor D is somewhat confusing: it is usually hard to see the shadow getting sharper as the light is moved farther away, because at the same time, the light's intensity also falls off with distance. So, if you move a lamp away from an object, the increased sharpness of the shadow is somewhat negated by the reduced light intensity (which reduces the intensity of the shadow). The one exception here is the sun, which is the only light source that is extremely far yet still strong enough to produce visible shadows. Indeed, sunlight shadows are sharp, but that sharpness is of course affected by factors B and C, and, most importantly, by the atmosphere.

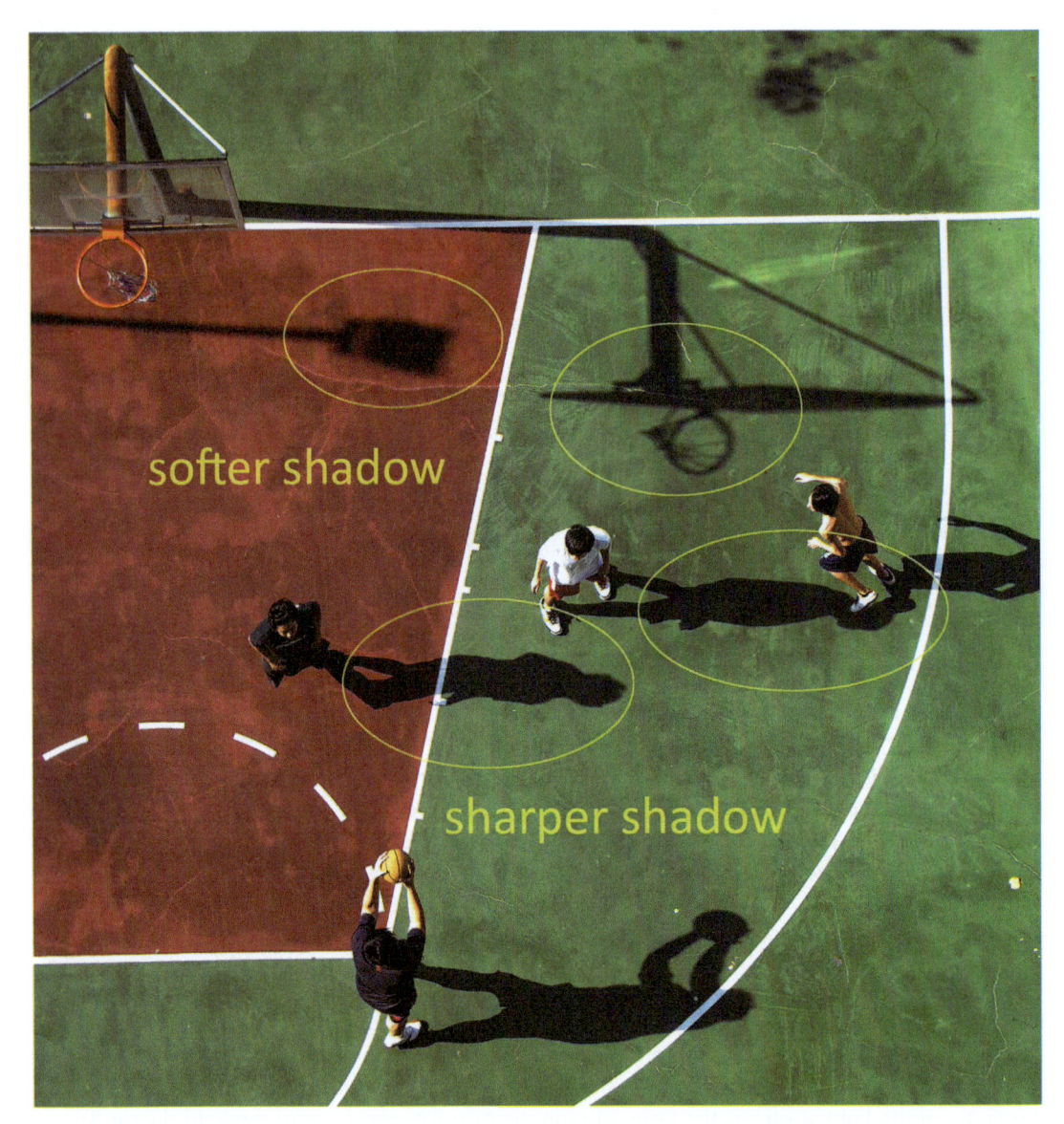

The shadows of the basket and the light pole are softer than the shadows of the players, because their top is farther away from the ground (factor C, the distance between the occluding and shadowed surfaces).

Shadow Color

Since shadows represent the relative lack of light, their color is determined by the balance between the occluded and non-occluded lights in the environment. In other words, it is the sum of all lights in the scene, minus the occluded light/s. On a clear sunny day, our own shadow on the sidewalk is slightly blue, because the warm sunlight is occluded, and the shadowed area remains lit mostly by diffuse sky radiation. Shadow color in a daylight scenario is simple – there is only direct sunlight and diffuse sky radiation to consider. But in an environment with multiple lights of different colors (for example, an urban night scene), the color of the shadows represents a varied and complex balance between occluded and non-occluded light colors.

It is important to note that while the occluded area is darker than the fully lit area, it is not necessarily blacker. In any given environment, the darkest shades usually represent the areas with the highest amount of occlusion. On a sunny day, cracks in the sidewalk may already be quite dark even in the fully lit areas, because they occlude both the direct sunlight and some of the sky radiation. So, while our shadow on the sidewalk is darker wherever the direct light is removed, those cracks still maintain the same black value, because no additional light is removed from them. In other words, while a shadow is darker than its surrounding, it also has less contrast, as the midtones are reduced while the blacks are preserved (pushing the blacks too low while darkening to create a shadow is a common compositing and matte painting mistake, as discussed in Chapter 17).

On a sunny afternoon, lit areas are warm-colored while shadowed areas are bluish-gray. But the exact color of the shadow depends on the surface texture and amount of occlusion: darker and cooler in the most occluded parts (1), brighter in more exposed areas (2), and warmer where the shadow blends with reflected light (3).

Overlapping Shadows

What happens when shadows from two or more objects overlap? Do they add up to a darker shadow, or merge seamlessly? This depends on which lights are occluded. If both objects are occluding the same light source, then the shadows merge seamlessly. A group of trees on a sunny day all block the same light source (the sun), so their occlusion forms one continual shadow. However, if each object is blocking a different light source (for example, in a room with two lamps), then the overlap area represents the relative lack of both lights and is therefore darker.

Nested Shadows

Although the combined shadows of elements that occlude the same light source blend together seamlessly, additional occlusion can still happen within a shadow. A car that is parked in the shadow of a tree is not occluding any additional direct sunlight (it's already in the shadow of the tree), but its floorboard, which is much closer to the ground than the tree's canopy, occludes more of the diffuse sky radiation, and thus creates a darker shadow within the tree's shadow. If we now place a small rock underneath the car, the proximity area between the rock and the ground will be even darker, creating a third nested shadow, or more accurately, a third level of light occlusion. In a typical evening interior scene of a living room, the combination of several light sources with different characteristics and various pieces of furniture and other objects generates an intricate mosaic of multiple overlapping and nested shadows with different intensities, sharpness levels, and hues.

The potted plant and the railing (left) occlude the same source (sunlight), so their shadows merge seamlessly. The conch sits in the shadow of the box (right), but generates a nested shadow by occluding more of the diffuse sky radiation.

THE REAL WORLD

Contact Shadows

At the beginning of this chapter I suggested that there are no separate "types" of shadows. So why this separate discussion of contact shadows? Indeed, contact shadows are not different from any other shadows. However, when simulating photoreal imagery, there is a unique importance to proximity and contact shadows, especially when blending CG elements with 2D footage (or blending 2D elements from different sources in compositing and matte painting). When objects are at close proximity, the area between them is occluded from most of the light and is therefore strongly shadowed. It does not matter if the scene is dominated by a directional light or softly lit by diffused or scattered lights – when surfaces touch (or nearly touch) each other, the contact area is distinctly dark. We are particularly sensitive to such contact shadows, because we instinctively use them for spatial orientation (for example when we reach out to touch or grab something). Our eyes and mind are therefore quite unforgiving toward missing or mismatched contact shadows. When a CG table is composited onto an image without generating the appropriate contact shadows where the table's feet are touching the floor, the table appears to be floating. The innate importance of contact shadows to our spatial orientation makes them somewhat of an "Achilles' heel" in digital art. So, although technically no different than any other shadow, they do require special attention, and later in the book we will examine 3D and 2D procedure for generating and implementing contact/proximity shadows.

Examples of contact and proximity shadows. The photo on the left was taken during a fully overcast day. I could not see my own shadow on the sidewalk but the pigeon and leaf are generating a clear shadow, because the bulk of their occluding body is much closer to the surface (proximity shadow).

Chapter 9

Basic Material Properties

In Chapter 5 we discussed absorption, specular reflection, diffuse reflection, and transmission/refraction as separate outcomes of light interacting with surfaces. The visible attributes of materials are a combination of some (or all) of these interactions. Tinted glass, for example, absorbs, transmits, and reflects light both diffusely and specularly. A specific combination and balance of interactions defines the visual characteristics of each and every material. While these characteristics may vary widely, there are some common aspects that apply to all materials, or to a specific category of materials.

Dielectric Materials

The group of **non-metals** (**insulators**, **dielectrics**) encompasses an enormous range of materials: rocks, leaves, wood, skin, clay, water, plastic, paper, fabric, cement, glass, diamond, flesh, milk, to name but a few. While these materials greatly differ in their characteristics and appearance, they all share some key properties that make them distinctly different from metals:

Dielectric Diffuse/Specular Balance

All dielectric materials display a combination of diffuse and specular reflections. The material's base color is defined by the diffuse reflection, and in addition (and depending on the glossiness level of the material), specular reflections add the colors of the environment, independent of the diffuse color. Clear dielectrics like water or glass do not tint specular reflections, and the reflected environment retains its original colors. Likewise, most shiny dielectrics derive their glossiness from a thin, transparent coating (like the resin shell in some plastics, the lacquer finish of polished wood, the wax layer on an apple or the thin oily layer on human skin). In all these cases, the specularity happens at the outer transparent layer and is thus not tinted.

In CG shading, diffuse and specular reflections are usually separate parameters, but from a real-world perspective we can consider specular and diffuse reflections as two facets of the same thing. On a highly irregular surface, almost all of the incident light is scattered and reflected at random angles, while a more organized microscopic structure reflects at least some of the light back at

Left: different plastic materials displaying varying ratios of specular/diffuse balance. Right: Wood specularity is fairly rough, but the lacquer finish on this wooden duck adds a layer of clear specular reflection.

predictable angles. This mixed diffuse-specular balance characterizes all dielectric materials, from the very dull to the super-glossy. It is also distinctly view-dependent, as I will explain in the next section.

Fresnel Effect

Augustin-Jean Fresnel (the French physicist who was largely responsible for the widespread adoption of the wave theory of light), derived a series of equations (known as the **Fresnel Equations**, or **Fresnel Coefficients**) that established the ratios and relations between reflection, transmission, and refraction. While it is not necessary for the digital artist to delve deep into the math, the basic principle is crucial for the correct simulation of specular reflections in dielectric materials. This principle is often dubbed the "Fresnel effect" by CG artists.

At its essence, the Fresnel principle ties the prominence of specular reflection to the incident angle of the viewer's line of sight. At the shallowest angle (near parallel to the surface) reflection is strongest, and at the steepest angle (perpendicular to the surface) reflection is weakest. Here's the classic example: if you stand on the shore of a calm lake and look down toward the water at your feet, you notice that it's transparent, and you can see right through to the bottom. But as you shift your graze straight toward the opposite shore, you notice that the water gradually becomes opaque and reflective, with the reflection strongest further away. Your viewing angle is much steeper looking down at the water near you and becomes progressively shallower as you shift your gaze toward the horizon. This example demonstrates not only the effect of viewing angle on the intensity of specular reflection, but also the kind of inverse correlation between specular reflection and transmission: as the angle of incidence becomes shallower, the surface becomes less transparent and more reflective. Another typical example: the transparent glass cover of your cellphone screen. Look at it from the side, and it becomes more reflective and less transparent.

BASIC MATERIAL PROPERTIES

Fresnel Reflection

Less reflection   **More reflection**

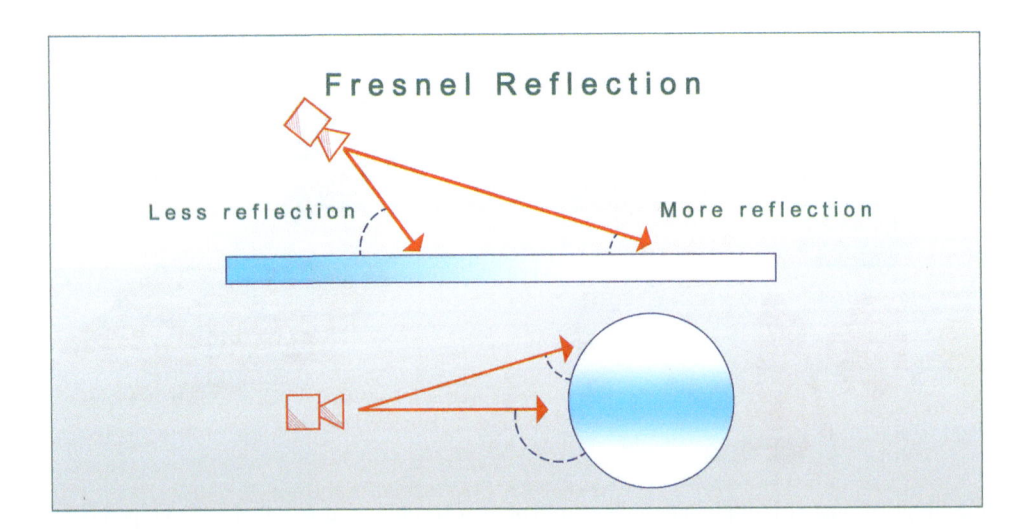

If we apply the Fresnel principle to a shiny plastic sphere, the part of the sphere that's facing the camera has the least amount of specular reflection (viewed from a perpendicular angle), while the sides of the sphere exhibit the strongest specularity (near parallel, grazing angle). Reflection in dielectric materials is therefore highly dependent on the viewing angle, and thus on the topology of the object in relation to the viewer. In the Fresnel equations, the amount of reflection attenuation is calculated based on the material's index of refraction. A lower IOR means less (or no) specular reflection at a straight angle, but at a higher IOR, reflections "expand" toward the straight angle zone, diminishing the Fresnel effect. There is a stronger influence of the viewing angle on reflection in water (IOR=1.33), than there is in diamond (IOR=2.4).

The water surface gets progressively more opaque and reflective as the incident angle becomes shallower.
© Google Street View.

Metals

The distinctly shiny and lustrous quality of metals is related to the looseness of the electrons in their molecular structure. The force of the atoms' nuclei is not strong enough to hold the outer shell of electrons, which causes them to float and interact freely. This "sea of electrons" acts like an imaginary impenetrable force shield around the molecule that either bounces photons back or "kills" them right at the surface. Because photons never penetrate the surface and never scatter, metals reflect all the light specularly, with no diffuse component. While some of the light energy is never reemitted, a strong, entirely specular albedo characterizes the shiny look of polished, freshly prepared metals. Many metals (like silver, chrome, aluminum, or platinum) reflect across a wide range of wavelengths, which gives them their neutral, silvery color. But some metals like gold, bronze, or copper do not reemit all wavelengths equally, and thus reflect with a specific tint, giving such metals their distinct color. Note that the diffuse color of all metals remains black (zero diffuse albedo), and their visible color is only affected by their specular tinting.

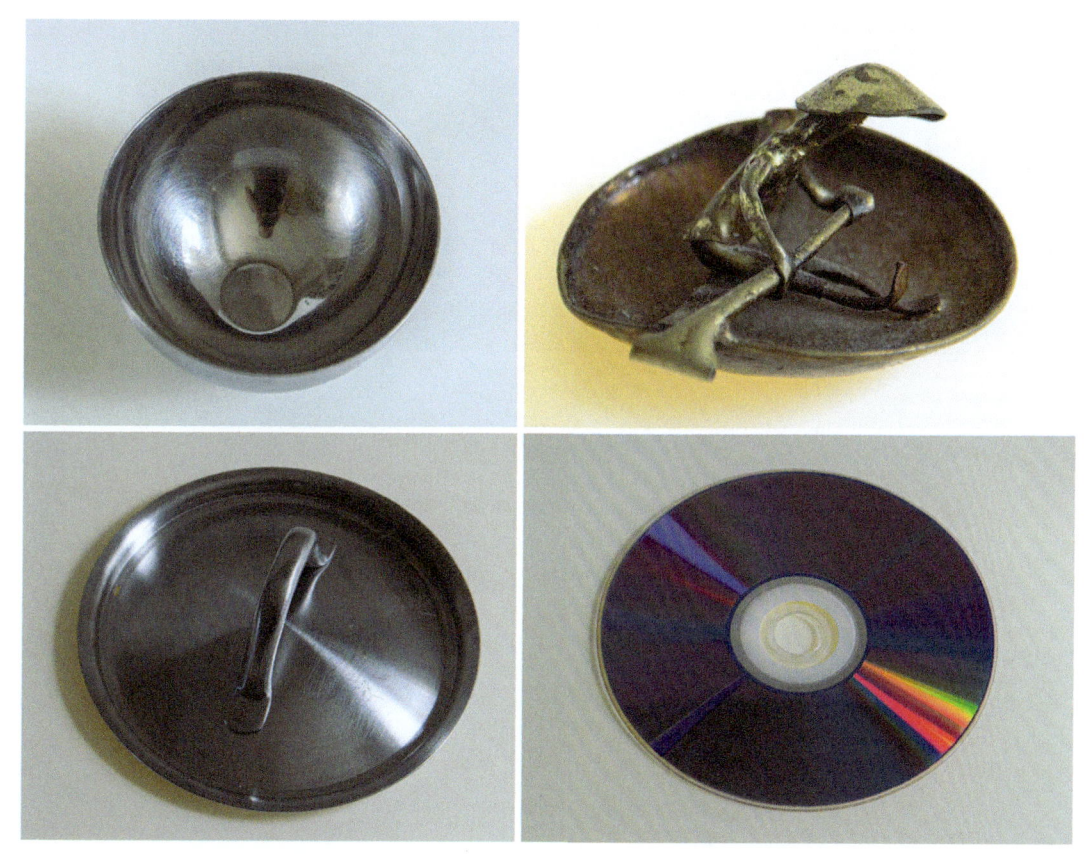

The mirror-like reflection on the stainless steel bowl (top left) is punctuated only be the scratches (notice how they are more visible around the reflection of the bright windows). Decay, wear, and dirt occlude much of the original bronze specularity (top right). The circular grooves on a pot lid (bottom left) generate distinct anisotropic reflections. The metallic reflective layer on a CD (bottom right) also shows anisotropic specularity, but the rainbow-like effect (thin film interference, see Chapter 12) is caused by the transparent plastic coating.

BASIC MATERIAL PROPERTIES

The Fresnel effect in metals is fundamentally different from dielectrics. Because of their unique molecular characteristics, the simple refractive index calculation described previously does not apply to metals. A **complex index of refraction** describes the relation between viewing angle and the attenuation of specular reflections in metals. Unlike dielectrics, metals do not show much reduction of specularity at straight viewing angles, and reflections are much more consistent across the surface. Mirrors, for example, reflect equally well from any viewing angle thanks to their metallic back coating. Also, because specularity in metals is not mixed with diffuse, the reflected image is much less attenuated (as it usually is in dielectrics), and thus shows much more distinct detail. **Anisotropy**, or the pronounced stretching of specular reflections, is usually the result of elongated or circular grooves in many types of processed metallic surfaces, such as brushed aluminum.

Chapter 10

Lens and Camera Characteristics

In the book's first chapter I wrote about the importance of making digitally created imagery look "photographic" to accomplish photorealism. In this chapter we will examine the most typical lens and camera characteristics and their effect on photographed reality. A good understanding of this subject is vital not only for VFX and visualizations – game engines now support various lens effects, which are used to instill a more cinematic look and enhance photorealism. The term "lens effects" is somewhat of a misnomer, since most lens and camera idiosyncrasies are the results of defects – lenses are not 100% perfect. Yet it is those defects that impart the kind of natural inconsistency to otherwise sterile digital creations. Visual lens imperfections (generally called **aberrations**), can be divided into monochromatic aberrations (all wavelengths affected equally) and chromatic aberrations (different wavelengths affected independently). Flares and blooms are the result of light being scattered by the glass elements in the lens, while film grain and digital noise are not related to the lens but to the characteristics of the light-recording medium (film or digital sensor).

Defocus

Of all the lens aberrations, defocus is the most significant, because it is used as a story-telling device as well as a visual and artistic instrument in photography and cinematography. It is also one of the most crucial aspects of photorealism and successful integration of 3D and 2D elements. Like atmospheric depth, defocus provides the viewer with vital spatial clues. Moreover, defocus helps establish the sense of an optical medium between the environment and the viewer, and subsequently imparts a photographic feel to digitally created content. Even a subtle sense of depth of field can elevate a CG render to a higher level of believability, while precise matching of defocus is of course a critical step in compositing.

Depth of Field

For every lens, there is a certain specific distance where a point of light is captured at maximum sharpness. That distance is the lens's **focal plane**. In fixed-focus lenses (like the ones used in webcams and surveillance cameras) this distance cannot be changed. However, almost all lenses used in photography and cinematography have a mechanism for moving the focal plane (**racking focus**) manually or automatically by changing the distance between the lens and the sensor/film.

The **depth of field (DOF)** defines the width of the area on both sides of the focal plane where the image is still sharp. Beyond those boundaries, the image starts falling out of focus. A wide (deep) DOF means that even points that are far from the focal plane are still sharp, while at a shallow DOF, only areas that are near the focal plane are sharp, and the rest of the image quickly goes out of focus. DOF is affected by several variables:

Aperture width: smaller apertures (higher f-stop numbers) generate a deeper DOF. A pinhole camera (which is essentially the equivalent of an extremely small aperture, f/100 or higher) produces an almost infinite DOF, or a uniform sharpness at any distance. Such an extremely small aperture is of course not practical for general photography and cinematography, since it lets so little light in. But even commonly used smaller apertures (f/8–f/11) have a decently wide DOF when focused at infinity. Small apertures are commonly used in landscape photography for maintaining sharpness across a wide depth. On the other hand, wide-aperture lenses (f/5 and downwards) produce an increasingly shallower DOF. Lenses with f/1.8 and f/1.4 apertures are popular for portrait photography and product shots because of the way they throw everything in front and behind the subject out of focus.

Focus distance: the farther the focal plane is from the camera, the wider the DOF. Given the same aperture, focusing on a distant subject results in a wide DOF, while focusing on a subject that is close to the lens produces a noticeably shallower depth of field (a fundamental characteristic of macro photography). Our intuitive perception of scale is tied to DOF exactly because of this principle. We instinctively associate narrow depth of field with small scale. A building feels like a dollhouse and a landscape like a miniature if the DOF is narrow and the focal plane distant. For the same exact reason, miniature models that are meant to appear much larger are filmed with the narrowest aperture possible, to maximize the depth of field (a narrow DOF would instantly give away the scale cheat).

Now, does **focal length** also affect DOF? In other words, do long lenses have a shallower depth of field than wide lenses? Yes, but to a lesser extent than what it seems at first sight. In fact, much

Left: with an open aperture of f/4, the background is thrown out of focus. Right: an aperture to f/22 keeps the background fairly in focus.

THE REAL WORLD

Both images were shot with the same lens and aperture, but the closer focal point (left) generates a narrower depth of field. Moving the focal point a few feet away widens the depth of field and, as a result, the distant background is much sharper.

DOF seems to be much narrower in the photo taken with a zoom lens at 200mm (middle), compared to the 56mm (left). But enlarging the 65mm shot (right) shows that the difference is actually not that big – the compression of depth contributes much to the illusion.

of the apparent difference in depth of field between wide and long lenses lies in the way longer lenses compress perspective and depth. Objects at a specific distance may have a similar amount of defocus when shot with a wide or a long lens. But with the long lens, these objects appear much closer to the focal plane, and their defocused detail much bigger. This creates an illusion of a shallower DOF because it seems like defocus happens over shorter distances. This compression of distance affects not only the appearance of DOF, but also the appearance of atmospheric depth, as objects seem to be much closer than the amount of atmospheric hazing suggests.

LENS AND CAMERA CHARACTERISTICS

Bokeh

Defocus blur is characteristically different from other types of blurring. For example, Gaussian blur (the most common blur function) blurs sharp points into soft-edged circles, and averages areas of sharp contrast into a smooth, consistent "mush". On the other hand, lens defocus blurs points into circular shapes with distinctly defined edges. As defocus increase, those circular shapes grow larger, but retain their edge sharpness. In addition, unlike Gaussian blur, areas of contrast are preserved even at high defocus levels.

The term **Bokeh** (from Japanese "boke-aji", or "blur-quality") is used in photography to describe the distinct character and quality of defocus. The shape of a defocused point is not necessarily a perfect circle. It is tied to the physical aperture mechanism of the lens. Simpler lenses use five or six straight blades to control the size of the iris. With such lenses, the resulting Bokeh looks like a pentagon or hexagon. More expensive lenses have nine or more blades, usually curved, to produce a clean, circular Bokeh. The fact that Bokeh is directly related to the shape of the aperture is particularly important in anamorphic lenses, which have an oval, rather than circular, aperture. Anamorphic Bokeh is therefore oval, like a circle squeezed on its horizontal axis. Because of the disproportionate shape of its Bokeh, an anamorphic rack focus has a very noticeable vertical squeeze/stretch effect.

Lens defocus does not grow infinitely with distance. There is a gradual increase in the size of the Bokeh shape from the DOF boundary to a point where defocus reaches its maximum level, after which it remains the same. The distance of the gradation and the actual maximum amounts depend on the lens type, aperture width, and focal distance. Another characteristic of lens Bokeh is **highlights bloom**. Unlike Gaussian or quadratic functions, which average colors, the Bokeh of most lenses accentuates highlights by keeping them relatively bright and larger in relation to the rest of the defocused image.

Circular Bokeh, notice how the highlights retain their brightness.

Lens Distortion

The amplified skew, or cornerstone effect on parallel lines is related to the way wide lenses exaggerate perspective, and is not lens distortion. However, when straight lines are bent into curves, this is the result of lens distortion, an aberration that is more typical of wide and zoom

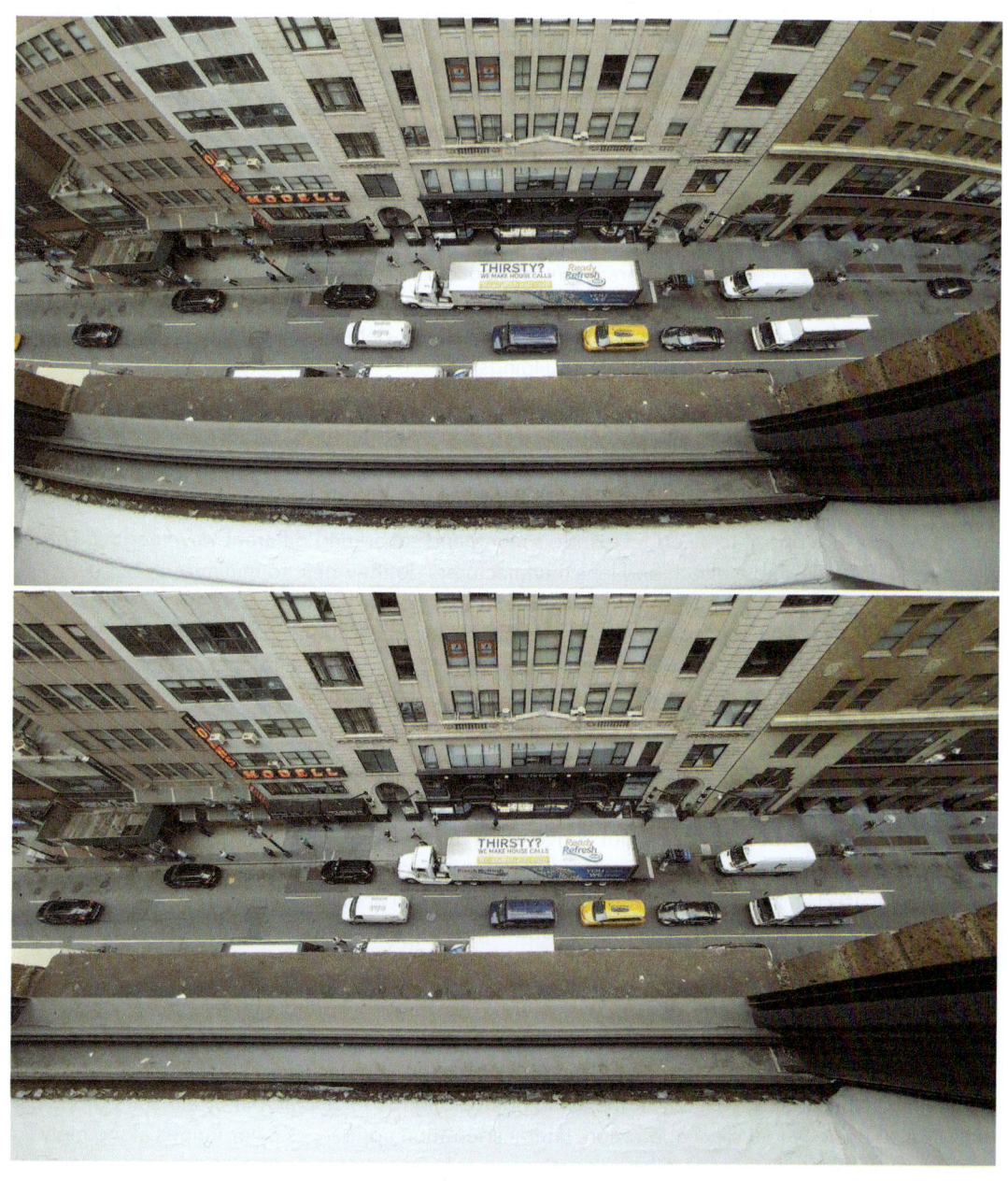

Top: the exaggerated perspective of a tilted-down wide lens generates a strong cornerstone effect of converging vertical lines. But the actual barrel lens distortion causes straight lines to curve, especially toward the edge of the frame. Bottom: when the image is properly undistorted, the curved lines are straightened out but the perspective distortion is kept.

lenses, but varies substantially between lens models. Lens distortion is a monochromatic aberration and affects all wavelengths equally. It is the only aberration that can be relatively easily undone because there is no degradation in the image quality, only displacement of pixels in 2D space. Undistorting footage is indeed a crucial step in VFX, as it allows for accurate camera tracking and integration of CG and 2D elements. However, the original distortion is usually reapplied at the end, and normally there's no attempt to "fix" lens distortion. This confirms the fact that, in most cases, photographers and cinematographers treat lens distortion as an integral part of the photographic language, rather than an undesirable defect. Lens distortion is not part of the CG rendering process and needs to be applied as a 2D effect in comp (see chapter 18). It is therefore not surprising that lens distortion is now offered as a post effect in game engines like Unreal and Unity. While not as dominant an effect as defocus, it is an important aberration that should be applied to final CG renders as part of the photoreal treatment, and must be matched precisely when elements are composited into live footage for proper integration and tracking.

In a typical lens distortion, lines are either bent outwards (**barrel distortion**) or inwards (**pincushion distortion**), though some lenses generate a mix of both. The exact amount and shape of the curvature varies between lenses and focal ranges but is normally stronger toward the edges of the frame than at the center. The effect of distortion is not depth-dependent, but it is more noticeable on elements that contain straight lines (like buildings).

Chromatic Aberration

Every lens acts as a prism, to a certain extent, shifting and separating different wavelengths. This is of course not a desirable effect, and lens manufacturers do their best to minimize it, but even high-end lenses may exhibit minor chromatic aberration (heavy chromatic aberration is typical of low-quality lenses). All chromatic aberrations stem from the fact that the refractive index of the lens is not equal for all wavelengths. As light passes through the lens, different wavelengths slow down and bend at slightly different rates, and thus hit the sensor at slightly offset positions. This causes some visible separation of color components in the captured image.

There are two main types of chromatic aberrations, depending on whether the wavelengths are separated on the depth (Z) axis or along the focal plane (XY axes). In **longitudinal** (or **axial**) aberration, different wavelengths do not converge at the same distance from the lens, which shifts the focal plane slightly for each wavelength along the Z (depth) axis. In other words, different colors are focused at slightly different distances. Longitudinal aberration appears as purple or green fringing along the edges of objects and high contrast boundaries, and can happen anywhere in the frame. It is typically more noticeable in areas that are out of focus. In fact, the color of the fringing is different when the area is in front or behind the focal plane (it usually shifts from purple to green).

In **lateral** (or **transverse**) aberration, all wavelengths are focused on the same focal plane and at the same distance, but not exactly at the same point along the focal plane (they are shifted on the X/Y axes). Like longitudinal aberration, lateral aberration appears as color fringes along high-contrast boundaries. However, lateral aberration never happens at the center of frame, and instead grows stronger toward the frame edges.

While photographers and cinematographers try to minimize chromatic aberration by using high-quality lenses, stopping down, or using post-process treatments, digital artists can (and should)

Two extreme zooms on a photo showing chromatic aberration at the edges of the windows, alternating between red–blue on the left and green–blue on the right.

add some artificial chromatic aberrations to the final image. This is usually a subtle effect (unless the goal is to mimic a very bad lens, or to achieve a stylistic effect), but can provide an extra touch of photorealism to CG renders by breaking up their sterile look a bit, and adding some lens "warmth". Obviously, when compositing elements into footage, the artist must match any chromatic aberrations embedded in the footage for seamless integration.

Lens Flares

That tacky wedding-video lens flare effect has thankfully gone out of vogue long ago, and even director JJ Abrahams, the "king of lens flares", admitted to overusing them in movies like and *Super 8* and *Star Trek*.[1] But putting their arguably inflated use aside, lens flares remain an important optical element that, when used judiciously, can add a substantial amount of photorealism to CG renders, VFX composites, and games. Lens flares do not only emulate lens behavior and add warmth and grit, they also help bind together separate elements in the composite into a cohesive environment. The combination of different lighting scenarios and different lenses produces such an immense variety of flares with complex features and behavior, that the subject can easily fill an entire chapter (or an entire book). Within the limited space here, I aim to highlight the main features of lens flares, in hope of providing a base for further exploration.

Flares are not exclusive to glass lenses. They happen in our eyes too. Just bring a small source of light (like your phone's flashlight) into your field of view – you can easily feel the haze-like flaring as the light scatters in your cornea and lens. If (like me) you are also wearing glasses, that hazing is augmented by the scattering in the glass lenses, and additional shapes seem to appear. If you are wearing glasses while driving toward the setting sun, you are experiencing triple flaring, as light is scattered in the windshield, your glasses and finally your cornea. This is essentially what happens inside a camera lens: at the basic level, light scattering causes a sort of hazy lifting of the blacks. But in most cases, additional separate elements are formed as the light scatters several times through the various glass elements that make up a lens assembly, producing those familiar yet complex chains of stars, circles, polygons, arcs, and various other artifacts. Zoom lenses, which contain more elements than primes, usually produce more complex flares. Here is an overview of the most common flare elements:

Simple Glow

When a camera is pointing toward a source of light, the scattering in the glass generates a glow around the light. When the source is near the center of the frame, the glow forms a circular halo around it. But when the light hits the lens from the side, the steeper incident angle causes a wider, more pronounced scattering that fans out from the light. If the light is relatively strong, it can create a noticeable glow even if the source is out of frame (for example, when the light is just off to the side of the camera). Photographers and cinematographers use lens hoods, flags, or even their hand to block light hitting the lens from the side and reduce flaring. When a flare glow happens in the lens, it lifts the blacks and lower midtones and reduces the contrast, but (like fog) does not brighten the highlights. A subtle flare adds a slight "haze" gradient, a strong flare can completely obliterate the frame.

Diffraction Spikes

Point your phone's flashlight toward your eyes and squint. Notice how, when your eyes are open, the glow is relatively uniform, but as you squint, numerous lines appear, emanating from the light's center – these diffraction spikes are caused by your eyelashes. A similar diffraction may happen when the lens aperture is not fully round. Since the aperture structure is much simpler than a person's eyelashes, the effect is also simpler – usually a distinct star shape, with the number of spikes either matching or doubling the number of aperture blades (for example, 12 spikes caused by a six-blade aperture). The length of the spikes can be uniform, but often, some spikes are longer. This familiar effect, often called **starburst** or **glint**, is generally well defined when the light faces the lens, but becomes more chaotic and less defined when light hits the lens at an angle.

Simple lens glow (left) and diffraction spikes (right).

Additional Flare Elements

Camera lens assemblies (zoom lenses in particular) are comprised of multiple glass elements with varied optical characteristics. When light enters the lens, it is not only scattered by the outer glass, but also by each of the internal glass pieces. This can generate an entire sequence of scattering effects, from glows and diffraction spikes to various shapes like circles, arcs, lines, and polygons (the latter usually matching the aperture shape and number of blades). When the light hits the lens assembly at a relative straight angle, the additional elements overlap in a way that makes them hard to discern. But when light hits the lens from the side, the various flare components spread along the direction of the light, starting from the origin position and ending at the opposite side of the frame, resulting in the classic elongated chain of flare components. The specific types of components and their order in the chain depend on multiple factors: the particular lens model, the angle of the light hitting it, the type of light source (focused or diffused), the amount of dirt on the lens, and the level of wear of the optical and mechanical components – potentially an infinite number of variations. However, the movement of all lens flare chains usually conforms to a simple principle: the elements are aligned along a straight line that starts at the light source and pivots at the center of the frame. For example, if the light moves from the top right corner to the bottom left corner, the entire flare chain rotates, and the end moves from bottom left to top right. Additionally, the brightness and visibility of the flare components varies according to the intensity of the light and its position in relation to the lens.

Dirt and Imperfections

Even the tiniest speck of dust or dirt on the lens becomes substantially more noticeable when light hits it from the side. This factor is often overlooked by artists as they strive to simulate realistic lens flares. No lens is absolutely clean or perfectly smooth. These inherent imperfections not only affect the look of the flare and its different components, they also contribute their own additional components – small circles or streaks that add to the complexity and irregularity of lens flares. Flare components are rarely consistent and change shape and appearance with the smallest movement, angle variation, or light fluctuation.

Different lenses produce completely different flares. The photo on the left was taken with a Sigma zoom lens on a DSLR. Notice the complex combination of different elements and the distinct heptagonal shapes generated by the seven-blade aperture. The photo on the right was taken at the same location with a smartphone, and shows quasi-anamorphic diffraction spikes and very few additional elements.

LENS AND CAMERA CHARACTERISTICS

Anamorphic Lens Flares

The oval aperture of anamorphic lenses and the fact that the footage is stretched horizontally makes anamorphic flares distinctly different and immediately recognizable. They are substantially wider on the horizontal axis, typically with one or two prominent, blue diffraction spikes stretching across the frame. This adds a uniquely dramatic visual component to footage and has been used effectively in movies (or, as some may point out, has become a bit of a cliché). Anamorphic flares should certainly be used when elements are composited into anamorphic footage but are better avoided with spherical footage or when the context of a CG scene does not call for an anamorphic emulation. For example, adding anamorphic flares to an architectural render may not be the best choice, as it is unlikely that such a render would be captured in real life with an anamorphic lens. This distinct and recognizable effect is best used only where it truly belongs.

Lens Bloom

The definition of bloom is quite fluid, as some use the term interchangeably with lens flare. Most commonly, the term is used to describe a lens glow that happens around bright highlights rather than actual light sources. Since highly specular surfaces reflect the light sources in the environment at relatively high intensity, such areas can scatter in the lens and produce a noticeable glow, or haze. Since lens manufacturers strive to minimize blooming, natural bloom is usually quite subtle and uniform, and rarely displays the complex flare elements associated with strong direct light sources. That said, photographers and cinematographers often exaggerate highlight blooms to achieve a soft, dreamy look, by using lens filters like Glimmerglass, or as a post effect.

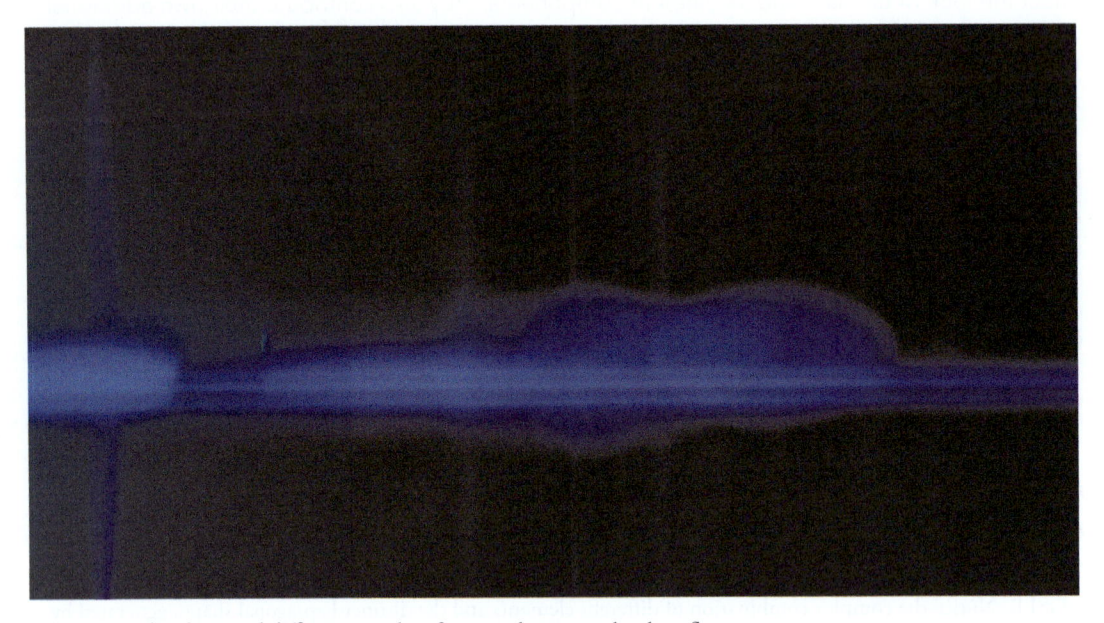

Closeup on the elongated diffraction spike of a typical anamorphic lens flare.

This extreme example of a bloom effect looks almost like a flare (as if the sun was visible in frame). Lowering the exposure (right) shows why: the sun is completely out of frame, but its specular reflection on the water is substantially brighter than anything else in the photo.

Motion Blur

Motion blur is a vital component of photorealism. A fast-moving object without motion blur does not only strobe, it looks extremely unnatural. Admittedly, motion blur does not play the same important role in visualizations and games as it does in VFX. Architectural and product renders rarely involve fast camera motion or fast-moving objects, and although motion blur is available in some games, so far it has not been universally accepted, partly because of technical limitations and partly because gamers tend to prefer visual clarity over optical realism. But in VFX, motion blur is crucial for integration with live action and cinematic believability.

Motion blur is not exclusive to cameras – it is also part of our vision. The amount of blur we see depends on the speed of the moving object. However, unlike our vision, camera motion blur is strongly affected by two additional parameters: shutter speed and frame rate. Assuming an object moves at the exact same speed, a longer shutter speed will produce longer motion blur. Sports photographers use wider aperture lenses and fast shutter speeds to minimize motion blur, for example. Movies are shot at 24 frames per second. But higher frame rates can reduce or eliminate motion blur. Interestingly, attempts to shoot entire films at high FPS have so far received mixed responses. The critical reaction to Ang Lee's 2016 film *Billy Lynn's Long Halftime Walk*, which was shot at 120 FPS, is a good example. While some critics praised its unprecedented clarity, others lambasted the effect as un-cinematic. As *Vox* magazine's Emily VanDerWerff put it: "At 120 fps, things look a bit like higher definition video – or, as many people put it, like a soap opera."[2] Over a hundred years of movies have left a mark on our cinematic perception, and the reduced motion blur of high frame rates can feel quite unnatural.

The word "blur" in motion blur is somewhat deceiving because the effect is markedly different from standard Gaussian blur or defocus. It should better be thought of as a trail that connects pixels between two adjacent frames, and unlike regular blur, it does not fade off softly but often ends abruptly at a defined line. While motion blur certainly smears details in the image, the smearing is always directional, and contrasted features in the image can be clearly seen as streaks. However, a complex fast motion like that of a shaky hand-held camera can produce an equally complex motion blur pattern that is not easily emulated with 3D or 2D software.

The camera's motion is clearly felt in the pronounced streaking, while the leopard's own motion generates a different streak direction on its back. Notice the general sharpness of the streaks – motion blur is more stretching than blurring.

Grain

Film grain is the result of the small particle of silver halide reacting to light photons. In digital cameras, noise is usually the result of the sensor's reaction to low light and high ISO settings, and is generally less prominent than film grain. Despite their differences, film grain and digital noise (which we will also call "grain" here for the sake of simplicity) are the very final layer of photorealism in digital imagery. Because grain happens uniformly over the entire image, it has an important role in compositing as a glue that binds together various elements. Grain adds a photographic feel to CG renders and is crucial for integrating CG elements with footage. Missing or mismatched grain, even if hard to detect without close inspection, can nonetheless cause composites to fall apart, especially when they are color corrected.

The exact appearance, scale, intensity, color variation, and randomness of grain and noise varies greatly between different film stocks and digital camera models. But there are some basic characteristics that apply to all types:

- Grain covers the entire image uniformly, but its visibility depends on the underlying colors. Generally, grain is more pronounced in the darker areas, and less visible in the brightest.
- Grain (both film and digital) is never equal in each of the RGB channels. Digital sensors are more sensitive to green and red light (same with the green and red layers in film), so the blue channel is usually considerably noisier.
- Grain is random, and changes on every single frame. It is never static.

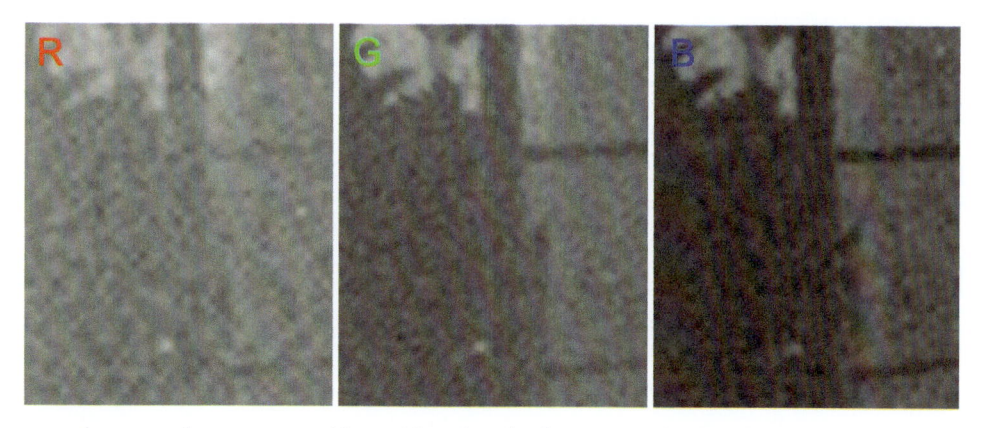

An extreme closeup on footage captured by an Alexa digital video camera, showing different grain pattern size, and intensity on each RGB channel.

Matching grain is an important (and often neglected) part of compositing and will be discussed in chapter 18.

Notes

1 www.theverge.com/2013/9/30/4788758/j-j-abrams-apologizes-for-his-overusing-lens-flares.
2 *Billy Lynn's Long Halftime Walk* is all technology, no movie, Emily VanDerWerff, *Vox* magazine, 2016.

PART 3
THE CG WORLD

Bicycle by Julian Sadokha.
© Julian Sadokha.

Here are the good news: it is easier today, more than ever before, to render convincingly photoreal CG imagery. Physically based rendering, BRDF shaders, IES lights, an extensive selection of smart lighting, shading and texturing tools, the widespread availability of scanned 3D models and textures, ready-to-use HDRIs, and advanced real-time technologies – all these factors contribute to the relative ease of generating believable CG content. What once required equal amounts of trickery and ingenuity to work around the many limitations of simulated reality is nowadays a much simpler affair: follow real-world paradigms in texturing, shading, and lighting – and you should end up with photoreal results.

And now the not-so-great news: the world has gotten used to physically plausible renders. Whether you create VFX for films and TV, architectural visualizations or product renders, your clients and your audience are expecting a level of photorealism that would have been considered very challenging, if not unattainable, just ten years ago. And talk about games ... yes, real-time rendering does not yet allow quite the same photoreal results as offline rendering. But the emphasis here is on the word "yet". The technology is consistently marching forward, and the gap is narrowing. With every new game that pushes the envelope of realism a little more, gamers are expecting the next one to go even further.

These lofty expectations certainly put the onus on CG artists, who must keep up with a higher than ever threshold of photorealism. The fact that contemporary shading and lighting works so much like the real world requires not only a deep familiarity with photography and physical light interaction, but also a mastery of contemporary CG tools. Lighting and shading are of course crucial for photoreal rendering, but so are textures, and to some extent modeling as well. To better emphasize how each of these tasks contributes to the final quality of photorealism, I chose to organize this part of the book in the reverse order of the CG process – starting with rendering and lighting, then shading, texturing, and ending with modeling.

Clover Field Test by Christopher Schindelar.
© Christopher Schindelar.

Chapter 11

Rendering and Lighting

When 3D computer graphics started evolving in the 1970s, the theory of light was already well established. The knowledge was there, the laws and paradigms were there, the formulas were there, the work of Newton, Huygens, Fresnel, Planck, Einstein et al. was there. What wasn't there? Computers that could handle the immense computational challenge of simulating physical light behavior and surface/light interactions. It is easy to forget just how much computing power has increased since the early days of CG rendering. Here's an example: the CDC 7600, one of the most powerful super-computers of the 1970s, a behemoth that occupied an entire room, had a computing power of 36 million megaflops. By comparison, the Samsung Galaxy S6 phone had a computing power of 36 BILLION megaflops. A 2015 consumer phone is still a thousand times (!) more powerful than the '70s' strongest super-computer.

The pioneers of CG rendering in the '70s and '80s had a mere fraction of the computing power we have today. With such extremely limited means, a true physical simulation of light was not even an option. The first CG light emitters, shading models, and rendering algorithms were never intended to faithfully emulate real-world lighting. Instead, they mimicked light behavior by way of crude approximations, using smart compromises that allowed CG artists to produce some surprisingly realistic imagery despite the hardware limitations of the time. Today's CPUs and GPUs are fast enough to support the type of physically based rendering that was a distant dream 30 or 20 years ago. But to better understand the contemporary tools we have at our disposal, it is important to see them in a wider evolutionary context, especially since many tools that have been with us for decades are still being used today.

From Scanline to Path Tracing

A render engine has one, and only one task: to determine what color a pixel is. At the end, after the scene is modeled, textured, shaded, and lit, it all comes down to this one question: what color is this pixel? And what color is the pixel next to it? And the one next to it? Even though the answer is just three numbers (RGB) per pixel, the road to it is a long and winding one, because those three numbers depend on a multitude of factors. To obtain an absolutely precise answer, the ideal render engine would need to examine everything in the CG scene that may, in one way or another, affect the RGB value of each specific pixel: all the light sources, every interaction of photons with any possible surface in the scene, the various material properties of every surface, and so on. Such an ideal renderer (let us call it **fully unbiased**) would be the closest thing to a true light interaction simulator. And while we are closer to this ideal renderer today, such a prospect was not a viable option in the past, and so rendering methods had to follow a much-simplified process.

Scanline/Rasterized Rendering

A scanline renderer gathers all the information about the geometry in the scene, then transforms that 3D information into a 2D projection based on the camera's viewing plane, a process called **rasterization**. Depth is sorted via a **Z buffer**, to ensure that only the front-most surface is rendered and the ones behind it kept hidden. The color of every pixel is determined by the shader applied to the surface. The shader calculates the color output at each point based on the material properties and the amount of light that hits that point. This process is then repeated until a color for every pixel is determined, which does sound like a lengthy affair (an HD image has over 2 million pixels, and a 4k image has over 8 million), but is in fact the fastest and most efficient rendering method for a 3D scene. Back in the beginning of CG, this was the only way to render in a feasible amount of time. Nowadays, this rendering process is blazingly fast, and forms the foundation of contemporary game engines, enabling smooth refresh rates at high resolutions.

Raytracing

Scanline/rasterization is fast, but very limited in its ability to generate photoreal renders. It cannot provide a truly accurate answer to the "what color this pixel is?" question because it ignores several key factors: much of the light–surface interaction depends on the surface's surrounding

These examples compare Blender's realtime *Eevee* renderer, and its offline full-on raytracing engine, *Cycles*. A: Eevee simple realtime render, B: Eevee realtime render with ambient occlusion, screen-space reflections and sub-surface scattering approximation (more accurate), C: Cycles render with path-traced reflections, true subsurface scattering and GI (most accurate). These lighting and shading aspects will be discussed in this chapter and the following one.

environment (as discussed throughout Part 2). The exact color of every point in the scene depends on specular reflections (what exactly is being reflected at this point?), transmission and refraction (what do we see through the surface at this point?), and, most importantly, bounce light (how is the environment contributing to the lighting at this point?). If we really want to find out how light behavior is affecting the color of every point in the scene, we need to start following photons around: shoot multiple rays from each source of light, and follow their path as they bounce around the scene and interact with surfaces. This, however, would be an extremely inefficient undertaking. As I mentioned in Chapter 1, the camera only sees photons that directly hit the sensor. If we started tracing light from the source, we would be spending an eternity following photons that will never even be seen by the rendering camera, and therefore will have little or no effect on the image.

Raytracing follows the path of light backward, starting from the camera and eventually ending at the light source/s. This ensures that only rays relevant to the rendered image are traced, substantially speeding up the process. Yet despite this smart approach, ray tracing is still painfully slow in comparison to scanline rendering. Imagine a single ray being traced from the camera to the first point of surface interaction. This single point may be affected by multiple lights, and reflect other surfaces, which in turn may also be affected by multiple lights and other surfaces, and so forth. One single ray needs to be split into multiple rays at the first point of interaction, and each of these rays may be further split into even more rays at subsequent interaction points, multiplying the ray number exponentially. In raytracing, rendering a single pixel may require millions of calculations (as opposed to just a few in scanline rendering), yet the added realism is well worth the longer render times. Indeed, ray tracing became a mainstay of offline rendering and elevated CG to a new level of photorealism by generating true specular reflections, realistic refractions, and accurate shadows. But raytracing remained too prohibitive for real-time rendering until recently: in 2018, Nvidia unveiled their RTX technology, and since then ray tracing is making a steady foray into games, VR applications, and realtime visualizations.

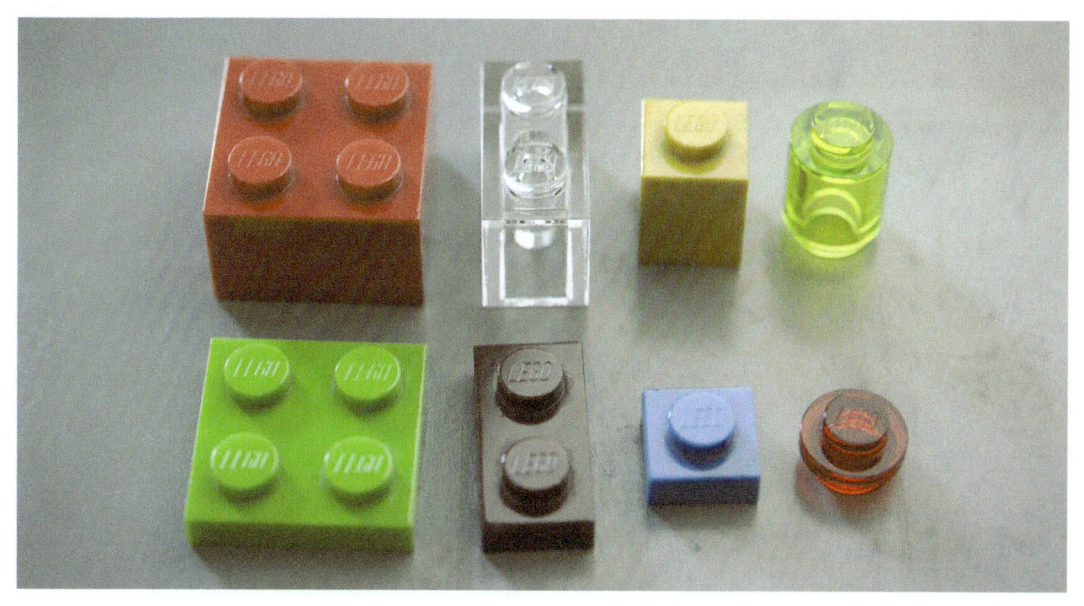

Lego Bricks by Raphael Rau. Created in Cinema 4D, rendered with Cycles 4D.
© Raphael Rau.

The Challenge of Global Illumination

Accurate reflections, refractions, and shadows are important for realistic renders, but the contribution of bounced light, or **global illumination (GI)** is the most crucial ingredient in the photorealism recipe. Only global illumination can faithfully reproduce all the intricacies of light interaction, and its effect, though often quite subtle, makes a tremendous difference. Global illumination is substantially more complex to calculate than other components and was not initially incorporated in raytracing renderers. In the history of CG, many brilliant animations, visual effects, and visualizations were created without any global illumination. Instead, they were masterfully lit by artists who used simple points and spotlights to create the illusion of reflected light and generate a convincing ambience. Several methods were consequently developed to cope with the challenge of global illumination, either by "faking it" (ambient light emitter, ambient occlusion) or by using more efficient calculation methods (radiosity, photon mapping).

AMBIENT LIGHT EMITTER

The ambient light emitter was used from the early days of CG as a quick and cheap way to crudely simulate the effect of reflected light or diffused sky radiation. Though in some

The image on the right shows only the indirect, or reflected light component of the path-traced render on the left. Notice the strong inter-reflectivity between the oranges and between the cooking utensils and the wall.

The old ambient light was a rather poor substitution for indirect illumination, as it only acted as a simple brightness multiplier.

applications (Maya, for example), the ambient light emitter has an optional basic directionality, it is not really a light at all, but rather a multiplier that uniformly raises the overall color gain of the scene. The ambient light was originally used to "fill in" for missing reflected or scattered light in both exterior and interior scenes. However, it produces an utterly flat and unrealistic "light" with no shading or occlusion, and although it can still be found in some rendering software, there is little reason to use it nowadays for offline rendering (and it is quickly becoming obsolete in realtime rendering as well).

AMBIENT OCCLUSION

Ambient occlusion (AO) is not a global illumination solution – it does not calculate reflected light at all. But it is a much-improved take on the crude ambient light emitter, and can be used as a very efficient "cheat" for GI. Ambient occlusion assumes multi-directional ("ambient") light emanating from a consistently white sphere around the scene, and then checks to see how much of that light reaches every point in the scene. Naturally, areas that are more exposed to the theoretical light dome are more illuminated than areas that are partially occluded, resulting in the soft shadowing characteristic of diffused sky radiation on a fully overcast day. This process is significantly faster than calculating a multitude of bouncing light paths and can add a substantial level of depth and photorealism by replacing flat ambient light with a shaded one. It is thus commonly used in game engines and realtime display of CG applications, and is an important component of texturing for enhancing bump/normal maps (see Chapter 13). In addition, an ambient occlusion render pass is used for adding contact and proximity shadows in the compositing stage (see Chapter 16).

RADIOSITY AND PHOTON MAPPING

As the first effective solution for GI, radiosity was an exciting development in CG rendering that was quickly adopted by ArchViz artists. Radiosity is view-independent and calculates reflected light energy over the entire scene. It divides the surfaces into small patches, and then checks each pair of patches for their **view factor** – essentially how much they "see" each other. Patches that are in close proximity and/or facing each other bounce more light between them, as opposed to patches that are distant or at oblique angles. Although radiosity was, for a while, the most efficient way of calculating the contribution of reflected light to a scene, it was limited by the fact that it could only calculate diffuse light (ignoring the contribution of specular reflections), and was detached from

An ambient occlusion pass (left) can be combined with the flat ambient light shown above to generate a "poor man's global illumination". This approach is used especially in games and other realtime applications.

the main raytracing process. Also, its reliance on dividing geometry into patches made it prone to errors and artifacts along hard edges and sharp angles.

Like radiosity, photon mapping works as a separate, complementary process to standard raytracing; however, photon mapping is view-dependent. In this two-stage solution, photons are first shot from a light source, and their interaction with surfaces is traced and recorded in a photon map. In the second stage, the renderer uses the projected photon maps to determine the radiance value of the surface at each point. This value is then combined with the direct illumination values obtained by raytracing. While photon mapping requires less computing power than path tracing, faster hardware made path tracing the preferred choice for fully integrated ray-traced global illumination.

Path Tracing

Almost every contemporary **physically based renderer** (PBR) uses a method called **path tracing**, which represents, to date, the most holistic (and physically accurate) approach to raytracing.

Green Tones by Javier Wainstein.
© Javier Wainstein

A path tracing renderer treats all light equally regardless of whether it is direct or reflected, incoming or outgoing. In conjunction with **BRDF shaders** (which will be discussed in Chapter 12), path tracers integrate global illumination seamlessly with diffuse and specular reflection and refraction. Although this requires heavier calculations than older GI approaches, reasonable rendering times are still possible thanks to the **Monte Carlo** approach. Monte Carlo is a wide term that applies to many fields, not just CG rendering, and refers to algorithms that speed up computationally intensive processes through random sampling. The concept is similar to statistical surveys: to find out which ice cream flavor is the most popular in the USA, for example, the surveyor would never interview the entire population (which will give the most accurate result but will take forever), but a much smaller selected group instead (which will give a reasonably accurate result in a manageable time).

A Monte Carlo path tracer uses a similar principle by tracing a limited number of random rays, in effect **sampling** the environment at various locations and for various light interactions, instead of methodically tracing every single possible ray. The quality and accuracy of the image depends on the number of samples. A low **sampling rate** results in noisy renders, because not enough information is gathered. In contrast, overly high sampling rates are counterproductive, as rendering times are increased for no substantial visual benefit. Each different CG scene therefore has its own sampling "sweet spot" of optimal quality/time setting. Reaching it is made easier by assigning separate sampling rates to different lighting components (diffuse, specular, subsurface scattering etc.). Usually, the noisiest components are the indirect ones (like indirect diffuse or indirect specular), and higher sampling rates can be set specifically for these components while keeping the direct illumination sampling values lower.

Unbiased vs. Biased Rendering

The "ideal render engine" I mentioned earlier is considered fully unbiased, because it diligently and meticulously checks every pixel for all possible light interactions, making no shortcuts on the way. This is bound to provide the most accurate "render solution" to a given scene, and, supposedly, the most photoreal results. The problem, of course, is that such a renderer can take a painfully long time to produce the image, and the outcome may not necessarily justify the long wait. By contrast, a biased renderer uses various shortcuts to speed up the process, making biased choices as to what is more important and what can be ignored. Does that mean that the result of biased renderers is less photoreal? Put in the correct perspective, the debate between "biased" and "unbiased" is rather pointless. The above mentioned "ideal renderer" does not exist, and even renderers that are considered unbiased still use an approximation of physical light behavior. Path tracing relies on sampled (not absolute) results, and often uses **importance sampling** that focuses the samples in areas that are likely to contribute more to the final output. This in itself is a biased process (physical light does not make such choices). In other words, all renderers are estimators of reality, not reality itself. Take, for example, two of the most powerful (and widely used) render engines: Arnold and V-ray. The first is considered unbiased, and the other biased. Both produce consistently excellent results and have a proven track record as production workhorses. Is one better than the other? Redshift, another popular renderer, is known for its blazing speed, which it owes to an array of smart shortcuts and optimizations. The fact that it is a clearly biased renderer does not necessarily make it inferior. Most contemporary PBR's are capable of similarly realistic results, whether they are considered biased or unbiased.

Winter in the Woods by Liam Cramb. 3D Studio Max and V-Ray.
© Liam Cramb.

Traditional Light Emitters

Point/Spot Lights

As its name suggests, the point light generates light from an infinitely small point, and a CG spotlight is essentially a point light with a restricted, adjustable cone of emission. The fact that the light emanates from a single point makes these light emitters considerably faster to calculate than area lights, and virtually immune to noise issues. But point/spot lights are physically incorrect because real-world light always originates from a physical, measurable surface. Point and spot lights therefore have several key limitations:

- Being infinitely small, point/spot lights cannot produce true, accurate soft shadows with an umbra and penumbra that relate to the shape, surface scale, distance, and angle of the light (soft shadows can only be "faked" through a global softness parameter).
- Since point/spot lights have no scale, they do not exist as visible entities in the CG environment, and therefore cannot appear in specular reflections. This goes against the very nature of specularity, where (as discussed in Chapter 4) light sources play a crucial role. The traditional representation of point/spot lights in specular shaders like Phong and Blinn is merely a "cheat", not a true reflection of a light-emitting entity.
- Point lights can only emit light in a spherical fashion. Elongated fluorescent tubes, rectangular fixtures, neon signs, and all other non-spherical light fixtures are hard (if not impossible) to emulate.

Point light (left) and spot light (right). Notice the perfect, harsh shadows and strong contrast.

Directional light (left). On the right, with a bit of shadow softness and additional sky dome for diffuse sky radiation (see below).

Directional Light

Like point and spot lights, the directional light has no surface or size, and light emanates from an infinitely small source. But unlike point/spot lights, the position of a directional light has no effect (only its direction), and it casts parallel rays and shadows, which makes it a basic but nonetheless effective simulator for sunlight. As described in Chapter 6, the sun is so distant that its light on earth (for all practical purposes) is parallel. The directional light is therefore still widely used in both real-time and offline rendering. Most render engines offer a shadow softness parameter (sometimes called angle). This is necessary to simulate the effect of the atmosphere (and time of day) on the softness of sun shadows.

Contemporary Light Emitters
Area and Mesh Lights

As computing power increased, **area lights** became the choice emitters for most offline rendering purposes. Their advantage over point lights is clear: area lights generate light from a

A small circular area light (left) produces a result that is similar to point light, but with softer shadows and a more natural light spread. With an elongated rectangular area light (right) shadows are even softer and the image is more pleasant to the eye.

surface that has a physical shape and scale, and thus solve the three crucial limitations of point lights: accurate soft shadows, true visibility in specular reflections, and non-spherical illumination. The visual characteristics of light fixtures are often derived not from the bulb itself but from the wider surface of scattering mediums like lampshades, reflectors, and diffusers, and area lights are well-suited to mimic such characteristics. Their disadvantage is that numerous rays must be shot from the surface toward every angle, as opposed to a single ray in point lights. This can introduce noise issues, especially in the shadows, which requires higher sampling rates and increases the render times.

Area lights usually come as a rectangle, disk, or cylinder – essentially the most common shapes of lighting fixtures. However, since PBR's use a holistic approach to lighting, any object with an emissive shader effectively becomes a light emitter. As a more efficient alternative to emissive shaders, most PBR's let you convert any mesh into a **mesh light**. This retains the shape of the geometry but adds the functionality and additional controls of area lights. Mesh lights are particularly effective for creating neon signs and other irregularly shaped light fixtures.

Image-based Lighting

As mentioned in Chapter 3, 16-bit HDR images can store a very wide range of luminance values, and thus capture real-world lighting at its fullest. **Image-based lighting** (IBL) constitutes an integral approach to CG lighting, not only because it uses real-world lighting snapshots instead of artificial emitters, but also because it creates a full environment around the CG scene, which can be used for specular reflections, as well as transmission and refraction. IBL is of course extremely useful in VFX, because it can capture the lighting on the set, which can then be applied to CG elements for optimal integration with the footage. It is also great for replicating real-world studio lighting for product visualizations, and of course to generate believable outdoor lighting (diffuse sky radiation in particular). It is important to remember that despite its effectiveness, standard IBL is not a three-dimensional environment – it is merely an "egg shell" that surrounds the CG scene. Therefore, it is only good for distant or background lights that do not interact with elements in the scene or

The same gray-shaded object, illuminated by six different spherical HDR images.

the camera (for example, it cannot replace street lights in a driving car scene, interior lights in an architectural walkthrough, or any light in a playable area in a game).

To successfully serve as an IBL source, an image needs to fulfill some key requirements:

- It needs to be a consistent, uninterrupted 360 panorama. This is usually done by shooting the environment with a very wide (or fish-eye) lens and rotating the camera three or four times (depending on the lens) on a nodal head to complete a full circle. The images are then stitched together into one spherical panorama that can be applied to a spherical **environment light** (also called **sky light**, **dome light**, or **sky dome light**).
- Even the best cameras cannot capture a full dynamic range in one shot. Therefore, several images must be taken for each angle, each at a different exposure. Usually 5 or 7 exposures are taken, both below and above the optimal exposure, and these are merged using dedicated software to produce a 16- or 32-bit image with an extremely wide dynamic range.
- If used for lighting only, HDR panoramas should be slightly or moderately blurred, to avoid any sharp peaks or artifacts that can create render issues. However, a sharp version should be used for specular reflection, and care must be taken to fix broken seams and clean up unwanted elements such as passing people. In most scenarios, only the upper hemisphere is used, as there usually is some kind of ground geometry in the scene that blocks the lower half of the HDR panorama.

A spherical HDR image from the sIBL archive.

Procedural HDR Environments

Instead of using photographic captures of real-world panoramas, spherical environments can also be created from scratch. This is an intriguing subset of IBL that covers a few different approaches: some programs (such as HDR Light Studio) let you design a virtual studio lighting environment by dropping 2D light elements that emulate lighting fixtures into a 2D spherical environment map. These are especially useful for product visualization. For outdoor lighting, many render engines offer a procedural sky map. These physically based sky simulations let you adjust the sun's position (or pitch/azimuth), the amount of sky turbidity (higher amounts simulate an overcast or hazy sky with less direct sunlight), sky color, and the sun's intensity and scale (for sun appearance in specular reflections). The color and gradation of the sky automatically shifts according to the position of the sun, simulating the effects of Rayleigh and Mie scattering. Finally, dedicated landscape-creation applications like Terragen and Vue have built-in atmosphere simulators that, in addition to providing procedural sun and sky interaction and volumetric clouds, apply a three-dimensional atmospheric volume to the entire scene that interacts with the objects and generates depth-based haze and fog (even crepuscular rays). Procedural IBL environments thus offer control and flexibility that is not possible with HDR images, and they do not require shooting, editing, and stitching photographs. But they often lack the realistic detail and irregularity of real-world environments, and, of course, cannot be used to match the set lighting in VFX).

Photometric Lights

The Illuminating Engineering Society (**IES**) instituted a digital format for storing the characteristics of specific real-world lights. CG photometric lights can read IES profiles and closely simulate the lighting distribution and color temperature of physical lighting fixtures. This is of course extremely valuable for architects and interior designers: not only do photometric lights accurately emulate the proposed lighting at the visualization stage, but they allow

Unlike standard IBL, Vue's atmosphere model is three-dimensional and truly volumetric. Tweaks to sun position, fog, haze, clouds, and other parameters can drastically change the look of a scene.

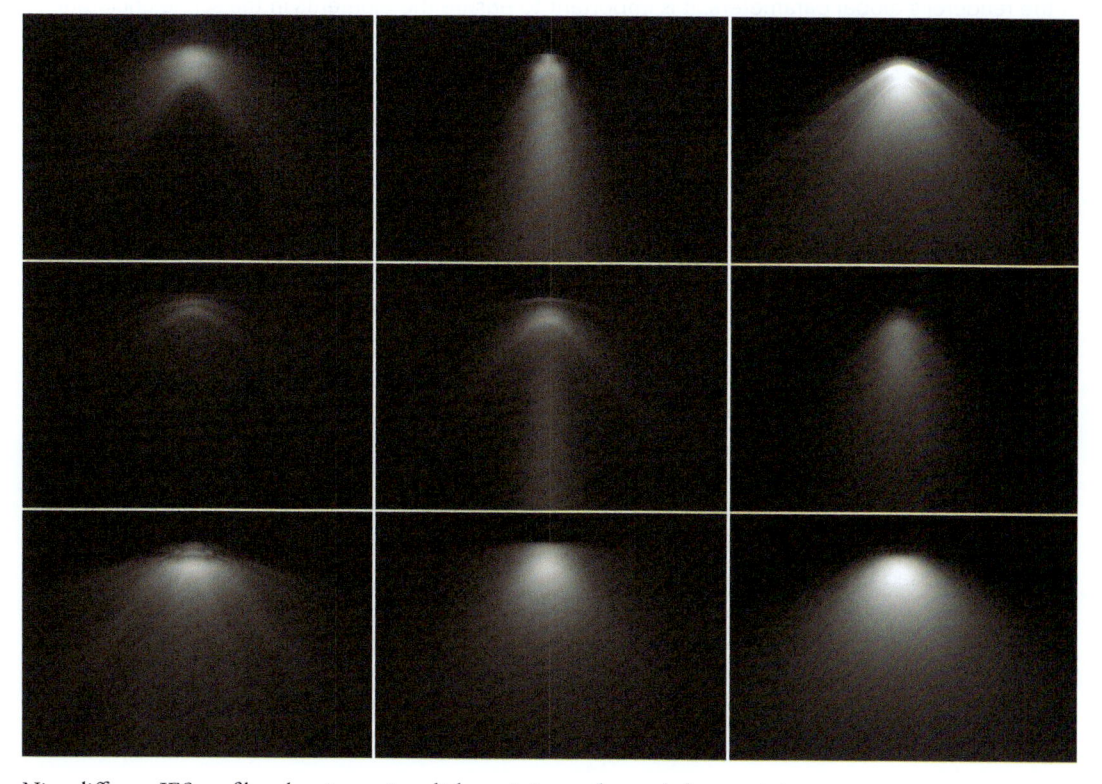

Nine different IES profiles, showing various light emission and spread characteristics.

RENDERING AND LIGHTING

experimentation with different lighting in a virtual environment, and pre-visualizing the results as part of the lighting design process. IES profiles can be directly obtained from different lighting manufacturers, and using a photometric light is as easy as dropping it in the scene and loading the IES profile.

Essential Strategies for PBR Lighting

Scale Matters

Scale is arbitrary in the virtual world of CG, where one unit can be an inch or a mile, a millimeter or a kilometer. In the past, when light emitters were limited to point, spot, and directional, and when global illumination was not an integral part of the raytracing process, there was little importance to the scale of surfaces or the light sources themselves. But with physically based renderers, scale matters: lights have a physical size and accurate quadratic falloff, and all surfaces and textures contribute to the global illumination. A light source with a 1 square inch surface emits considerably less energy than a 10 square feet light, and a one inch white cube contributes much less to the global illumination than a 10 feet cube. PBR's follow real-world paradigms and work best when real-world scale is preserved in the scene. While the intensity of lights can be increased or decreased to compensate for wrong scale, doing so tips off the physical balance of the scene. Moreover, the luminance of texture maps cannot be tweaked in the same way as CG lights, which can further push the lighting away from a photoreal equilibrium. It also goes without saying that photometric lights lose their accuracy when scale is not coherent. So, whichever base unit is set in the renderer's global parameters, it is important to ensure the elements in the scene (including area lights) match the scale of their real-world counterparts.

Natural Daytime Lighting

In the past, achieving convincingly realistic daytime light was a challenge, as it required careful placement of fill lights to simulate diffused sky radiation and occlusion shading. With contemporary PBRs, it is often as simple as dropping a spherical HDR image into the scene and hitting the render button. The combination of Monte Carlo-based fully integrated global illumination and BRDF shaders ensures that light energy emanating from the sky dome is distributed and propagated accurately within the scene. However, sometimes there is a need to further control the balance between direct sunlight and sky radiation. Thus, it is a common practice to erase the sun from the spherical HDR image with a clone-paint tool, and use a directional light instead. While the light's angle, intensity, and hue should roughly match the captured sunlight in the image, there's still some leeway that allows more precise control over intensity and even exact angle. As mentioned previously, most PRBs offer some form of built-in physical sky simulation which can be used to quickly generate accurate sky radiation with varied hued and intensity based on the position of the sun. But such simulations usually lack the real-world detail and variance that is captured in an HDRI, so are better used as look development tools for experimenting with different lighting conditions. There are numerous online libraries of high-quality sky, environment, and interior HDRIs (many for free), so finding a suitable one for a desired lighting is easier today than ever before.

Quarry by Christopher Schindelar.
© Christopher Schindelar.

Skylight Color

The color of diffuse sky radiation is not as blue as the sky itself, but HDR images of clear skies tend to cast an overly saturated blue light, because the light color is derived directly from the deep blue pixels in the image. Some desaturation of the HDR image is useful to achieve a more balanced and realistic result. Also, even though HDRIs have a wide dynamic range, their brightness often needs to be boosted because the merged exposures do not represent the true luminosity of the captured environment. Finally, the color (and especially the white balance) of HDR images is subjective and depends on the camera type and camera settings. When shooting HDR photos, it is very helpful to include a color card (ideally at the bottom of the frame), so that color balance can be corrected and optimized for lighting purposes.

Ambient Occlusion for Outdoor Scenes

As mentioned earlier, ambient occlusion can be used as a cheap and fast alternative to global illumination, especially for real-time rendering. This "cheat" is particularly effective in exterior scenes because the role of bounced light is much less critical outdoors than it is indoors. In an enclosed space, the contribution of bounced light is crucial for the render result (without GI, a room lit by a single window would be much too dark). In exterior scenes however, a large portion of the incident light is reflected back up toward the sky and contributes little to the illumination of the environment. The ambient occlusion alternative works especially well for natural scenes with a lot of small detail and variations (trees, plants etc.), but is less effective for large, uniform surfaces (such as building exteriors) where the lack of true light reflection and color bleeding is more apparent.

Franz Liszt by Hadi Karimi. Maya, Substance Painter, Xgen, rendererd in Arnold. © Hadi Karimi.

Daytime Interior Scenes

Indoor settings that are illuminated by daylight can be problematic: while the exterior environment is a full 360 degrees hemisphere, the light that reaches the interior space through the window/s is restricted to small areas. Most of the sampling is thus wasted on parts of the environment that do not contribute to the lighting, while the lack of samples in the critical regions causes noisiness. Some rendering applications offer a **light portal** tool, basically a plane that is placed in front of the windows and focuses all the exterior light sampling toward that area. Another often-used option is to ditch exterior IBL altogether, and instead place large, bright area lights in front of the windows. This is how interior sets are lit in real life, and it works particularly well when the view out the windows is a simple 2D background image rather than a 3D environment (as it often the case in architectural interior renders).

Man-made Lighting

Chapter 7 provided an overview of the principles of light intensity (Lumen/Lux), and Kelvin color temperature, as well as a rundown of the most common emitters. As mentioned, the type of light modifier (lamp shade, diffuser, reflector, filter, lens, barn doors) often affects the characteristics of the light more than the lamp itself. Rectangle, disc, and cylinder area lights work for most light fixtures, with mesh lights supporting emitters of more complex shape. Some render engines provide an option to set light temperature in Kelvin units, and photometric lights offer an even closer approximation to real-world fixtures. However, the believability of the scene (especially interior renders) depends not only on the right shape, intensity and color of the light, but also on its interaction with the different elements in the light fixture, so even when using photometric lights, it is often necessary to model and shade fixture elements like casings, lamp shades, and diffusers separately. While this may slow down the rendering, the added level of realism achieved through physical fixture elements is worth the price, especially in interior architecture and design.

Case Study: Rendering Interiors in Unreal Engine

© Pasquale Scionti.

I introduced Pasquale Scionti previously in the book, in a case study comparing his render to the photograph he used as reference. It is especially impressive to know that he uses Unreal Engine masterfully for his photoreal visualizations. Here, he briefly describes his work on that particular scene, which was nominated for the 2019 *CGarchitect* award in the Unreal DXR category:

"This scene was inspired by a real photograph – my goal was to recreate that realism using raytracing technology in Unreal Engine. I first modeled the leather sofa in 3D Studio Max starting with basic poly cubes. I used cloth simulation for adding softness, sculpted additional detail and creases in Zbrush, created the leather texture using Substance Source directly in Unreal Engine, and made the pillows and throw in Marvelous Designer. I also modeled and textured the dining storage and coffee tables and added other assets from my 3D library. For lighting, I placed rectangular raytrace lights outside the windows, and used all the raytracing features in Unreal, such as global illumination, ambient occlusion with soft shadows, and realistic reflections."

© Pasquale Scionti.

Chapter 12

Shading

A Brief Overview of Shader Evolution

The most fundamental function of a shader is to calculate the amount of illumination at every point on the surface. The term "shader" itself comes from the traditional art technique of shading areas of partial light occlusion to simulate a three-dimensional look in a 2D painting. Like all other aspects of CG rendering, the development of shaders has been tightly linked to the growth in computing power. A **Lambertian reflectivity model** calculates only diffuse reflections, a much simpler process than calculating specular reflections, because there's no need to reference the environment. Earlier shading models combined a basic Lambertian diffuse component with a simplified specular component.

The most primitive shading model in the evolution tree was the **flat shader**. It checked the angle of each face on a CG model relative to the light source, to determine how much it receives. Since each face was shaded separately, rendered surfaces had a distinctly faceted look. While this could work for a cube, for example, it was unsuitable for any curved, smooth surface. The next evolutionary step, the **Gouraud model** (first published in 1971), calculated the color value at each point of a triangle face, based on the normal vector of that point, and then interpolated those values linearly between vertices. This produced a smooth shading across the surface. While the Gouraud model was good enough for Lambertian shading (and faster to render than subsequent models because it only calculated the color on vertex points), it did not work well for specularity – any highlight that happened to fall at the center of a polygon was simply not "seen", since only vertices were calculated.

Moving on – Bui Tuong Phong published a paper about his light reflection model in 1975. The **Phong** model provided a better alternative to Gouraud shading but required heavier calculations. Unlike Gouraud, which interpolated the color value between vertices, the Phong shader interpolated the vertex normal vectors first, and used this averaged vector value to assign a color for each pixel. This ensured a per-pixel accurate shading, and solved the specular limitation of the Gouraud model. The Phong model was thus more suitable for shiny surfaces. A few years later, Jim **Blinn** developed a modification to the Phong model that reduced rendering time by calculating half-way normal vectors. The Phong/Blinn model became the pillar of CG shading for many years and was used in numerous animation films, VFX, visualizations, and games. However, it is now made obsolete by the more capable **BRDF** model.

A: faceted lambert shader, B: smooth lambert shader, C: Blinn shader.

The BRDF Shading Model

Most physically based renderers use the **Bidirectional Reflectance Distribution Function** model as the basis for their surface shaders.[1] This latest step in the evolution of CG shaders provides the most effective simulation of realistic surface–light interaction, and represents a number of important advantages:

- BRDF shaders use microfacet models like GGX or Cook-Torrance to accurately emulate surface roughness not only for diffuse reflections, but also for specular reflection and transmission.
- BRDF shaders calculate true isotropic and anisotropic specular reflection for dielectric as well as metallic materials.
- Fresnel effect is always factored in reflection/transmission, and is based on either simple refraction indices (for dielectrics) or complex refraction indices (for metals).
- BRDF shaders behave according to the law of conservation of energy. The specular, diffuse, and transmission components are always balanced to prevent any situation where the amount of light leaving the surface exceeds the amount of incident light. For example, specular intensity is automatically reduced with higher roughness values so that the same amount of reflected energy is maintained over the wider specular spread.
- Multiple specular layers are possible within a single material (for example, many BRDF shaders have a second specular layer for clear coat and glossy paint effects).
- True depth-based transmission color is possible (color gets more pronounced as light travels deeper through the surface).
- Complex effects like transmission scattering, dispersion, and subsurface scattering are possible.

Magnifying glass by Raphael Rau. Rendered with Cycles (Blender).
© Raphael Rau.

This impressive list shows why a BRDF model acts as a sort of "super-shader" – it is capable of realistically simulating almost any type of solid and liquid surface and provides a comprehensive and flexible foundation for physically based rendering. While BRDF shaders in various rendering engines differ in some respects, they largely share a similar feature set, which makes it much easier for artists to transition from one application to another, or to create cross-platform materials and texture sets. Below is an overview of the most common BRDF features and how to approach them from a photoreal perspective:

Diffuse

Most BRDF shaders include (in addition to the basic diffuse color and diffuse weight parameters) a **diffuse roughness** setting. This uses a microfacet distribution function to simulate the variance in diffuse reflectivity and light falloff on rougher surfaces. Small roughness values are suitable for materials such as coated plastic, water, and glass, while higher values work well for fibrous or grainy materials like concrete, plaster, sand, or paper.

Dielectric/Metallic Toggle

This parameter (also called "**metallic**" or "**metalness**") is found in all BRDF shaders and has a vital role in the photoreal simulation of materials. While real-world materials are either metallic or dielectric (there is no in-between), in most applications this toggle is a range slider, to accommodate texture maps that drive this parameter and may have intermediate values. As noted in chapter 9, there are some fundamental differences between dielectric materials and metals, so toggling from dielectric to metallic changes some key aspects of the shader:

- The model for specular reflection is changed to properly represent the characteristics of metallic specular reflection, and simple index of refraction is switched to complex index of refraction for correct metallic Fresnel effect.

Left: no diffuse roughness, right: maximum diffuse roughness. The difference is subtle, but when diffuse roughness is high, the surface reflects less in the illuminated areas and the diffuse reflection is more evenly spread out.

- Since metals do not reflect diffusely, the diffuse color parameter effectively controls the specular tint. Setting the diffuse color to yellow, for example, causes all specular reflections to be tinted yellow (as in gold). This is consistent with the principle that the perceived color of a metal is derived from its specular tinting.
- In some applications, certain parameters that are no longer relevant are either grayed-out or ignored. These may include: diffuse roughness, specular intensity/weight (the metallic model assumes 100% specularity for metals), index of refraction, and transmission (again, as the assumption is that metals are never transparent).

Specular

Since BRDF specular reflection maintains energy conservation, the rougher the specularity, the lower its intensity. So, by simply varying the **specular roughness**, one can effectively cover the full range, from highly reflective materials to the dullest surfaces. The **specular intensity** (or specular weight) control is therefore redundant and should normally be kept fixed at 100%.

The **index of refraction** in BRDF shaders does not only affect refraction. It is also linked to the Fresnel effect of specular reflections. As discussed in Chapter 9, a higher IOR increases reflectivity at facing angles. The IOR of most liquid and solid dielectric materials lies between 1.3 and 2.4, so the difference in the Fresnel effect is rather subtle. While it is possible to achieve a crude pseudo-metallic look by raising the IOR much higher, it is completely unnecessary – switching the BRDF to the metallic option is a much better way for simulating metals, for all the reasons described above.

As in older shader types, BRDF shaders include controls for **Anisotropy** amount and direction. But unlike Phong or Blinn shaders, energy conservation in the BRDF model means that the amount of stretching is also affected by the specular roughness parameter (the higher the roughness, the farther anisotropy stretches the highlights). For example, a roughness setting of 0.05 would yield minimal stretching, even if anisotropy amount is set to 100%. This prevents a situation where

A: Shader set to non-metallic (dielectric), B: shader switched to metallic (notice the increased reflectivity and luster), C: roughness is increased, but the metallic feel is maintained.

A: a dielectric shader with specular roughness of 0.05 looks smooth and shiny, B: with roughness increased to 0.3, specular reflection is still visible, but the surface feels duller, C: with roughness of 0.7, the surface looks completely matte. Note that specular intensity has remained at 100%.

extremely bright highlights are stretched over a wide area, resulting in an albedo value that exceeds one. This is also a more photoreal approach: real world anisotropic highlights are almost always the result of tiny elongated grooves or bumps on the surface (for example, brushed metal), and thus are rougher by default.

Coat

Most BRDF shaders come with an optional second specular layer called **coat** (or **clear coat**). This additional layer helps simulate a very wide range of materials that have a thin, clear coating,

A: rough dielectric base layer, B: clear coat with a low roughness value is added, C: sheen effect (see later).

SHADING

lacquer, or resin finish, like many types of plastic, lacquered wood, and coated metals. Coat is also effective in simulating wet surfaces, especially when modulated by a texture. Usually, the main material has a relatively higher specular roughness, while the coat layer provides a shinier, sharper specularity. The combination of a duller base surface and a glossy outer layer creates a complex look that is simply not achievable with a single specular setting.

Transmission

Glass, liquids, gemstones, and other transparent (and semi-transparent) materials were never easy to emulate with Phong and Blinn shaders. BRDF shaders, with their adherence to energy conservation, accurate Fresnel effect, and microfacet transmission distribution, can generate extremely photoreal transmission, refraction, and scattering. Exact transmission parameters differ between applications, but the following description should cover the most common ones.

Most shaders provide control for **transmission weight** (or **transmission amount**), but it is generally better to keep it at 100%, and avoid using in-between values. This ensures that diffuse color has no effect on the appearance of the material (some applications automatically disable diffuse color when transmission amount is set to 100%, others use the diffuse color as the transmission color). Just like with specular reflections, the **transmission roughness** should be used instead to control the amount of transparency, or how clear or "cloudy" the material is. In most BRDF shaders, the transmission roughness is tied to the specular roughness, so increasing the roughness respectively reduces the clarity of the material's transparency. This simulates real-world material properties, where clear transparent materials are also quite shiny, while half-transparent, cloudy materials are duller. However, some BRDF shaders also offer a separate transmission roughness parameter. This is useful when a material needs to be only semi-transparent but still maintain sharp highlights (for example, murky water).

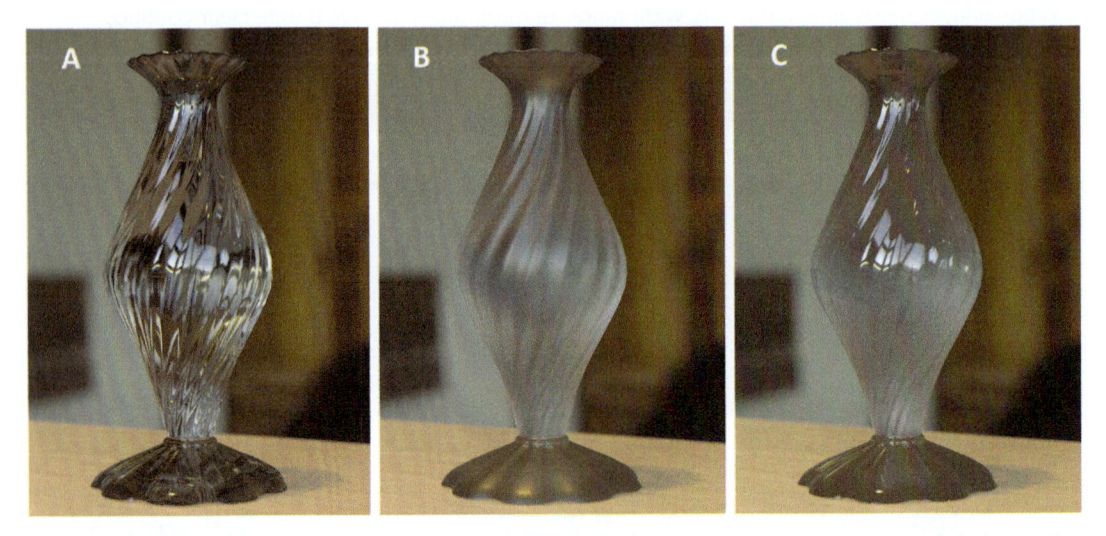

A: 100% transmission with low specular roughness (clear transparency), B: 100% transmission with high specular roughness (cloudy transparency), C: 100% transmission with low specular roughness but high additional transmission roughness (cloudy transparency with sharp highlights).

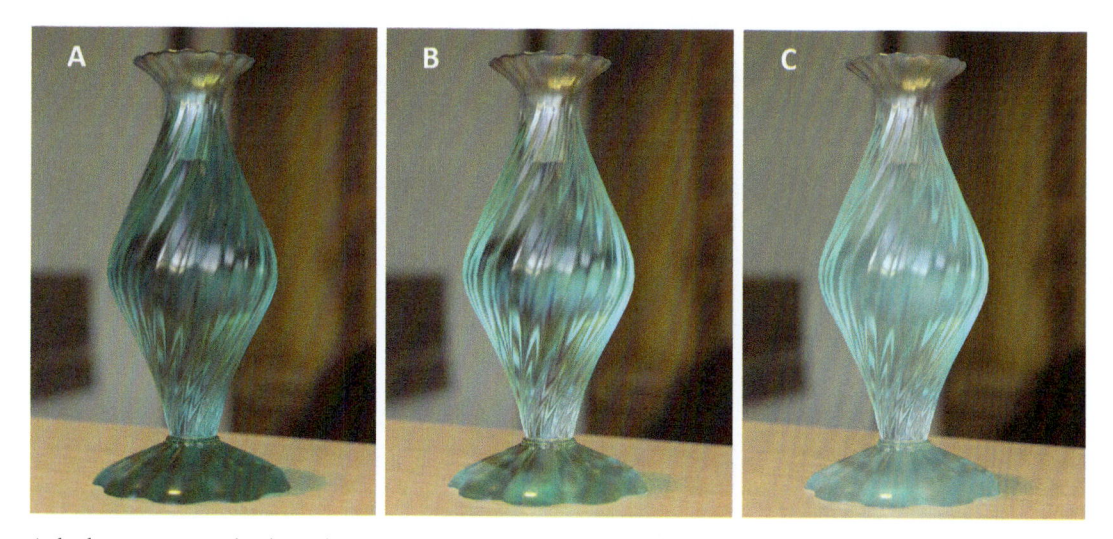

A: high transmission depth result in deeper coloring in thicker areas, B: low transmission depth, C: the same depth amount with increased scattering, causing the transmission color to spread more evenly.

In transparent and semi-transparent materials, **transmission color** (**Fog color** in some render engines) replaces diffuse color to define the base hue of the material. There is a significant difference here: diffuse reflection happens at (or just below) the surface, while transmission color happens as light passes through the object. Transmission color varies with depth – brighter and less saturated in thin areas, darker and more saturated in thick areas. BRDF shaders faithfully recreate this variance of color, which greatly increases the photorealism of transparent and semi-transparent materials. Some shaders offer a separate control for **transmission depth**, which can be used to increase or decrease the apparent thickness of the transmitting material regardless of the real-world scale of the object.

Transmission scatter, another parameter found in some BRDF shaders, is especially handy for emulating thick, murky liquids like honey or certain gemstones. Increasing scattering causes light to spread more evenly through the volume, which works particularly well when specular/transmission roughness is fairly high (clear liquids have minimal scattering). A **scatter anisotropy** parameter allows for a more precise control of the direction of light scattering.

Subsurface Scattering

Most diffuse reflections involve at least some minimal light scattering just below the surface. For practical purposes, many dielectric materials can be emulated in BRDF shaders without using the more computationally intensive subsurface scattering. However, even the smallest hint of scattering can substantially enhance the look and feel of a wide range of non-metals: many types of plastic, foam, stones, rocks, clay, plants, thick liquids, and more. The enhanced photorealism is often worth the extra rendering times, especially for close-up renders where even a subtle effect can make a big difference. Of course, subsurface scattering is a must for materials that are characterized by a deeper penetration of light under the surface: wax, skin, marble, thick leaves and stems, certain types of plastic, gemstones and minerals, etc.

A: no subsurface scattering, B: subsurface scattering with a small radius (notice the "waxy" feel), C: subsurface scattering with a large radius, resulting in a quasi-translucent look.

When the subsurface scattering amount is set to 100%, the diffuse color loses its role, and instead, the **subsurface scattering color** becomes the material's base color. The most important parameter for controlling subsurface scattering is **radius,** which defines how deep the scattering happens under the surface. A small radius generates a subtle, almost imperceptible effect that nonetheless greatly affects the "feel" of the material, giving it a softer, milky look. This is particularly suitable for marble and some types of plastic and stones. A wider radius creates a noticeable sense of translucency, important for materials like wax. As the radius is increased even further, the material may start feeling almost semi-transparent. However, transmission and subsurface scattering are fundamentally different: no matter how large the subsurface scattering radius is, the material always remains opaque (you cannot see through it). Subsurface scattering and transmission, therefore, serve different purposes, and are normally mutually exclusive. That said, unusual and interesting shading effects can be achieved by lowering the subsurface amount below 100%, and creating a mix of diffuse, transmission, and subsurface scattering, with each component assigned its own color map.

Emission

When emission is above zero, the surface acts as a light source. Render engines offer better light emitters (like area and mesh lights), which are optimized for the task and have dedicated controls. But emission is useful for self-illuminated surfaces that contribute little light to the scene (like distant light sources, stars, or neon signs) and effects like phosphorescence and bioluminescence. It is not advisable to use emission as a way of making a surface brighter or to make it stand out in the render. Doing so breaks the law of conservation of energy and damages the photoreal coherence of the render. It can also slow down the render because the surface is now treated as an additional light source in the scene. Emission should only be used for self-illuminating surfaces.

Additional BRDF Features

Beyond the basic features described above, different BRDF surface shaders may have one or more of these extra features:

SHEEN

Although this word is often used to describe glossiness or shininess, in CG terminology it relates specifically to the characteristic velvety effect of microfiber in textiles (and other fuzzy surfaces). Sheen is not specular reflection but rather a soft luster that is related to the facing direction of the microfibers. It is therefore a distinct effect that is particularly useful for emulating garments, upholstery, rugs, carpets, bed linens, and even skin.

THIN-FILM INTERFERENCE

Thin-film simulates the diffraction that happens when light hits a very thin, clear layer like the wall of a soap bubble, an oil slick, or some types of glass coating. This wave interference creates a rainbow-like appearance that shifts pattern and color depending on the angle of the surface and the light.

DISPERSION

The separation of frequencies as light that is refracted in transparent materials is the cause of chromatic aberrations in lenses. The amount of dispersion in different types of glass is indicated by their **abbe number** (also called the **V-number**). The higher the abbe value, the lower the dispersion. Some render engines provide a dispersion feature that is especially useful for accurate visualizations of glass and jewelry. The abbe number of most glass types is somewhere between 100 and 20, so the effect of dispersion is normally very subtle and hardly perceptible. It is possible to achieve prism-like results by pushing the abbe number below 20, though the results become more stylistic than photoreal.

A: an abbe value of 30 produces a subtle, realistic dispersion that makes the glass feel slightly yellowish, B: an abbe value of 1 generates an exaggerated prism-like effect, C: thin film interference is a completely different effect, suitable for soap bubbles and oil slicks.

SHADING

Other Common Shaders

Since a shader is merely a description of how light interacts with a surface, shader-writers can create an almost endless variety that ranges from specific material types, to shaders that simulate complex systems like grass or ocean waves. While it is impossible to cover every type of shader here, the following is a brief overview of some of the most common shader types available in rendering packages:

Car Paint Shaders

Cars are a ubiquitous subject in many types of renders, from VFX and commercials to product visualizations, so it is not surprising that most rendering packages offer a dedicated car paint shader. Generally, such shaders are an elaboration on the clear coat principle, and offer extended control over the color and specularity of the base and coat layers, as well as an emulation of the tiny flakes that are a characteristic feature of metallic car paints. These additional features help create a rich, multi-layered look that is useful not just for cars, but for many other types of painted surfaces.

Volumetric Shaders

Voxel-based fluid simulations are used to simulate volumes of small particles like fog, smoke, dust, and fire. To successfully emulate their unique scattering and absorption characteristics, the shader needs to have specific material attributes that are quite different from solid or liquid materials.

McLaren/720S Ludus-Blue by Carlos Colorsponge.
© Carlos Colorsponge.

Most physically based renderers offer volumetric shaders with dedicated controls for features like density (or thickness), scattering, opacity, and even emission and temperature (for light-emitting volumes like fire).

Hair/Fur Shaders

Because hair is a collection of numerous thin strands, it reacts to light in a markedly different way than solid or liquid surfaces as well as volumetric entities. Hair and fur display a distinct combination of reflection, transmission, scattering, and sheen that is difficult to simulate using standard surface or volume shaders. While in the past, some VFX companies developed their own proprietary hair and fur shaders, nowadays most renderers offer a hair/fur shader out of the box. Unlike standard BRDF shaders, which share similar parameters across different applications, features and terminology in different hair shaders is quite varied. However, most hair shaders provide detailed control over melanin (natural hair color) or dye (artificial color), as well as glossiness, backlighting, and sheen (or glint) amounts. Randomizing color and other parameters is important for achieving a complex, photoreal hair/fur look, and most hair shaders offer some control over randomness and subtle variations.

Bengal Tiger by Massimo Righi. Modeled in Maya and Zbrush, fur generated with Shave and a Haircut, rendered with Arnold.

© Massimo Righi.

Case Study: CG Portraiture

The Forever by Maxchill Patiphan.

© Maxchill Patiphan.

Like all living beings, humans are a complex and challenging subject to create realistically in CG. But what makes humans even tougher is the fact that we are so intimately familiar with our own kind. We rely on visual cues to read emotion and intent and are inherent experts of the human face and body. Thus, we are all strict critics when it comes to CG people. *The Forever* by Maxchill Patiphan is not just a superb photoreal portrait, it also stands out in a world full of young CG heroes and heroines with a perfect physique. It is, in my opinion, a brave and touching rendition of the beauty and tenderness of old age, and is thus much more than well-done CG. Yet, beyond the unusual subject, it is the artist's admirable attention to detail that shines here: the finely sculpted wrinkles, the blemishes on the skin, the detail on the sweater (down to the tiniest wool fibers), the fine hair work – the combination all of these factors contributes to a believable, warm, and, well, human rendition.

© Maxchill Patiphan.

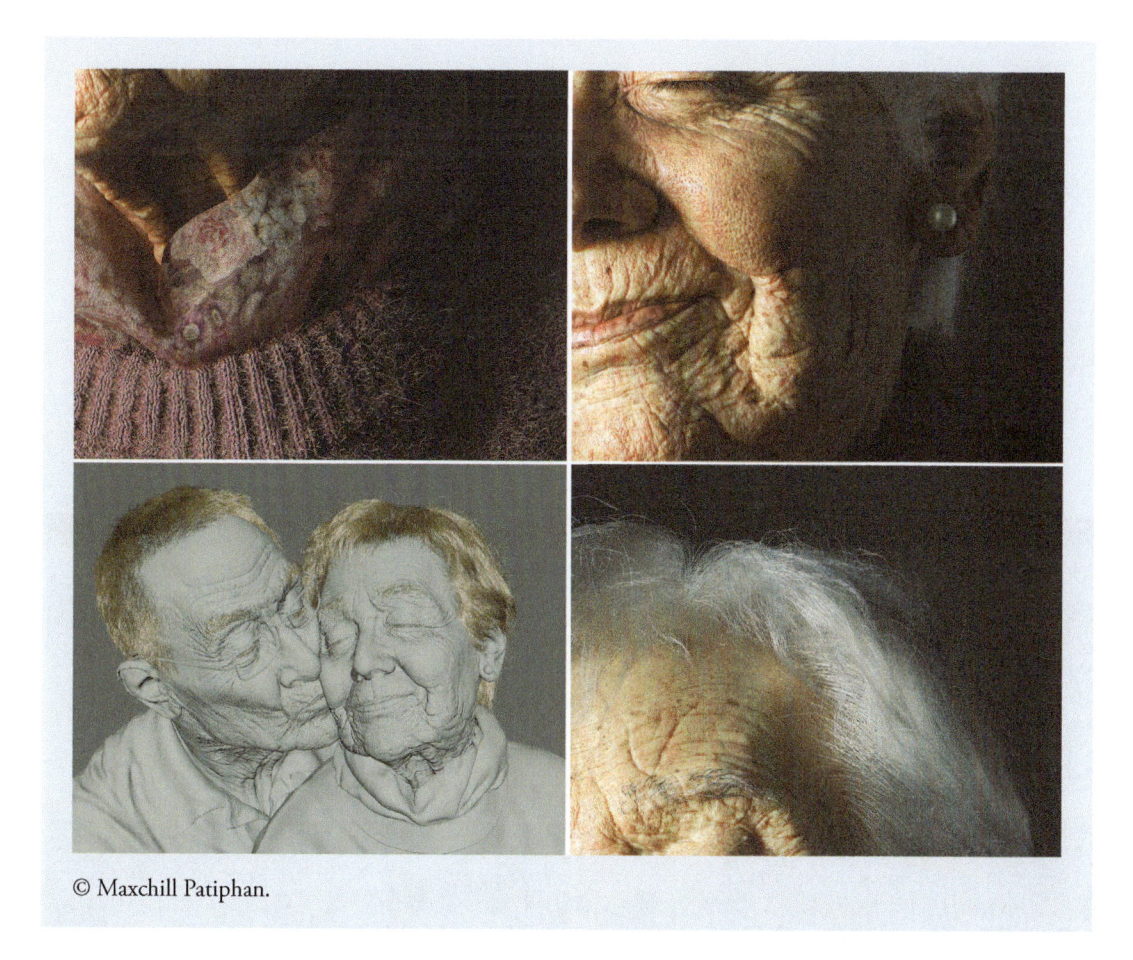

Note

1   Some 3D applications use the term BSDF (Bidirectional Scattering Distribution Function). In general, the principles of BRDF discussed here apply to BSDF as well.

Chapter 13

Texturing

Racing Hovercraft by Jose Iuit. Maya, Zbrush, Substance Painter, Mari, Marvelous Designer, V-Ray.
© Jose Iuit.

Textures add surface detail that is crucial for believable imagery. One can say that texture mapping has greater impact on photorealism than modeling, shading, or lighting, because our eyes are instinctively drawn to color variations and patterns that define surfaces. Simply switching the color texture on a cube can instantly transform it from a stone wall to a concrete slab, a cereal box, a metal container, or a book. But texture mapping is of course much more than just colors and patterns. By definition, a texture is something that you can feel, not just see. A wooden table feels different than a towel, and the smooth surface of a plastic box feels different than the surface of a stone. So, while we cannot physically touch surfaces in a CG render, it is the role of texture maps to visually recreate that "feel" by modulating shader properties like bumps, displacement, ambient occlusion, roughness, metalness, or transmission. Texturing can substantially raise the level of believability but can also do the exact opposite: no matter how good the models, lighting, and shaders, common texturing mistakes like noticeable repetition, implausible grime maps, or over-the-top bumps can easily ruin a render. This chapter focuses on the contemporary PBR texturing workflow, and aspects of texturing that are most pertinent to photorealism.

PBR Texturing

Physically based rendering is a wide term and does not necessarily indicate a specific category or method of rendering. But it is often used in CG talk to describe a texturing workflow that is based on a set of maps that drive the most common shading parameters of BRDF shaders (diffuse color, specular roughness, dielectric-metallic definition, bumps, displacement, and ambient occlusion). Depending on the material, this base set may be augmented with additional maps (like transmission, opacity, and subsurface scattering). PBR texturing now works with the vast majority of renderers, including most game engines, and this makes it easier to create materials that can be used in different applications. In this section we will look at the role of each texture type within a PBR map set, and discuss ways to maximize the texture's contribution to the photoreal appearance of the material.

Stages of PBR texturing. 1: untextured model, 2: base color texture, 3: specular roughness map, 4: bumps/normal map, 5: metallic/dielectric map, 6: closer angle, showing how the roughness and bump maps are used to add subtle imperfections.

TEXTURING

The Linear Workflow

A few words about the linear workflow: there are no color spaces in nature – the interaction of light and surfaces is universally linear. Physically based renderers must operate in linear space for light interaction to be calculated properly. Unfortunately, different display technologies make it necessary to add color curves to digital images. By default, computer images are saved in sRGB color space (they have a sRGB gamma curve baked in) so that they display correctly on computer monitors. But when sRGB images are used in linear color space, they are much too dark. Global illumination in PBRs depends on the color values of textures in the scene, so overly dark textures completely skew the lighting solution, forcing the artist to boost the light energy of scene emitters, which throws the render off the photoreal path. Initially, texture artists had to manually convert images to linear color space, but nowadays most 3D and rendering applications provide a color management system that automatically linearizes images (reverses their color space curve), based on the specified source color space and format. While most color maps are based on sRGB images, many of the secondary maps described below are not feeding color data into the shader. For example, the color values of a normal map define XYZ vectors, and a roughness or metallic texture is a zero-to-one grayscale map. To work properly, non-color maps should always be set to linear (raw) color space at input to maintain their values.

Base Color Map

Also called **diffuse color** or **albedo**, the base color texture is the most important in the PBR map set, for two main reasons: first, our eyes instinctively focus on color patterns to make out what we see. Therefore, color textures are the front-line "delineators" of the material and are scrutinized more than, say, bump textures, because we are so sensitive to implausibility in color. Second, color maps in a PBR system do not only represent the material's diffuse colors – they define the way a surface reflects light and how it affects the environment. Whether you are using photographs, procedural functions, texture painting, or some combination thereof, the base color map has a crucial role in the final render result. Consequently, there are some key issues to be aware of:

DIELECTRIC/METALLIC DIFFERENCES

The base color map has a different role in metallic materials. In dielectrics, the base color texture represents the color of the diffuse reflection color (the diffuse albedo), and defines which

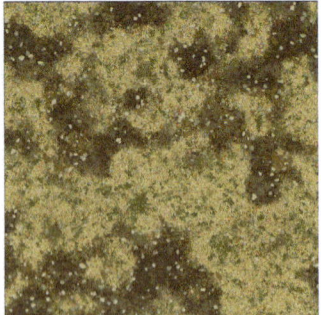

The color map for a wet ground material, showing the different sand, mud, water, moss, and pebbles colors.

wavelengths are absorbed and which are diffusely reflected. In metallic materials, the base color map affects the specular reflection color (metals derive their colors from tinting the specular reflection). This is important to understand in the context of PBR-safe colors described below.

PBR SAFE RANGE

Physically based rendering abides by the law of conservation of energy. Since the base color texture defines the albedo values of the surface, extreme bright or dark values may cause the surface to react unnaturally to incoming light by reflecting or absorbing too much of it, in essence breaking the rule of conservation of energy. While there is no precise definition for a "good" color range, the common safe range for diffuse color maps lies around 30–240 (using a standard 0–255 sRGB scale), while the range for metallic color is around 180–255. Most texture authoring applications provide tools for checking the brightness of color textures. Ensuring that values fall within the PBR safe range can eliminate lighting and rendering issues down the line.

CONTRAST AND SATURATION

Regardless of PBR safe ranges, extreme contrast and saturation in base color textures should also be avoided. Color textures need to react well to any CG lighting setup in the scene, and sharp differences in luminance values, as well as pitch-black areas or overblown highlights, may cause parts of the object to pop out unnaturally in the render. Extreme saturation is also problematic, as it makes it hard to balance the lighting in the scene (later in this chapter we will discuss ways to avoid these issues when shooting and sourcing material for textures).

AVOIDING OVERLY BUSY COLOR

There is a tendency to cram all the texture information into the color map. While sometimes this is necessary, it often leads to an overflow of color information on the surface, and a noisy, unrealistic feel. Take a look around you – many surfaces have a rather flat color, and some of the variations we detect are due to roughness or reflectivity, and not necessarily the base color. It is therefore good practice to delegate some of the detail to secondary textures like specular roughness, bumps or even displacement.

Scanned textures test render.
© Cristopher Schindelar.

Roughness Map

In a PBR/BRDF setup, it is assumed that the specular amount is constant, and only the specular roughness varies between shiny and dull materials. A roughness map is necessary for complex, layered materials. For example, on a partially painted wooden beam, the roughness value should be higher where the underlying wood is revealed, and lower in the painted areas. In a wet pavement material, roughness is higher in the dry parts. But simple single-layered materials can also benefit from differences in specular roughness, which can hint at areas of smudges or dust. A roughness map is a great way to add subtle imperfections to smooth, clean surfaces like glass windows or polished metal.

Extracting a roughness map from photographs can be tricky since the color values in a photo do not necessarily represent specular roughness. Texture authoring applications offer some smart functions to simplify the process, but sometimes it is better to paint the roughness values manually when using a photo as a base texture.

Metallic Map

The metallic (or metalness) map is a grayscale texture that defines which areas in the material have metallic properties. This is an essential map for any layered or mixed surface that combines

The roughness map is brighter in the sand and pebbles (rougher surfaces), and much darker in the water puddles (reflective areas).

Rust areas are darker (dielectric) in the metallic map of this simpe rusty metal material.

metallic and dielectric elements. Rusted metal is a classic example – while the clean non-oxidized areas are metallic, the rust itself is not. Without a metallic map, the rusty parts would look strangely reflective and metallic, and the material's layered feel will be lost.

With procedural or layered textures, it is usually easy to derive the metallic map's values from the relevant layer/s. When processing a single photo, it is of course harder. Often, the metallic map can be derived from differences in hues. For example, in a photo of a rusty surface, the rust may have a more saturated warm tone than the underlying metal, and a similar difference in hue is likely to happen with painted metal. Regardless of the method used to create the metallic map, it's important to crank the contrast and values of the map so that they are close to either zero or one, and avoid too much gradient gray shades: areas should be either metallic or dielectric, and the transition should be fairly sharp.

Bump (Normal) Map

From the very beginning of CG, bump maps were used to create the illusion of surface roughness and small-scale detail. The emphasis here is on "illusion" and "small scale", because unlike displacement, bumps do not affect the actual geometry, and are nothing more than a shading trick of the eye. Bumps are therefore somewhat of a double-edged sword: when used correctly they can add a remarkable amount of subtle detail to any surface by breaking up specular reflections and adding dimension and depth. There is, however, a certain tendency to push bump mapping too far in an attempt to increase realism by emphasizing surface features. This often causes the opposite result, because real-world surface roughness is generally only noticeable up close, and quickly loses its definition with distance. When bumps are too strong, their prominence from a distance harms the realism of the image. And when viewed up close, exaggerated bumps reveal their "fakery", especially along the outline of the object. It is therefore a good practice to combine bumps and displacement, relying on displacement for the larger features and using bumps only for smaller detail.

Originally, simple grayscale height maps were used for bumps, but today normal maps are preferred, because they use RGB to represent a three-dimensional relief rather than just an up–down value in a grayscale map. Traditional game modeling relies heavily on normal maps, which are first extracted from a detailed, high-poly model and then reapplied as bumps/displacement to a low-poly version of the same model. This technique also works well in VFX and visualization, especially when dealing with scanned or sculpted models that contain a massive amount of

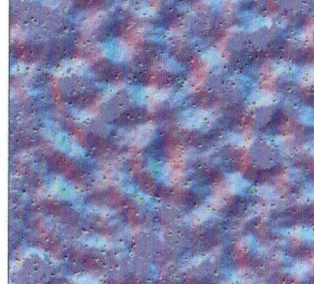

The normal map uses RGB to represent XYZ relief values.

surface detail. That said, bump maps are a crucial component in practically every material, as very few are perfectly smooth. The relationship between bumps and specular reflections is particularly important. A subtle bump texture that is hardly felt as surface roughness can nonetheless break specularity in ways that hint to fine irregularity. For example, even a clean glass window can feel more realistic with a few scratches or some unevenness of the glass. When used well, bump mapping can add a level of complexity to evenly colored surfaces, and thus contribute to a richer and more photoreal look.

Generating a normal map from a photograph can be quite challenging, because dark and bright values do not necessarily represent height. For example, the roughness pattern of a rug may be completely different from its color pattern. The process of generating bump maps requires image manipulation skills in order to isolate the roughness-relevant color differences from the rest (material authoring applications like Substance Alchemist have some useful tools to help with the process). Sometimes, when there's not enough information in the color image to produce meaningful height detail, it makes more sense to create the bumps through texture painting or procedural generation, separate from the color image.

A fully procedural workflow greatly simplifies the creation of normal maps because height detail is separate from color detail. But even with procedural textures, it is important to choose the right balance between larger and smaller features. When the bump values of a tiny dent and a deep fissure are similar, the material looks overly noisy and the amount of detail feels unnatural. Large-scale and small-scale bumps maps need to be sensibly mixed with this relative balance in mind.

Ambient Occlusion (AO) Map

In physically based rendering, ambient occlusion is calculated as an integral part of the global illumination process. However, the renderer can only detect light occlusion based on geometry – it cannot calculate occlusion for bumps. The AO texture is thus a useful companion to the bump (normal) map. It reinforces the illusion of nooks and crannies on the surface by shading cavities and partially occluded areas in the material itself, adding depth to an otherwise flat texture. The AO texture is usually applied as a multiplier to the base color texture, so darker (more occluded) values in the AO map darken the colors while white areas have no effect.

In games (which rely heavily on normal maps for surface detail), AO maps are a necessity, but they are useful in any type of render situation where surface detail is conveyed through bump maps.

Areas that receive the least amount of light are darkest in the AO map (under pebbles, for example).

In a procedural workflow, the AO texture is directly derived from the height information. With photos, the process is tied to generating a grayscale bump map: the same values that are used to define lower (recessed) parts in the bumps are used to define a stronger occlusion. As with bump maps, AO textures should be kept subtle: over-cranked occlusion can tip the lighting balance in a scene by shifting too much emphasis toward small-scale shading detail. In the final render, the darkest values in the AO texture should not be darker than true geometry-based occlusion in the scene.

Displacement (Height) Map

Unlike bumps, displacement effectively modifies the underlying geometry. This makes the displacement texture somewhat unique among PBR maps because it is, in fact, a modeling tool (rather than a shading tool). For displacement to work properly, the affected geometry must have enough subdivision at render time. The finer the displacement detail, the denser the subdivision must be. For this reason, displacement maps are used when height detail is prominent enough in the context of the scene. For example, it is quite an overkill to use displacement for a carpet texture (bump will suffice), unless the carpet is viewed at extreme close-up. On the other hand, displacement works best when height differences are not too extreme, and the geometry is not overly stressed. Displacement and bumps work well together, especially when displacement is used for the largest features in the material while bumps fill in the smaller detail. Therefore, when generating displacement maps from images, it is advised to mask out (or blur) small features in the image and keep only the larger detail.

Transparency Map vs. Opacity Map

A transparency map controls the transmission amount in the material – it is useful for varying the transparency of a surface, or to differentiate between opaque and transparent areas in a layered material. A transparency map does not affect reflection and bumps, which may still be visible in fully transparent areas (for example, on a clear window glass). However, sometimes the goal is to simply make parts of a surface invisible. In such a case, an opacity map should be used. The opacity map does not control any physical transmission properties of the material, it simply causes

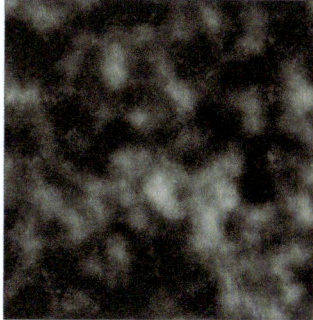

The displacement map is a simple altitude map, usually representing larger surface features.

the surface to completely disappear wherever the opacity value is zero. Opacity maps are mostly used as "cookie-cutters" for thin elements like leaves or twigs, for creating objects like fences or nets without actually modeling the fine detail, or as a mask in layered materials.

Texture Generation Workflows

Essentially, there are three basic workflows for creating a texture map:

- Using one or more photographs (captured, scanned, or sourced)
- Generating the map procedurally, using a dedicated procedural texture authoring application
- Hand-painting the map, either in a 2D application (usually with the unwrapped UVs as a guide), or directly on the model, using a 3D paint application.

There is no superior methodology, since the choice of workflow depends on the specific material, model, and context. Each of these texturing approaches has its merits and limitations, and often the most practical and efficient solution is a combination of two or three approaches. In the following sections, we will examine these texturing workflows and look at ways to maximize their advantages and improve photorealism.

Image Textures

The main advantage of photo-based textures is of course the fact that they are inherently photoreal. Image textures retain all the complexity and subtlety of the real world and can add a remarkable amount of realism to even the simplest CG scene. Photographing or sourcing photos for textures is a more straight-forward process then procedural generation, and image textures carry the kind of intricate, natural detail that is hard (and sometimes impossible) to emulate artificially. The increased popularity and availability of quality 3D scans has redefined image textures as an inseparable and organic part of the model. This further strengthens the role of image textures as the most effective means of connecting CG to the real world.

That said, image textures have some significant disadvantages:

- Photographs are two dimensional, so image-based textures need to be wrapped around objects. This requires meticulous UV mapping and applying multiple textures to different sections of the mesh to avoid stretching or tearing.
- Image textures often need to be tiled to cover large surfaces. While there are many tools that facilitate tiling, photographs may need substantial retouching work to achieve seamless tiling (and some simply don't tile well).
- Lighting is baked into every photograph, and photos with strong directional lighting can be extremely problematic for texturing. This substantially limits the choice for sourced images and forces some strict limitations on shooting photographs for texturing.
- Generating secondary maps (like specular roughness, bumps or ambient occlusion) from a photograph can be very challenging, because the color information does not necessarily represent height, occlusion, or specularity.

Conifer forest scanned ground textures test by Christopher Schindelar.
© Christopher Schindelar.

Shooting and Prepping Photos for Texturing

CG artists have access to an enormous selection of free and commercial generic photographic texture maps, and the higher-quality ones are often preprocessed for optimal lighting and seamless tiling. But many situations call for specific textures that can only be obtained by photographing or scanning surfaces. This section offers some advice for minimizing the issues listed previously, while shooting and prepping materials for texturing.

Resolution

Texture size is important – a resolution that is too low may result in degraded, soft, pixelated, or aliased look, which can hurt the believability of the material. 2K texture maps are the norm for generic materials, but not every texture needs to be 2K. For example, a texture map that is intended to cover a small area or to be tiled multiple times (like a single bolt or a single bathroom tile) can, and should be, smaller. On the other hand, textures that are meant to cover a large surface with no tiling (say, an entire brick wall) may need to be 4K or even higher, depending on the final render resolution. When shooting photos for textures, it is best to use the highest available resolution, to allow cropping and further editing down the line.

Baked-in Lighting

The rule is simple: avoid direct light. For example, direct sunlight produces harsh shadows, bright specular reflections, and extreme differences in luminosity between lit and shadowed arears. This does not only limit the texture's usability in different CG lighting scenarios, it makes it extremely hard to generate subsidiary maps like specular roughness, normal, or displacement. Outdoor photos and 3D scans should always be captured under overcast sky or in full shadow. Indoor photos should be lit as flatly and diffusely as possible, avoiding any noticeable effect of direct light sources, or strong cast shadows. Even a gradual color change due to soft shadows can make it hard to tile the texture. Inconsistencies in lighting and luminosity must be corrected and "flattened" in an image-editing software or a dedicated texture-authoring application.

Angle, Perspective, and Focus

Ideally, texture photos should be taken at a straight angle. For the same reason, it is also better to use medium or long lenses to minimize the distortion of wider lenses. When shooting large or tall objects, it is not always possible to find a parallel vantage point (for example, shooting the trunk texture of a large tree from the ground). Perspective and distortion can be corrected in an image-editing application. Sharpness, on the other hand, cannot be restored in post, so photographs should always be captured as sharp as possible, by avoiding a shallow depth of field (using a smaller aperture and keeping the focal point at a reasonable distance).

Exposure

Brightness and contrast can be easily changed as the image is prepared for the texture. But muddy blacks or clamped highlights cannot be salvaged. It is important to ensure that enough detail and color information is captured at both extremities of the color range. Photos should always be saved as raw in the camera, never JPG, to preserve the full dynamic range and allow

Garden Scene Scanned textures test by Christopher Schindelar.
© Christopher Schindelar.

for extensive image manipulation in the texture prep stage. If possible, three or five different exposures per angle can really expand dynamic range and help produce a texture with consistent lighting and clear detail.

Optimizing Photographs for Tiling

As mentioned, avoiding directional or uneven lighting goes a long way toward smoother tiling. Color and luminosity across the texture should be equalized, to avoid a noticeable repeated gradient. Another area that needs careful attention is repetition: singular or unusual detail (like a knot in a tree bark or a lone bolt in a concrete wall) can add a great deal of realism if the texture is used as-is, but will look conspicuously repetitious once the texture is tiled. Such detail can be easily spotted when tiling the image and should be removed (usually with a clone-paint brush).

Procedural Textures

Procedural texture maps are generated from scratch using a combination of different mathematical functions like noise, fractal algorithms, and pattern generators. 3D applications have always included a basic selection of procedural functions (for example, Maya's Brownian, cloud, or marble functions). But procedural material creation received a serious boost in recent years with the introduction of dedicated material-authoring software like Substance Designer, which provides powerful procedural tools coupled with a streamlined system for exporting materials as texture map sets for contemporary PBRs.

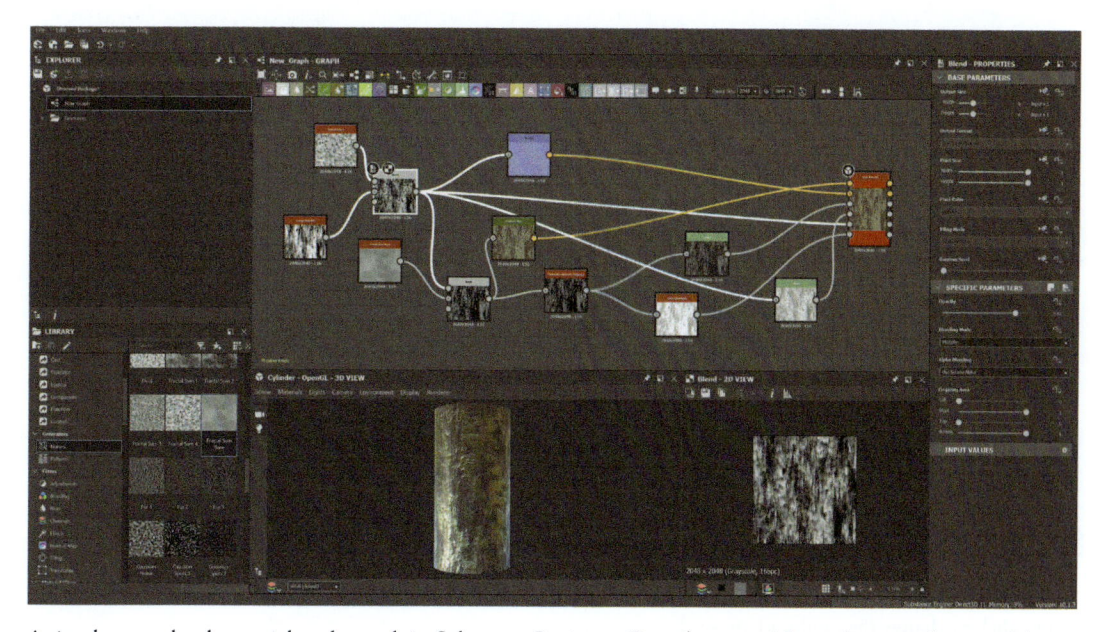

A simple procedural material node graph in Substance Designer. Complex materials can have much more elaborate graphs.

TEXTURING

Procedural textures have some significant advantages over image-based textures:

- They are fully editable and controllable, with full flexibility at every level and over every aspect.
- A single "master" texture can be easily and quickly randomized or tweaked to create a range of variations on the same look.
- Procedurally generated maps are not hampered by baked-in lighting and work with any lighting setup.
- A procedural workflow makes it easy to generate secondary maps for bump, occlusion, roughness etc.
- Tiling is easy and seamless.

Being a mathematical product, procedural textures lack the inherent real-world realism of photographic textures and tend to feel somewhat mechanical and generic. It is of course possible to create intricately rich textures with a purely procedural workflow, but successfully implementing the typical real-world imperfections and detail requires meticulous work and expertise. However, this downside must always be weighed against the power of procedural textures. Take, for example, a leaf texture: while it is possible (but not easy) to emulate such a texture procedurally, it makes a lot more sense to just scan or photograph the leaf (or find a photo of it) to get the exact, real look with very little effort. But what if this texture needs to be applied to thousands of leaves on a tree? This is where a procedural workflow shines, because it can easily generate multiple variations of the same texture, avoiding the cloned look of repeated image textures.

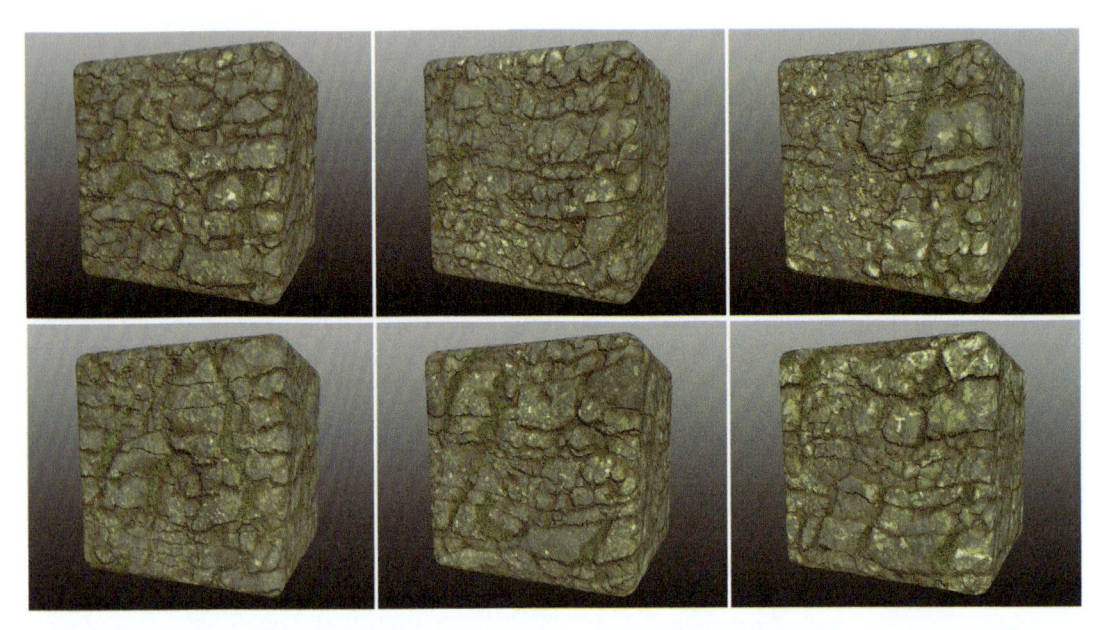

Six variations of a procedural stone wall material, all similar yet each uniquely different, generated with a single mouse click to change the random base seed.

Combining Workflows

Texturing workflows have changed in the past few years. Look at games for example: the introduction of new texture authoring applications opened up the vast possibilities of procedural texturing. Expansive 3D environments in many games require a huge library of textures and a fast workflow, and the fact that a single procedural texture prototype can be easily changed and repurposed is a boon. Procedural texturing brings the promise of infinite variation, but ironically, the results are often quite the opposite: many games suffer from a sort of generic "procedural look" that makes everything feel nearly identical. It is almost as if you're seeing the same rusted metal/peeling paint material everywhere. Like any other aspect of digital art, texture authoring is a craft that requires creativity, imagination, and attention to detail. The best results can often be achieved by mixing images, procedural functions, and hand painting. Here are some tips for combined workflows:

- Texture maps that need to cover wide areas (for example, ground textures) often suffer most from repetitious tiling. One way to dodge this issue is to tile the base image texture a few times first, then use the tiled result as a base, to which additional large-scale procedural and/or hand-painted maps are added. This helps breaking (or masking) the repetition while preserving the underlying photographic quality.

Marabou Stork by Jose Iuit. Created in Zbrush, Maya, and Xgen, textured in Mari, rendered with V-Ray. © Jose Iuit.

- Procedural functions are great for creating patterns and tiles for pavement, walls, structures, etc., and can be combined with a base image map that provides the fine color detail and variation. In general, using images for the color and procedurals for bump and displacement makes it much easier to produce effective secondary maps. For example, a brick wall can be created by first generating the brick pattern procedurally, then adding color detail for the bricks and the mortar from image textures. The procedural pattern is then used for clean and precise bumps, AO, and roughness, while the diffuse map benefits from the realism of photographic detail.
- One way to avoid a "procedural look" is to mix several different noises or grunge maps (using overlay, screen, or multiply) to break up the familiar patterns of Perlin noise and other commonly used functions. Varying the scale and intensity of the noise layers can help create a rich, natural texture. Another option is to break up procedural patterns with image textures. This can add irregularity and randomness to function-based patterns.
- Texture authoring applications offer smart procedural functions for applying dirt, wear, and tear in certain areas, based on the height, ambient occlusion, or curvature values of the underlying layers. This is useful for quick, basic dirt/gunge layers, but specific, topology-based wear and dirt should be hand-painted on the actual object using a texture paint application.
- Hand-painted wear and dirt effects look best when added in physically correct areas. Finger smudges and spots normally happen in the areas of higher interaction (such as doorknobs, touch buttons, or touch screens, levers or handles); scratches appear around areas of friction, or areas that are exposed to the elements; dust usually collects in areas of least interaction, under objects, and in cracks and nooks; water marks follow paths downward along the curvature of the surface, and so on. Topology-specific texture painting can truly boost the believability of texture maps by tying the features to the model in an organic, interactive fashion, and is a good way to avoid the above-mentioned generic grime look.

Case Study: Creating Bark Textures for SpeedTree

Sarah Scruggs is a painter, photographer, and lead artist at IDV (the developer of SpeedTree). I asked Sarah about IDV's proprietary process for acquiring and editing realistic bark textures for SpeedTree's plant library. Here is her description:

Bark and foliage of a SpeedTree conifer model.
© IDV Inc.

"I was approached by IDV because they needed a bark photographer and I was recommended as a 'tree geek' by a current employee. With the arrival of SpeedTree version 8, IDV wanted to deliver a significantly improved texture asset library, which meant starting from scratch on the texture bank. So, my first part-time hours were offsite, gathering photos of trees in the woods. We moved from an experimental stage to determining a method for gathering these textures. One of the IDV engineers built the scanning rig and system that we currently use at the office. That led to the creation of our photo-scanning process and the birth of the version 8 library.

To create bark textures, we usually use one of these three methods:

Outdoor photography:

This method is available while traveling deep in the woods and works well for getting surprisingly high-quality scans. I set a control ball on the bark to mark the shadows for the computer to read and work with an SLR camera. The trick here is to photograph early mornings when the shadows are not as harsh. In the woods, you have to deal with many variables like branches crossing and leaves obstructing the shot. You need a certain distance from the tree trunk to your camera on all four sides, to enable using your flash without casting shadows. The scan that you get from this method is curved, so the images must be artificially corrected after shooting. SpeedTree's proprietary software allows us to do bending as well as normal facing adjustments.

Scanning in a controlled environment

We break off bits of bark from the tree in two- to four-inch sections. For a long section like a gnarl from top to finish, we break off a large strip of the tree and cut it in two workable sections where the seam is easy to hide. Our leaf/bark scanner is a DSLR camera set up on a rig. A few factors help us completely control the light. We use a dark room with a polarized light setup to reduce highlights.

Photogrammetry

Our newest adventures have sent us gathering photogrammetry models using a rather in-depth process. The "stitch generator" can generate a blend between the unwrapped mesh and the procedural SpeedTree parts. We often take chunks from a photogrammetry scan and use them to build that procedural bark so that the two will blend even more easily.

Creating seamless bark textures

We create a tiled texture using scanned bark chunks and pieces and make sure the ends and sides wrap. It's partially procedural where we spawn a bunch of the same chunks with some repetition, but this part is often hand-hooked together like a puzzle, especially when a texture has a long linear pattern. For those I might create a chain of chunks that need to fit together. Our in-house software allows us to make adjustments across all of the maps.

Not all barks are created with the same approach and there is a good bit of art involved here in assessing how it is all put together. On special trees that are the focal point of the scene, SpeedTree lets you connect and blend several textures. With this feature, we can make a more custom texture for the base of the tree and apply the regular wrapping textures farther up the tree.

Textured Sago Palm SpeedTree model.
© IDV Inc.

Chapter 14

Modeling

It goes without saying that a disproportionate human figure or a grossly inaccurate car model reduce the believability of a render. But assuming 3D elements are modeled correctly and match their real-world counterparts, does modeling really affect photorealism? Much of this book is focused on light and its interaction with surfaces (and, consequently, color). Modeling is thus a unique subject in the context of this book – it has nothing to do with light and color. Or does it? This chapter is not an overview of modeling techniques – there are many books about that subject. Instead, this chapter focuses on two specific modeling aspects that particularly affect photorealism: modeling for lighting, and procedural generation of complex natural detail.

Modeling for Lighting

Modeling is traditionally split into two main types: technical modeling and sculpting. The first includes mostly man-made objects, from furniture and cars to spaceships and buildings, while sculpting is most commonly used for modeling creatures of all sorts, from humans and animals to monsters and aliens. Both categories require accuracy and an understanding of the subject, whether it is mechanics, construction, or anatomy, and both benefit from careful studying of reference material, images, or blueprints. The main difference (at least in the context of this chapter) is that humans and animals are sculpted as one continuous surface, and are naturally curved and flowing, while technical models, just like their real-world counterparts, are usually built from multiple separate pieces. The vast majority of those pieces are derived from simple geometric forms: a table, for example, is essentially five boxes (or one box and four cylinders), and a building is one big box made out of multiple smaller boxes (doors, windows, balconies, stairs, railings, etc.).

Herein lies the issue of light interaction, and the need to model for lighting: in the mathematically perfect world of CG, box-like objects have perfectly sharp corners, but in reality, that is hardly ever the case. The edges of the five boxes that make up a table have been cut and sanded, leaving the corners slightly rounded. As discussed in Chapter 5, rounded corners and edges act as "highlight magnets", displaying noticeably stronger specular reflections. Such beveled corners can be found practically everywhere, and even when they are extremely thin, rim highlights still contribute substantially to the way objects catch light. When a CG model has perfectly sharp corners, the effect of rim highlights, which we normally take for granted, is sorely missing – renders feel dull, flat, and "CG". Modeling for lighting means addressing sharp corners and edges by judiciously applying bevels or chamfers. That extra bit of detail is extremely important for

Meters by Raphael Rau. Notice how almost every edge is slightly beveled, catching highlight and giving the render a rich, photoreal feel. Cinema 4D and Octane.

© Raphael Rau.

photorealism and is usually well worth the additional modeling time (and poly count). That said, the necessity of beveled edges must be weighed for each particular case. Take, for example, two scenes: an architectural render of an office building and a render of an interior apartment. In the first, beveling the corners of the building or various architectural elements would probably be an overkill – the building is too large and too far from the camera for rim highlights to even be noticeable. But the apartment interior could certainly benefit from beveled edges on furniture and even wall corners. Beveling in games and other realtime rendering is often limited by poly count restrictions, but rim highlights can still be achieved by applying the bevels to low-poly models as normal maps like other fine detail.

Procedural Modeling

While standard modeling and sculpting techniques work well for man-made objects as well as humans, animals, and imaginary creatures, they are not the most efficient for terrains, rocks, and plants. The realism of natural elements not only depends on the amount of detail – it relies on a seemingly contradictory combination of randomness and order. Nature's chaos can only be successfully simulated by subjecting it to natural laws: the way that water, wind, and ice shape mountains and valleys; how plants of the same species share structural and visual characteristics; or the way vegetation grows only in specific areas on a terrain.

Procedural modeling methods provide a better alternative to standard modeling or sculpting. Using fractal displacement and algorithmic erosion, an artist can quickly generate vast, highly detailed terrain surfaces which would otherwise be extremely tedious to sculpt. And by using a combination of random generation with deterministic algorithms like L-systems, artists can "grow" an infinite number of plant variations from a single species, or a large set of individual rocks that share specific characteristics.

Terrain Modeling

The concept of height-map based terrain generation is simple: a polygonal plane is displaced with a black and white image (height map). Precise elevation data like the USGS DEM maps[1] has been used for many years to create real-world 3D terrain for a variety of applications, from geological survey presentations to architectural and environmental visualizations. But accurate scientific height maps are not necessarily the best solution for creative VFX and games scenarios that require the ability to design and generate terrains with specific features and detail from scratch. Game engines like Unreal have some basic tools for terrain creation, while specialized terrain-generation apps like Vue, Terragen, World Machine, World Creator, and Gaea offer extended functionality by using different combinations of one or more of the following modeling procedures:

Snowy Terrain by Jeff Heral. Generated in Gaea, textured and rendered in Clarisse IFX. © Jeff Heral.

FRACTAL-BASED ELEVATION

Many natural elements display fractal characteristics as the progressive recurrence of larger patterns in smaller ones. The key here is to introduce a random factor, usually by shifting the center point arbitrarily through each subsequent subdivision. Perlin noise is the most used in fractal terrain functions (Voronoi is another common noise type). Attributes such as scale, amplitude, and roughness affect the overall look of the displaced terrain, while the number of subdivided iterations, or "octaves" affects the amount of detail (fewer iterations produce smoother surfaces with fewer small-scale features). Some terrain generation applications offer specialized fractal functions that better emulate the highly varied topology of large-scale terrains.

EROSION SIMULATION

Despite the complex and highly detailed look of iterative fractal functions, the resulting terrains still feel somewhat repetitive and mechanical. Real-world terrains are shaped by erosion – millions of years of water, wind, and ice that sculpt mountains and hills and give them their distinct, familiar look – the crisscrossed fluvial marks on the slopes, U-shaped glacial valleys, alluvial deposits at the foothills. What makes specialized terrain generation applications unique is the tools they provide for simulating natural erosion, which add a level of realism to fractal terrains that is extremely hard to recreate with standard modeling and sculpting techniques.

FREE SCULPTING AND TERRAIN FILTERS

While procedural modeling and erosion simulation are capable of producing a staggering amount of detail very quickly, they are still procedural – based on random functions or a set of rules – and offer little localized control over the shape of the terrain. The most powerful terrain generation applications offer the best of both worlds: the ability to use the power of procedural generation along with the hands-on sculpting. The artist can then choose to start a terrain by sculpting the general shape and features and then apply procedural displacement and erosion effects, or work the other way around, by first generating a procedural terrain and then sculpting specific detail. The new generation of terrain modeling software (like Gaea or World Creator) provides a wider toolset that includes procedural filters for quickly adding unique terrain features like terraces and balconies, stratified rocks, sand dunes, plateaus, and scattered rocks.

A Quiet Place by Terje Hannisdal. Terrain generated in Gaea, layout and render in Terragen.
© Terje Hannisdal.

Case Study: Erosion Algorithms in Gaea

Dax Pandhi is a CG environment artist, nature aficionado, and co-founder of *QuadSpinner*. Read his fascinating description of the R&D process behind Gaea, *QuadSpinner's* terrain generation software:

"*QuadSpinner* co-founder Cynthia Najim and I conducted research trips to the US Southwest and Pacific Northwest, Central America, Mediterranean, Iberian North Atlantic coast, and the deserts of Western India over the course of seven years. The mission was to understand geology in a new light and distill it into algorithmic form, striking a balance between geological realism and artistic requirements. Nature is beautifully complex. But when attempting to recreate it in algorithmic form, it becomes frighteningly challenging. Since our goal was not to replicate, but to approximate nature for artistic use, we began adapting some of the oldest tricks in the history of art. For example, a simple white dot on a pencil-shaded sphere hints at a smooth, reflective material. The position of this highlight is paramount to conveying the effect. Similarly, applying certain shapes and soil/rock modifications along specific curvatures, ridges, and deposits could convey a broad spectrum

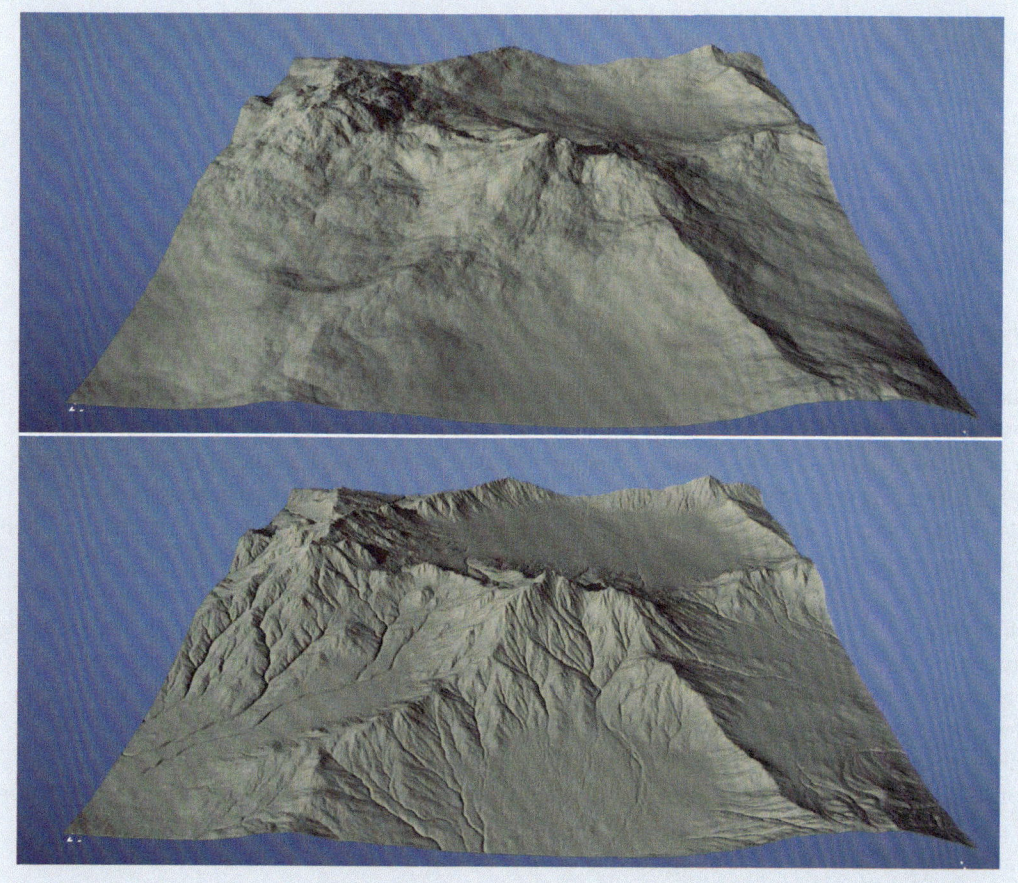

An erosion algorithm in Gaea faithfully replicates the effect of water and other elements on a base terrain.

of terrain features. This was our way of translating immensely complex geology into 2.5D heightfields and polygonal meshes. This is a methodology we call geological minimalism.

Back then, all procedural terrains were built with a shader-like model. You create noises, filter them to look like random geological features, and then erode. If modeling software had spheres, cubes, and teapots as primitives, we needed a similar language for making terrains. We started to create meaningful procedural shapes such as mountains, faults, valleys, ice floes, mesas – essential geological building blocks. Industry wide, digital terrains were fatigued from the overuse of fluvial erosion. If a terrain did not look realistic enough, artists tended to throw more erosion at it. To combat this, we started to craft new algorithms for alluvial deposits, terrain folding, stratification, anastomosis, and a range of other processes. Only by applying multiple processes would terrains look more realistic and diverse.

Our new R&D Lead Daniil Kamperov augmented our work with his groundbreaking research on hydraulic and thermal erosion. Unlike other models during that period, this erosion model was resolution-independent, struck a new balance between erosion and deposition, and was both particle and grid based. In practical terms, artists would be able to modify erosion properties to give the terrain unique personalities and escape the limitations of previous models. Over time, this research has expanded to include snow simulation, hydrological features, and other natural phenomena.

We completed our toolset with a set of simulations called Data Maps. They analyze terrains – even static terrains such as DEM data – and simulate natural properties such as water flows, rainfall velocity, vegetation growth patterns, and even quasi-random geological shapes for both processing and texture propagation. With this workflow, color production is enforced through systematic elements rather than on slope, randomness, and flow lines."

Plant Modeling

Plants have a complex structure, but this structure follows a set of rules that is specific for each species. Individual plants of the same species share the same characteristics and visual traits, yet a certain factor of randomness within those rules makes each individual plant uniquely different. In 1968, Botanist Astrid Lindenmayer developed a system that defines the parent–children relationship that characterizes plant structures and can be used to model their growth. This system (known as the L System) is used today as the mathematical basis for procedurally generating plants. Plant modeling applications such as SpeedTree, Plant Factory, or the venerable Xfrog let artists define a set of parameters like length, diameter, curvature, and angle through the recursive structure of a plant – starting from the trunk (or stem), through the main branches, to smaller branches, twigs, and leaves. Each subset inherits characteristics from its parent while introducing new ones, and for each parameter, a certain margin of randomness can be set. This provides not only a quick and efficient method for creating a wide range of plants, it also gives the artist the option to "roll the dice" and let the random deviations kick in, which produces an infinite number of plant models of a single species, each uniquely different. These can then be exported to the main 3D application for populating scenes.

The leading specialized plant creation applications offer a complete toolset that includes not just core L System modeling but also shading, texturing, and mapping tools, various modifiers,

An Acacia tree model in SpeedTree. Notice the complex procedural hierarchy on the left, which includes nodes for trunk, branches, twigs, leaves, and special features like knots, and the PBR leaf texture set on the right.

poly count and LOD control, and specialized animation tools for wind, growth, and even physical reaction to objects. Applications like SpeedTree became ubiquitous in the games, VFX and visualization industries because they offer a one-stop shop for 3D vegetation. However, some generalized 3D applications like Houdini provide L System tools that allow stripped-down plant modeling within the core application. A similar approach to plant modeling (though not necessarily with L-systems) can be used to quickly generate libraries of stones, rocks, bricks, minerals, or even animals and humans.

Note

1 www.usgs.gov/core-science-systems/ngp/3dep/about-3dep-products-services.

PART 4

THE 2D WORLD

Everything You Can Dream of by Marvin Funke. Blender, Photoshop, and Nuke.
© Marvin Funke.

2D workflows are undoubtedly more prominent in visual effects, which rely heavily on compositing. Many of the most common bread-and-butter VFX shots start and end with compositing, and do not involve any type of CG work. The same can be said about matte paintings – a substantial chunk is done solely in 2D. Visualizations are certainly more 3D-centric, but many architectural models are composited into photographed environments, and 2D processing is used to add finishing touches to product renders and clips. Games and VR are based on 3D realtime rendering, yet despite the seemingly pure 3D nature of these fields, compositing techniques are increasingly being used to augment the game's cinematic experience, and 2D matte paintings are created for distant backgrounds. So, while this part of the book applies first and foremost to VFX artists, many of the subjects discussed here are useful to visualization and games artists as well.

Compared to 3D, the 2D workflow may appear extremely limiting – there is no lighting, shading, texturing, or modeling, and transformations are restricted to just two axes. But the notion that 2D is limited contradicts hundreds of years of prodigious artwork by numerous artists who managed to successfully convey depth, light, texture, atmosphere, and scale with nothing more than a brush and a canvas. They did it (and still do) through masterful use of color, and a deep understanding of three-dimensional space. For digital artists, the 2D process is essentially the same – in compositing and matte painting, photorealism is achieved through meticulous color work and a three-dimensional approach to a two-dimensional workspace.

The first advice I give to my students is that mastery of color is the key to successful compositing and matte painting. The second advice is to never, ever, think of compositing or image manipulation as a process of stacking layers, as "A over B", or "layer 5 over layer 4". Every image

City of Silence by David Edwards.
© David Edwards.

or piece of footage represents a three-dimensional world, and every 2D element that is added to that world should be approached as a three-dimensional entity placed within a three-dimensional space. In essence, the key to photoreal 2D is to never think of it as 2D: the seemingly unattainable third dimension should always be accounted for through the thoughtful use of scale, perspective, atmosphere, and depth of field.

Working in 2D has some significant benefits for a photoreal workflow. First and foremost, it is faster: compositing, matte painting, and image manipulation are not nearly as computationally intensive as 3D modeling, lighting, and offline rendering. The ability to view the end result in real-time as the artist interacts with the scene makes continuous tweaking and fine-tuning a much easier and intuitive process. This is why the final lighting and color adjustments of CG renders, as well as the addition of lens characteristics like depth of field are often left for the compositing stage. However, the most important advantage of 2D is the benefit of working with photos and footage. The inherently photoreal quality of such material allows compositors and matte painters to manipulate realism (or create realism from scratch) without the need to mimic or simulate reality by relying on mathematical rendering algorithms. The detail, the imperfections, the wear and tear, the subtle shading, the warmth of a physical lens – all the aspects that are difficult to produce in CG are already embedded in footage. The challenge, nevertheless, is in combining different photographic elements: it is akin to combining puzzle pieces from multiple unrelated puzzles into one, coherent image.

Chapter 15

Integrating 2D Elements

Color Matching

The ability to tweak the colors of an element to make it "sit" well within a new environment is one of the most crucial skills for compositors and matte painters, and arguably one of the toughest to master. Say you composite the same tree element over five different backgrounds. The tree's leaves will remain green, but it will be a different green in each of the five cases. How different? That depends on a variety of factors. Back in Chapter 3, I presented my six-layer approach as a way of simplifying the process of color matching. The green of the leaves exists as an absolute color only in a virtual world with no external influences. In reality, that green is already affected by the lighting and the camera's own color interpretation. When extracted and placed over a different background (or, to word it more appropriately, within a new environment), that green needs to be adjusted with respect to that environment's particular lighting, atmosphere, and camera color interpretation. The color operations I described in Chapter 3 (gain, gamma, lift, offset, saturation) are the essential tools in this process – mastering them and understanding the factors that affect color are the keys to achieving seamless integration and photoreal results.

There is no single methodology for color matching, and it is more a matter of personal preference. Some compositors start by matching the black and white points, others start with the brightness or the hue. Some use value sampling and others rely solely on their eyes. I like to start with the big brush strokes – adjust the gain and the gamma for general brightness, contrast, and overall tint, then proceed to finer adjustments for blacks and highlights, and finally (if needed), tweak specific ranges like shadows, midtones, and highlights, or use a hue correct tool to modify specific hues. I like to rely on my eyes more than on sampling or automated tools, because I believe that color matching is context-sensitive and relative, rather than absolute science. Then again, this is merely a personal preference, and the process depends on individual experience. In the end, the goal is to be able to quickly and easily match colors to achieve seamless integration.

I often give my students two versions of the same photo, an original and a color-corrected one, and ask them to adjust the colors of the original version to match the second as closely as possible. Depending on how the colors have been tweaked, this can be an easy introductory exercise or a mind-twisting puzzle. It may initially seem like a rather mechanical drill, but so is practicing scales for a pianist or doing jumping jacks for a soccer player. Color matching is an acquired skill, and the more you practice it, the more you train your eye to see color precisely and strengthen your grip on color tools and operations.

Three stages of color-correcting a tree element to better integrate with the footage.

Edges: Problems and Solutions

Unlike CG elements, which are normally rendered on a clean black background and come with a built-in alpha, every 2D element needs to be cut out or extracted from its original background before it is composited into a different footage. If all elements had sharp, well-defined edges, this process would have been rather straight-forward. But that is hardly ever the case: edges are often comprised of complex sub-pixel detail (hair, fur, fabrics, tiny irregularities), or are fuzzy and semi-transparent because of translucency, defocus, or motion blur. Such edges make the extraction process challenging even if the original background is a perfectly clean and well-lit green screen. And extraction is only half of the challenge – integrating the elements into their new environment becomes tricky when edges are soft. The reason lies in the fact that any edge that is not 100% opaque carries with it some of the original background. This is obviously a problem if that background is busy and detailed, but even clean backgrounds (like a green screen) can be problematic: chances are that the luminance level of the original background does not exactly match that of the new background. This difference in luminance shows up as dark or bright edges around the composited element, killing the believability of the comp.

This problem presents a tricky compositing dilemma: whether to preserve the detail and softness of the edges and risk ugly bright/dark outlines, or to tighten the extraction and end up with unnaturally sharp and harsh edges. Both options can damage photorealism: unnaturally sharp edges or dark or bright fringes around edges inevitably lead to composites that "look Photoshopped". The goal is to preserve as much of the edge detail and its original softness while also treating any bright or dark outline and making sure that the semi-transparent edges blend seamlessly with the new background. Easier said than done, but crucial for seamless integration. In this section I will discuss some key methods that can help achieve photoreal integration of extracted 2D elements.

Matching Background Luminosity

If you know in advance what type of environment the element will eventually be composited into, you can match luminance values already at the shooting or sourcing stage, eliminating edge issues down the line. For example, when I am on set shooting a green screen element for a nighttime shot, I ask the cinematographer to reduce the lighting on the green screen and take it down a notch or two below optimal level. While it is important to keep the green screen bright enough for proper chroma keying, slightly dimming the lighting in such a case can mitigate unnatural bright edges (or light spills) when the element is composited over a darker background. A similar principle can be used when selecting elements for a matte painting – those with backgrounds of similar luminosity to the target background will transfer and integrate much better and will require much less edge work. For example, a tree extracted from a bright sky background and composited onto the dark forest environment is bound to show unwanted bright edges. In this case, it makes sense to look for tree elements that have a similar, darker background.

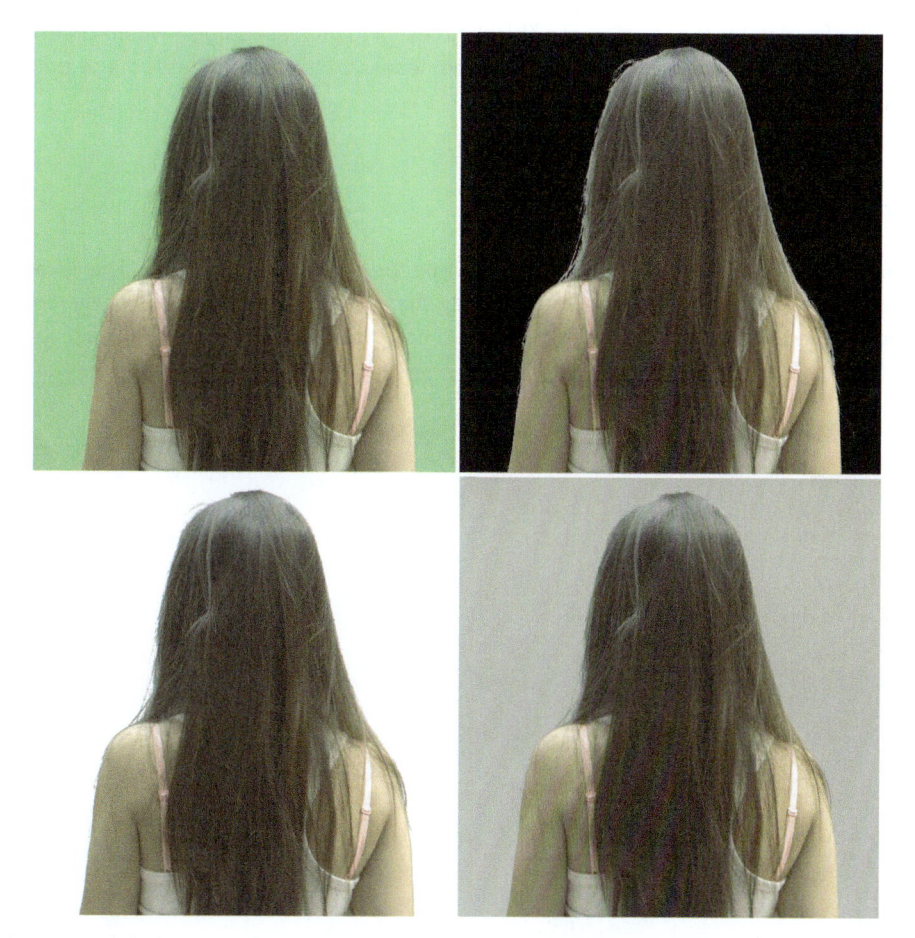

Bright edges around the hair are visible when the background is darker than the green screen (top right), while dark edges form along the arms when it is brighter (bottom left). A background with a similar luminance to the green screen produces the best results (bottom right).

Footage courtesy of fxphd/Eduardo Abon.

INTEGRATING 2D ELEMENTS

Spill Suppression

Green and blue screens must of course be highly saturated to serve their purpose, but this does not help with edge integration. Semi-transparent edges carry not just the background's luminosity, but also its hue (in this case, extremely unnatural green or blue). To be clear, spill suppression is required not just for edges – areas on the subject that receive bounce light from the screen or specular reflections are also susceptible to spill. But soft edges often require a separate spill suppression process, because they reveal the actual screen, not just its reflection.

A wide variety of despill tools are available for compositors, and many have controls that allow fine-tuning the spill sensitivity and output color. Some despill algorithms go even further: Nuke's IBK algorithm, for example, uses a dedicated screen color node that, when set up correctly, creates a clean version of the green/blue screen. This is used as a color "roadmap" for subtracting green spill. It is a more accurate method because it takes into consideration the different color values on a typical green screen (green and blue screens rarely have uniform color, due to wrinkles, smudges, and uneven lighting). Spill suppression is a relatively straight-forward aspect of keying and integration, as long as it is used judiciously and with attention to the results. For example, heavy despill of grainy footage can create "black holes" and increased noise where green pixels turn black by the process (in which case, it might be necessary to degrain the footage prior to despill and then re-grain it).

Edge and Core Extractions

Junior compositors often attempt to generate a single, perfect extraction matte. This is rarely the best approach (unless the element has perfectly sharp, solid edges) because of the constant tug-o'-war between achieving a clean matte with no holes or noise and preserving soft and semi-

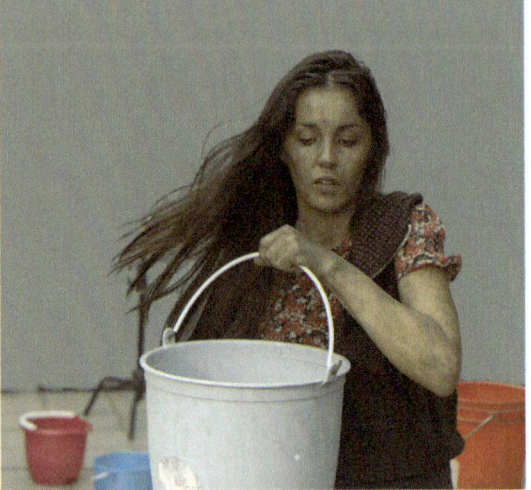

Spill suppression removes unnatural green spill from wispy areas like the hair or reflective areas like the floor. Care must be taken, however, not to despill areas that are naturally green, like the bucket in this shot.

Footage courtesy of fxphd/Eduardo Abon.

Nuke's IBK extraction algorithm does not use pre-multiplication, and generates noticeable background noise (left). But it uses the background luminosity and hue (middle) to camouflage the noise for a clean background (right).
Footage courtesy of fxphd/Eduardo Abon.

transparent edges. It is much more effective to create two separate extractions – a hard-edged, solid matte for the core of the element, and another, softer extraction solely for the edges. If the element is a person, for example, then the core matte ensures there are no unwanted holes in the body and face, while the softer semi-transparent matte preserves hair and fabric detail, as well as any motion-blurred or defocused edges.

While a core matte is easier to extract with most keying tools (even the elementary ones found in editing software), edge mattes are trickier, and require skill, effort, and good keying tools. Some extraction algorithms like Nuke's IBK are especially suited for edge mattes because they do not use pre-multiplication, which can shrink the matte and make the edges crunchy. Instead, they "camouflage" the noise and extraction artifacts outside the matte borders by matching their luminosity and hue to the background. This method is especially suitable for integrating semi-transparent edges, and dynamically adapts the color of the edges to changing colors in the background.

Edge Reconstruction

When an element is heavily motion-blurred or defocused, it is vital to preserve its soft edges. Failure to do so results in a visibly awkward mismatch between the element's blurry detail and its unnatural hard edges. In addition, the lack of soft motion-blurred edges causes fast-moving elements to strobe. The problem, however, is that extended areas of heavy motion blur or defocus are so transparent and wispy that they contain too much of the background. This is of course undesirable with a green or blue screen, and especially tricky if there's detail in the background. The latter situation is a typical issue with rotoscoping: attempts to include motion-blurred and defocused edges within the roto shape generally fail, because there is no way to separate the background from the element in such semi-transparent areas. For that reason, enabling automatic motion blur in the roto shape usually does not provide good results.

Initial extraction fails to pull the fine motion-blurred hair edges. With some additional edge reconstruction, they feel softer and more natural.

Often, the best approach is to not even try to extract such areas, but instead to recreate them artificially. With this method, roto shapes or extractions follow the last solid pixels along the edges to create a tighter matte. Then a copy of the extracted element is dilated, blurred, and placed underneath itself, to replicate the missing soft edges. Directional blur (or vector blur) can simulate the typical streaking effect of motion blur. Using the original footage as reference, the compositor can recreate soft and semi-transparent edges through a clean process that does not carry any of the original background and blends seamlessly with the new environment.

Matte-less Extractions

The notion of compositing an element without a proper alpha matte may sound odd at first, but think of it this way: it's really all about color. When you composite an element over a background you are in fact changing the color of the background pixels. The matte is merely used to define where those color changes happen, not to delineate any physical "thickness". But when it comes to thin and wispy sub-pixel detail like hair, fur, or grass, standard extraction techniques often result in a chunky, sticky look. Instead of containing the color channels within an area defined by an alpha channel, it is sometimes better to modulate the background color with the foreground color directly, using either an additive (brightening) or a multiply (darkening) operation. This method requires enough contrast between the original background and the detail you want to preserve. With dark hair over a bright green screen, the color channel with the most contrast should be isolated, then the whites should be brightened just enough so that non-hair pixels reach a value of 1 (and are clamped to 1 to prevent artifacts). When the target background is multiplied by this image, the darker hair values darken the background, while white areas (no hair) do not affect it. Sub-pixel detail can thus be added to the background, bypassing the normal chroma extraction and pre-multiplied alpha channel. The method for bright blond hair over a darker blue screen is similar, but this time non-hair areas are darkened down to zero, and the image is then added to the background, brightening only areas where hair exists. These methods are normally used as a

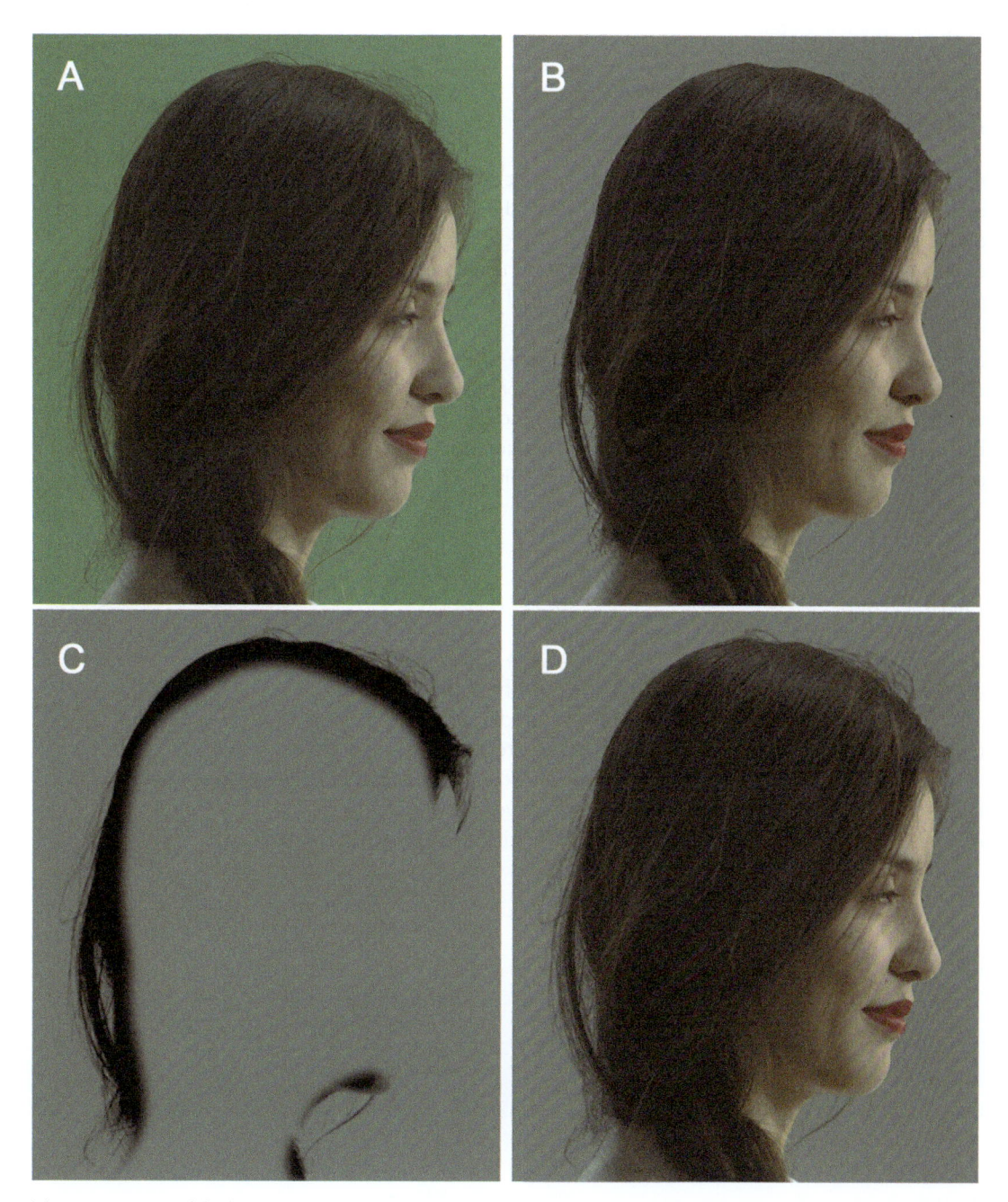

The wispier parts of the hair (A) are lost in the extraction process (B). Instead of pulling a hair matte, the background is multiplied by the darker hair (D), and the extraction is comped on top, with the detail now preserved (D).

Footage courtesy of fxphd/Eduardo Abon.

complementary process to standard keying and roto, but their contribution to the photorealism of the comp is often substantial, as they help mitigate the cutout "Photoshopped" look by bringing back the very fine detail.

Edge Blur and Edge Color

A slight blur to the edges of an extracted element usually helps alleviate noise and improve the blending. An edge blur affects both the alpha and color channels, which softens harsh transitions and adds a photographic touch (lenses tend to slightly soften boundaries). Edge blur is most effective when used very subtly – depending on the resolution of the image, a blur value of 1–3 pixels is usually enough (higher values are useful if the element is out of focus). It is helpful to reference the footage for the amount of softness of real edges at a comparable focus level. Since an edge blur operation uses a mathematical edge-detect algorithm, some edge blur tools also offer edge color tweaks. Nuke's edge blur filter, for example, includes brightness and tint controls, which can be used as an effective last-resort remedy for bright or dark edges. Because edge blurring affects the color channels, it also affects grain. Missing grain along the blurred edges can call unwanted attention, but this issue can be easily fixed by using the edge-detect matte to add back grain only where it is missing.

Light Wrap

When a subject is located in front of a light source or an area of substantial brightness (such as a window), a certain amount of light bleeds over the subject's edges. Light warp is unfortunately often misused by compositors as a remedy for bad edges. It is important to remember that in most cases, objects display a rather solid silhouette, even when backlit. Light bleeding is limited to extremely bright areas (mostly light sources). Exaggerated light warp can result in unnaturally fuzzy, ghost-like edges. Light warp is most effective and realistic when used sparingly and always in direct relation to areas of strong luminance behind the subject.

Chapter 16

Integrating CG Elements

In VFX, CG elements are usually composited into live action footage. Similarly, architectural and product visualizations often combine CG elements with background photos or footage. Even when perfectly textured and lit, CG elements rarely drop right in the footage without the need for some fine-tuning. The compositing stage is where this happens, and in this chapter we will look at the most essential tools and techniques for integrating 3D with photographic footage.

Compositing with Render Passes

For photographers, the ability to separate a photo into different lighting passes or various components would have been a truly astonishing concept. Just imagine the incredible breadth of post-processing possibilities that photographers and cinematographers could have had, if only they could separate their footage into direct and indirect light, highlights, shadows, transparency, refraction, and depth (or even by individual lights). While this is not (yet) possible in the photographic realm, it is practical reality in the CG world. Indeed, render passes are an integral part of the VFX (and visualization) workflow, because they provide a flexible, fast, and interactive way to adjust, improve, and integrate CG elements at the compositing stage, without the need to go back to time-consuming 3D rendering. Even the most perfectly lit renders need some adjustments at the finishing stage, and good strategies for using render passes help pave the way to photoreal results. Render passes (also called **AOVs**, **render elements**, and **render channels**) can be output as separate stills or image sequences, or combined into a single multi-channel EXR image or image sequence. Generally speaking, render passes fall into two main categories: **lighting passes** and **utility passes**.

Lighting Passes

The final, complete rendered image is typically called the **beauty pass** (or just "beauty"). That image encompasses the full accumulation of all light interactions in the scene. Those interactions can be separated and output as distinct lighting passes, each representing a single component of the beauty render: diffuse, specular, transmission, subsurface scattering, and so forth. In addition, the influence of different lights in the scene can be separated into specific lighting layer passes. Most rendering applications provide the option to separate the direct and indirect aspects of

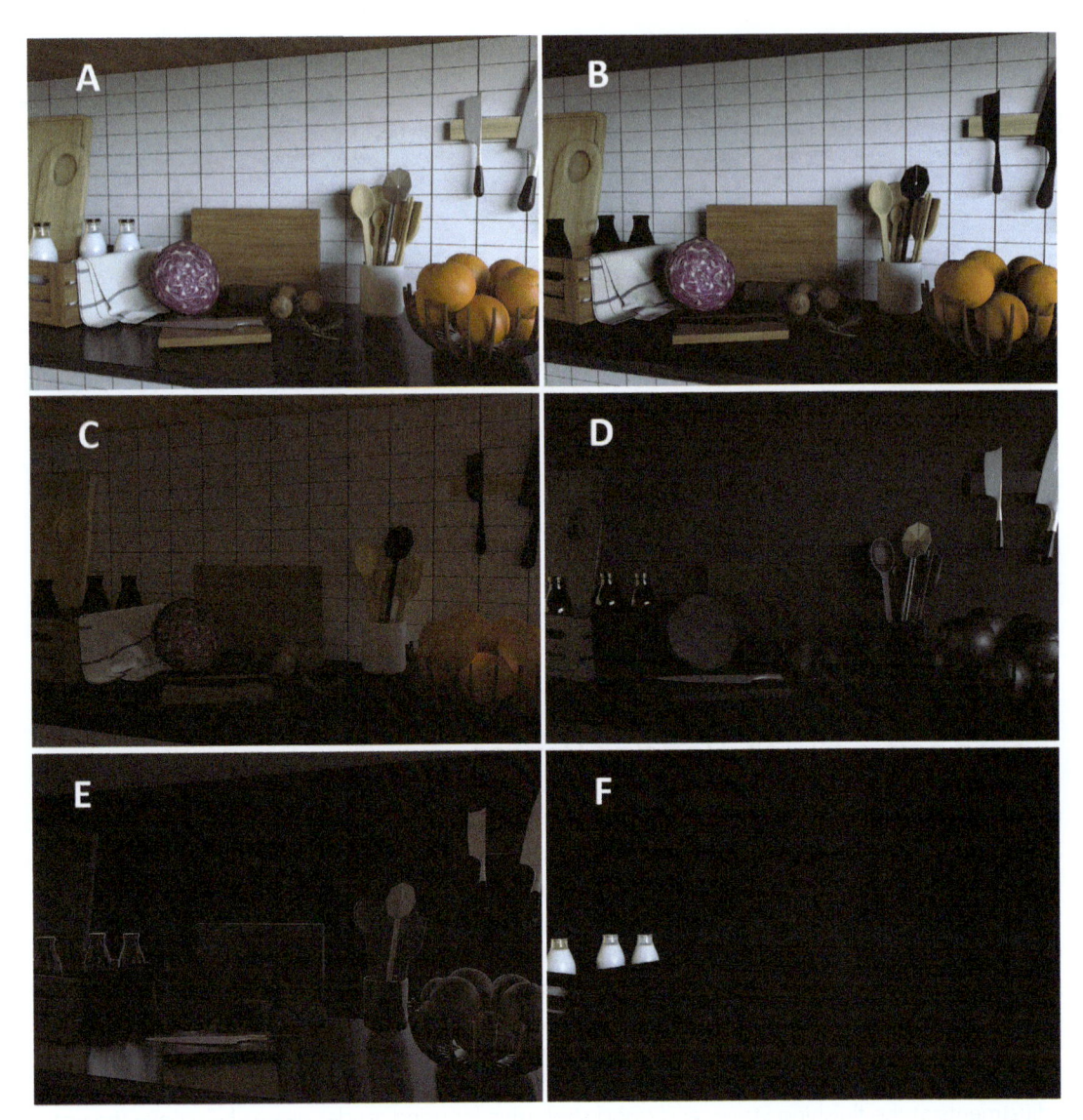

A: beauty, B: direct diffuse (notice how metallic surfaces turn black), C: indirect diffuse (notice the strong color bleeding between the oranges), D: direct specular (showing mostly the reflection of the window light), E: indirect specular (showing object inter-reflectivity), F: transmission (the milk bottles are the only transparent objects).

some components: a direct diffuse pass includes only the illumination of light sources, while indirect diffuse shows only illumination from reflected light. A direct specular pass shows the reflection of light sources (including sky and environment domes, which are considered lights), while indirect specular shows the reflection between objects. This type of separation is of course completely artificial – in the real world, there is no difference between reflecting the sky or a nearby tree – but it is nonetheless extremely helpful for achieving better real-world emulation.

There are two basic approaches for working with lighting passes in comp. The first is to start with the separate passes, then re-combine them by adding their values together (since light components accumulate, an additive operation of all the passes produces an exact replica of the

The raw render (left) is somewhat bland and murky, but by boosting the indirect light components, the lighting feels more natural and the image looks more pleasing (right).

beauty render). Like an audio mixing console, this approach gives the compositor full control over each component, its color and its relative amount in the "mix" and is suitable for situations where the original beauty needs to be substantially tweaked and modified. However, recreating the beauty by separating and recombining every single pass can be an overkill in situations where only minor tweaks are needed. In such cases, it is simpler to start with the beauty, and add (or reduce) only specific components. For example, increasing the specular level can be done by simply adding a bit of the direct specular pass to the beauty using an additive (plus) operation, while reducing specularity can be done with a difference operation.

Regardless of the approach used, it is important to remember that changing the balance between lighting components may affect the energy conservation principle of PBR. That is not necessarily bad – the goal is to make the image look convincing and sit well in the comp, even if it means breaking physical rules. But it is helpful to keep this in mind, especially with heavy modifications. I have often found myself tweaking render components ad nauseam, only to go back to the beauty at the end. Sometimes the well-balanced results of PBR work best unaltered.

In most cases, the use of the basic lighting passes is a straightforward process of balancing the look of the rendered element: reducing the specular highlights a bit, tweaking the color of the diffuse refection, etc. Here are some tips for additional uses of lighting passes:

- Increasing the indirect diffuse presence produces a "poor man's subsurface scattering" effect, by reducing the contrast and softening the object's features. It can be used to subtly take the edge off of elements that feel too harsh and "CG".
- Although technically incorrect, boosting the indirect specular component is a sort of "cheat" to make a surface feel more metallic, because it enhances the illusion of increased reflections at grazing angle.
- As mentioned in Chapter 11, indirect components (like indirect diffuse or indirect specular) are usually the main culprits in noisy renders. When re-rendering at higher sample settings is not an option, one way to reduce the noisiness is to separate the indirect passes, run them through a denoise or degrain algorithm and then plug them back in comp.
- Transparent objects are usually rendered with the intended background included for proper transmission and refraction. The problem is that at the compositing stage, the colors of the background may change (subtly or drastically), in which case the rendered

transparency will no longer match. By using the transmission pass, the compositor can adjust the transparency to match the modified background without affecting the other lighting components and surface properties.
- Separate per-pass color-correction is an extremely effective way of grading CG elements in comp without generating a blanket effect on all the components that can hurt photorealism. The classic example is changing the diffuse color without affecting the specular color. As explained in Chapter 9, specular reflections are not tinted in dielectric materials, so keeping the specular component unaffected while grading the diffuse maintains the correct look of the material.

Utility Passes

Unlike lighting passes, utility render passes do not represent any of the visual content of the beauty pass. Rather, the pixel data of utility passes provides additional information that can be used to manipulate the rendered image or diagnose render issues. The most common utility passes are **Z depth** and **facing normals**, but different render engines allow for a wide variety of utility passes, including fully customizable ones. Utility passes are indispensable tools for compositing CG elements and enhancing photorealism. Here is a brief look at the role of the most common ones:

SHADOW MATTE AND AMBIENT OCCLUSION

While shadows are calculated as part of the rendering process, they only apply to the existing 3D geometry in the scene. Rendered elements that are composited into footage need to interact with the 2D environment in the footage, and shadows are a primary factor in that interaction. This is where shadow mattes and ambient occlusion (AO) passes come in handy – they help bridge the gap between 3D rendering and 2D compositing. For example, if you need to composite a CG chair onto a photo of a room, you must create the illusion that the chair is actually standing on the (photographed) floor. This requires contact shadows underneath the chair's legs. Depending on the room's lighting, the chair may also need to cast shadows on the floor (and possibly on other elements in the footage).

To create these shadows, the CG artist needs to model the interacting elements in the footage (like the floor and nearby objects) as accurately as possible. These are added to the rendering scene, but only as shadow casting/receiving objects. They are not visible in the beauty render, but they are active in the AO and shadow matte passes. Ambient occlusion is perfect for contact and proximity shadows because it is completely independent of the actual lights in the scene. By multiplying the background image/footage with the AO pass in comp, the areas of contact or proximity (which have values lower than 1) darken the image, while non-affected areas (fully white at 1) remain unchanged. When the CG element is comped over, all areas of occlusion are properly darkened underneath (or behind) the element.

When the scene includes lights that also cast defined shadows, a shadow matte pass is used in addition to the ambient occlusion pass. Unlike an AO pass, a shadow matte pass is derived directly from the specific lighting of the CG scene, and represents the softness and intensity of each shadow in relation to the occluded light. This allows the compositor to set a global shadow grade for the scene, and then use the shadow matte as a mask for applying this grade to the footage, resulting in shadows that have the correct intensity and softness.

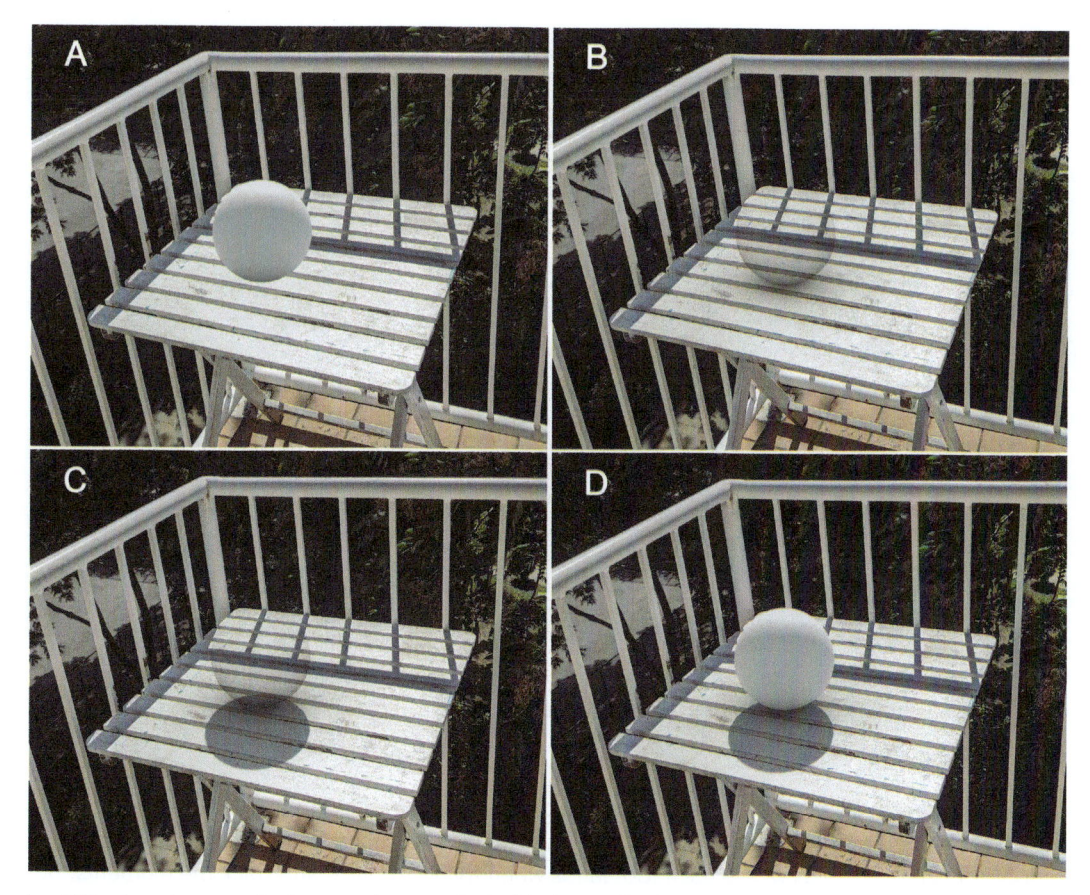

A: a CG sphere is composited over a photographed table, but is clearly missing a shadow and contact shadows. B: an AO pass is multiplied with the image to darken the areas of contact. C: A shadow matte pass is used to create the shadow through color grading, D: The sphere is added back.

POINT POSITION AND NORMAL PASSES

These two standard utility passes are used as 3D to 2D translators, and together they form an accurate two-dimensional map of the three-dimensional geometry. The **Point Position pass** (aka **Position pass** or **P pass**) denotes the location of every surface point in actual 3D space, using the RGB channels to represent the XYZ position values. Because the value range is huge and precision is paramount, position passes only work in a 16- or 32-bit floating point format such as EXR. The **Facing Normal pass** (aka **Normal pass** or **N pass**) shows the facing direction of each point in the 3D geometry. Like the Position pass, it uses the RGB channels, but with a range of −1 to 1. For example, in a CG model of a room, the facing values of any point on the floor would be 0,1,0 (the floor surface is facing straight up on the Y axis), while a point on the right side wall would be −1,0,0 (facing left). Note that the facing direction is in relation to the world 3D coordinates, not the camera.

Modern compositing applications offer the ability to work in 3D space, but they are not built to handle heavy geometry sets. The Position pass is used together to create a 3D **dense point cloud** that accurately represents the scene's geometry within the compositing application, directly from the rendered image and without the need to actually import any geometry. This provides an extremely useful reference for compositing additional elements in 3D space. For example,

INTEGRATING CG ELEMENTS

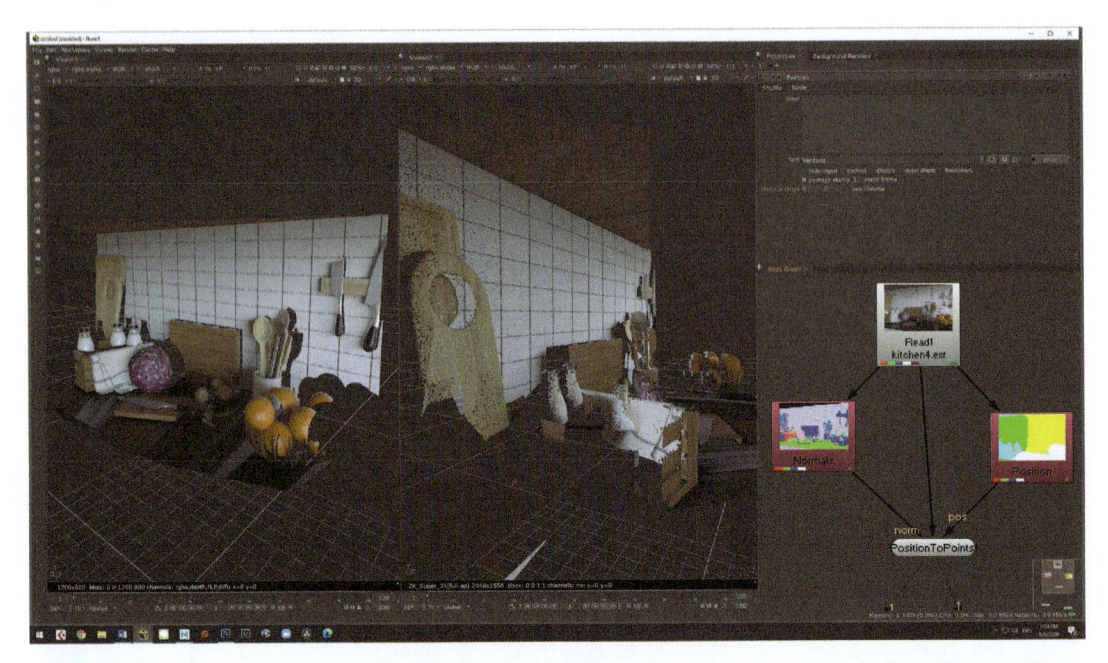

A Nuke screen grab, showing how the position pass is used to generate a dense point cloud of the 3D scene. The normal pass is also factored in, to enable relighting in Nuke.

imagine a shot with a CG character running on a dirt road, where one of the compositor's tasks is to add 2D elements of dust as it is kicked off by the character's feet. In a 2D only workflow, the compositor can only guess where each foot lands when trying to place and track the elements. But with an animated point cloud derived from the Position pass, the compositor can clearly see where the feet land in 3D space and place the 2D dust elements on cards in 3D space to match those positions.

Position and Normal passes can also be used for projecting textures onto rendered geometry at the comp stage, or to make three-dimensional selections within the render. Some compositing applications even offer relighting tools that are solely based on the information of the Position and Normal passes. This hybrid method requires placing CG lights in 3D space and using the compositing software's own 3D renderer. As a cheap and quick 2D alternative, the Normal pass can be used to increase or reduce the light in the rendered images based on direction. For example, to increase top lighting overall, the Y channel of the Normal pass can be used as a mask for brightening only up-facing areas in the render.

MATTE AND ID PASSES

One of the clearest advantages of working with CG renders is the ease of isolating specific elements or areas for separate treatment. Mattes can be generated at render time for individual objects (or a combination of objects), as well as materials or shaders. Colored mattes only work well as pure red, green, or blue, because mixed colors cannot be accurately isolated in compositing. A single matte pass can therefore have up to three separate mattes, one in each RGB channel. However, new tools like the excellent Cryptomatte plugin make the process of rendering mattes and selecting them in comp much more efficient. Cryptomatte automatically assigns a unique ID to every object and/or every material in the scene (along with a unique color), which allow the compositor to easily isolate any object or material (or any combination thereof) with a simple point and click process, and eliminates the need to render multiple matte passes.

Z DEPTH

Z depth is an important utility pass, as it serves two essential purposes: applying accurate depth-of-field in 2D and applying depth-based atmospheric effects (see Chapters 17 and 18). Despite its important role in compositing CG elements, the depth pass has some notable limitations:

- Most current render engines output a non-normalized depth pass, which can represent any distance to infinity. While this is generally advantageous, it does pause some difficulties when a non-normalized depth pass is used as a mask for atmospheric depth effects (especially when dealing with small distance differences) and may force the compositor to increase the contrast in the depth pass by pushing the black and white points.
- Transmission/refraction cannot be represented in a depth pass. All transparent or semi-transparent surfaces appear as fully opaque, and any see-through element is not visible in the depth pass. This may cause serious issues with refracted objects. For example, an out-of-focus element may suddenly jump into focus when it moves behind a glass object, because at that moment it simply disappears form the depth pass.
- Volumetric CG elements such as smoke and fog are similarly problematic, since the depth pass cannot accurately show multiple layers of semi-transparent pixels (some advanced render engines provide volumetric depth options, though these are not ideal).
- Reflected elements are not represented, so it is impossible, for example, to use the depth pass to focus on a figure reflected in a mirror (only the mirror itself is visible in the depth pass).

Deep Compositing

Most renderers can output **deep data** in a deepEXR format. Unlike the standard depth pass, which can only represent surfaces that are visible to the camera, deep data provides an array of multiple values per pixel at varying depths, and thus includes surfaces that are hidden behind foreground objects. Deep compositing provides an entirely new level of functionality because the

Left: a non-normalized depth pass (color-corrected to show the values). Right: Z-defocus in Nuke, displaying the depth of field settings (green is in focus, red and blue out of focus).

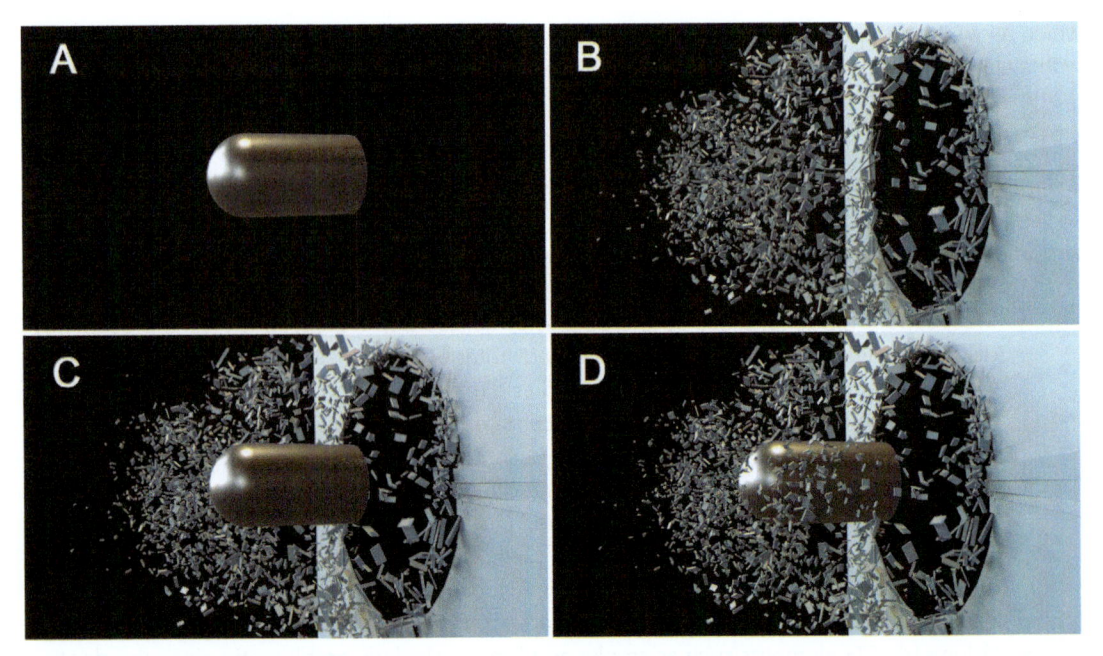

When the bullet element (A) is composited over the shattered surface element (B), the bullet is simply on top. But with deep compositing, the bullet is automatically placed in the correct depth.

rendered elements are treated as three-dimensional entities rather than 2D layers. When you layer standard 2D elements, the order of the layering defines which element goes in front. With deep compositing, the layering order does not matter at all, because the elements are automatically arranged at the correct depth in 3D space. Standard 2D operations like transform, crop, and even color correction can be done along the Z axis in addition to X and Y. Deep compositing allows true 3D depth-based layering which is especially useful with complex scattered elements like particles or volumetric smoke, because the deep data automatically sorts which parts of one element go in front or behind other elements in the composite. Deep compositing can significantly enhance the process of compositing complex CG scenes, but because deep data can only be generated through a 3D rendering process (not live-action footage), and deepEXR file sizes are substantially larger than regular EXRs, it is not used as frequently in bread-and-butter VFX compositing work.

Improving CG in Comp

Computer-generated imagery is purely mathematic, and thus inherently perfect. Such perfection often stands in the way of photorealism. In Part 3 we discussed ways of adding complexity and randomness in the modeling, texturing, and shading processes. Such methods are of course necessary to create plausible CG scenes. But the 2D process provides an opportunity for additional treatments that can reduce the "curse of perfection" of CG renders and help their integration with live-action footage. One thing to consider is the fact that CG is rendered through a virtual camera, not a physical one. The light that hits the virtual camera's "sensor" does not travel through layers of glass. Emulating specific lens characteristics like flares, defocus, or chromatic aberrations will be discussed in Chapter 18. In the following short section, I will offer some simple, basic "CG sweetening" tips that can work for almost any scenario.

Render Resolution

The logical assumption is that the render resolution needs to match the final output or source footage resolution. Sometimes it is necessary to render at the full resolution (or even higher). For example, if a scene contains a lot of thin straight lines (like the wires of a suspension bridge), high resolution is necessary to avoid jagged, aliased edges. But in many cases, rendering at a lower resolution is not only a time-saver, it actually helps the CG look more realistic. CG renders are almost always too sharp compared to photographed footage, and very often need some softening to sit well in the comp. Rendering at 80% or 75% of the full resolution, and then resizing back to 100% with a cubic or quadratic filter produces the same effect as softening, with the additional bonus of cutting down render times and file size. The exact render resolution reduction can be decided on a per-case basis, by rendering a test frame at full resolution and seeing how much softening is needed in comp, then reducing the render size to match.

Hazing Effect

This effect has nothing to do with depth-based atmospheric hazing (to be covered in Chapter 17). Rather, I am referring here to a very subtle, almost imperceptible effect. It is easily achieved by blurring the CG element a little (10–40 pixels, depending on the resolution), and then merging back that blurred version of the element over itself, while setting the mix (opacity) just high enough to slightly soften/smear the features of the CG render. It is a very simple yet effective trick to take the edge off of CG, as long as you keep the mix relatively low and avoid a cheesy "dreamy photo" look.

Highlights Bloom

As described in Chapter 10, highlights blooming is essentially a "mini-flare" that happens when very bright areas scatter slightly in the lens. The procedure is essentially the same as the hazing effect, but a max (maximum) operation is used instead of an over or screen operation. This ensures that only the brightest areas in the render get hazed, mimicking real-world highlights bloom. This too works best as a subtle effect – lens manufacturers strive to minimize lens scattering, so overdone blooms tend to look distracting and unnatural.

Albedo Pass and Contrast

One recurring issue with CG is that the render looks terrific on its own, but somehow does not feel quite right in the context of the comp. Contrast, in particular, is elusive. Renders may look like they have just the right amount of contrast when viewed over clean black, but often feel much too punchy when integrated with the target footage. There are of course ways to adjust contrast through color operations like lift and gamma, but it is tricky to adjust lighting-related color without affecting texture-related color. In other words, flattening the contrast caused by the lighting also flattens the contrast in the textures. The diffuse albedo pass is useful for this purpose because it contains all the texture color information minus the lighting and shading. Blending the beauty with a bit of the albedo pass is an effective way of reducing light–shadow contrast without flattening any of the texture color detail.

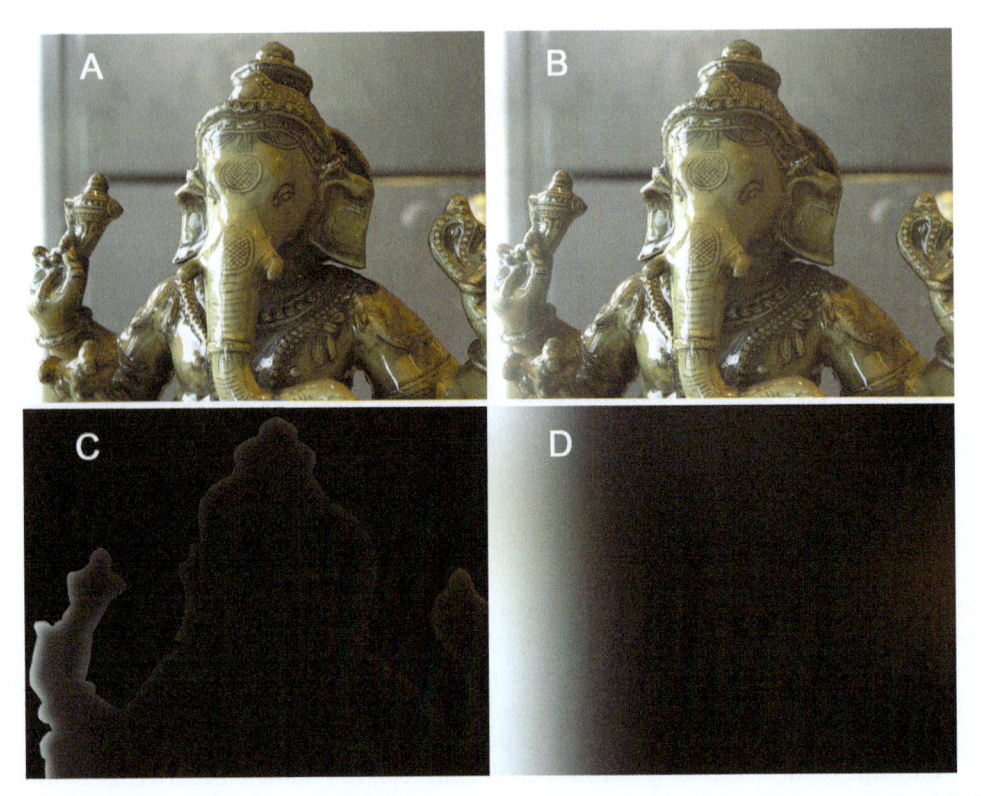

The CG render feels a touch too crunchy and clean over the background image (A). Adding some light wrap (C) and some light bleed/flaring (D), while also mixing in a bit of the diffuse albedo pass and adding subtle bloom, helps the element "sit" better in the comp (B).

Edge Treatment

CG elements are normally rendered over a black background (or over the target footage), and are thus free of the issues associated with extracted or rotoscoped elements, such as bright/dark edges, and green or noisy fringes. The relatively pain-free process of adding CG element to footage, however, does not mean that edge treatment is not necessary. Overly sharp, clean, or consistent edges and boundaries are often tell-tale signs of CG. Successful integration therefore requires one or more of the following treatments: subtle edge blur, blooms on rim highlights (making sure the blooming bleeds into the background), light warp, chromatic aberration (see Chapter 18), and, in some cases, breaking the edge consistency by subtly modulating the alpha with noise. Like everything else described in this section, subtle touches are usually more effective than heavy treatment – good CG renders require minimum comp intervention, just enough to break the curse of perfection.

Chapter 17

Lighting in 2D

Relighting with Color

When working in 2D, artists have none of the convenience of CG lighting: they can't place lights at selected locations in the scene and control their intensity and color; there are no shaders or surfaces that can be set to react to light in specific ways; accurate shadows and reflections are not generated automatically; and perhaps most importantly, lighting is already pre-baked in the image, and often needs to be undone before it can be modified – a challenging, sometimes even impossible task. Just like a traditional painter, the only way a digital artist can create or change lighting in 2D is through the selective use of color. In matte painting, traditional techniques are used to create lighting by coloring areas of light and shadows, and in compositing, the paint brush is replaced with animated roto shapes when coloring is applied to moving and shifting elements.

The pre-baked lighting in the source material is a defining factor on how effectively that material can be relit in 2D. If an element is shot in direct sunlight, changing the direction or intensity of the light requires removing the baked light and shadows first – a difficult, or sometimes impossible challenge. Even the highest quality imagery may not contain the kind of super-wide dynamic range that allows grading highlights down and lifting shadows up to such an extent. In many cases, there is little or no information in the highlights or deep shadows, and extreme grading results in clamped, flat areas or ugly artifacts. It is of course best to source material with lighting that already matches the target environment. But if no such material can be found or used, it is far preferable to start off with overcast/flatly lit material. As in texturing and 3D scanning, 2D material lends itself best to relighting through color when it is captured under overcast sky, or is evenly lit by non-directional, diffused lighting.

The Challenge of Reflections

Up to this point, we approached specularity as a single type of light interaction, whether it appears as simple specs of highlights, or discrete mirror-like reflections. In 2D, this distinction does matter. Our visual perception is not particularly sensitive to the top of the color range and we are pretty lenient toward misplaced or inaccurate specular highlights. So, without the need to represent a specific reflected image, generic highlights can be painted in with relative ease – even a few

It took Luke Panayiotou a week to paint this image, using just a single brush in Photoshop. Every aspect of photorealism in this work is achieved solely through color.

© Luke Panayiotou.

THE 2D WORLD

scattered daubs are often all it takes to hint at reflectivity (this is clearly manifested in numerous traditional paintings). That said, film and video add the factor of motion – the effect of specularity is lost if the painted spots do not move in tandem with the movement of the object, light, and camera. Without proper movement, static highlights read as texture rather than specular reflection.

Clear reflections on smooth surfaces like windows, mirrors, water, or polished metal represent a much greater challenge in 2D and deserve a closer look, especially since "faking" reflections is a common compositing and matte painting task. This task can be tricky, mainly because what is visible in the reflection is not necessarily seen by the camera. In other words, **the reflected image represents the point of view of the mirror**, which can be different (or in fact the complete reverse) of the camera's point of view. Let us examine two VFX scenarios:

Scenario 1: a matte painting of a serene mountain lake. Such a setting obviously requires a reflection of the environment in the water. It seems like the reflection can be easily created by grabbing the background above the lake's distant shore and flipping it 180 degrees down. But is this really an accurate method? Is the reflection of the lake a simple flipped image of the environment? While the camera's line of sight is more or less horizontal, the lake is "seeing" the environment vertically from the bottom up. This 90-degree difference in POV hardly affects the appearance of the distant elements, but anything close to the water edge may look different in the reflection than in the camera. A deer standing on the lake shore is viewed face-on from the camera, but the reflection is "seeing" the deer from the bottom up, showing more of its underside. It is of course difficult to recreate this change in perspective in a 2D matte painting workflow without resorting to hand-painting or 3D. Yet for most practical purposes, this level of

What the reflection "sees" is not necessarily what the camera sees. From the camera's point of view, most of the colorful lights are hidden behind the tarp roofs. But the water is "seeing" those lights fully from below, reflecting a view that is hidden to the camera.

LIGHTING IN 2D

accuracy is not needed. The viewer is unlikely to notice anything wrong in the reflection, and the simple flip can work just fine. The discrepancy becomes noticeable only in close-up views, where there is distinct focus on elements close to the reflecting surface.

Scenario 2: in an interior set on a soundstage, an over-the-shoulder shot of an actor standing by a window, looking at the "view" outside. A green screen is placed behind the window, to allow adding the exterior in post. While the actor is keyed out and the green screen replaced, a proper sense of window glass can only be achieved through reflections. The problem is that the camera is shooting the actor's **back**, while the mirror is reflecting the actor's **face**. In a traditional painting, the artist will simply paint the reflection. But in a photoreal VFX situation, the compositor must use real footage of the actor from the reflection's point of view.

The simplest solution would be to have a physical glass on the set window. Even though the green screen will be removed later and replaced by an exterior view, the compositor could still use luma-keying techniques to extract the reflection and screen it back on the added BG. This is a common practice, but not always feasible: often the glass reflects unwanted elements like the camera, the crew, or an unbuilt section of the set. Another option is to shoot a separate "witness camera" take from the direction of the window toward the actor's face. This ensures a clean footage but works only if the actor is not moving much (syncing could be a problem). The point here is that not every reflection can be created from scratch at the VFX phase. Sometimes the necessary material must be shot on the set or location.

Fresnel Effect

When adding reflections in 2D, the artist needs to be aware of the Fresnel effect discussed in Chapter 9, especially on non-metallic surfaces. The reflection should be stronger at shallow viewing angles, and gradually disappear as the viewing angle increases. In the above lake example, the added 2D reflection would look rather unnatural if it were consistently strong. Rather, it should gradually fade out toward the camera, in correlation with the change in viewing angle (Translated to 2D, this fade happens from "top to bottom"). The same principle applies to any horizontal reflective surface (say, a shiny floor or table surface), and to curved surfaces where the reflection is stronger at grazing angles (on a sphere, reflection would be stronger toward the sides).

Breaking up Reflections

As the irregularity of the surface becomes more pronounced, the reflected image loses its definition, and at a certain point only the areas of highest intensity and contrast (light sources, the sky) are visible as broken highlights. The lake surface is a good example: small ripples on the surface break the reflection to a certain extent, but the reflected image is still recognizable. The approach for creating such a reflection in 2D is to modulate or distort the reflected image with animated undulating noise. The noise pattern should match the scale and intensity of the ripples and should also match the perspective (ripples getting smaller with distance). However, when the waves are stronger, their height and complexity break the reflected image beyond recognition. In such a case, the reflected image should be blurred before being modulated. This ensures that only the strongest differences in illumination (like the sun) are noticeable in the broken reflection, but finer detail (like clouds in the sky) is not.

A simple noise pattern (right) is used to distort the reflection image to simulate a rougher water surface.

Creating Shadows

In Chapter 16 we looked at shadow mattes and ambient occlusion passes as tools for generating interactive shadows in comp. But these techniques only work with CG elements that are lit and rendered in 3D. When elements are extracted from 2D footage and comped into a new environment, shadows must be created solely in 2D. This is certainly more challenging, because the angle, perspective, falloff, and softness must be approximated and generated manually as in traditional art. The first step when compositing a 2D element into footage is to study the shadows in the footage and estimate the location and character of the light sources (even if they are not visible in the frame). This is easier to achieve in an outdoor daytime scene, as it only requires assessing the position of the sun, but can be much more difficult in a nighttime or interior footage with multiple light sources of varying characteristics.

Shape, Angle, and Stretching

The alpha channel of the comped element can be used as a starting shape for the shadow's silhouette, and can then be transformed, scaled, rotated, and skewed to achieve the correct perspective and shadow stretching. This is easier to do on a still frame, but much harder when the element is moving. For example, if the element is a green screen extraction of a walking actor, care must be taken when manipulating the shape of the shadow so that the shadow always sticks to each of the actor's feet whenever they touch the ground. It is usually more important to ensure that the shadow sticks to the contact areas than to emulate every small detail in the shadow's shape – we are much more susceptible to "floating" shadows than to missing detail.

The angle and length of the shadow needs to correlate to the position of the light source as well as its size. For sunlight, the shadow angle and length can be assessed by gauging the position of the sun in an imaginary half dome and tracing a straight line from the sun's position through the subject at its point of contact with the ground. The angle and length should be kept consistent across the scene regardless of where the elements are. With any other light except the sun, the angle needs to change depending on the position of the subject relative to the light source. The straight line can be animated with its origin tracking the light and its pivot tracking the subject, and the result used as a rough guide to the shifting direction of the shadow.

Shadow Softness and Falloff

As shown in Chapter 8, the softness of the shadow (or the relative size of its penumbra) depends on a combination of several factors. While physically based renderers faithfully calculate shadow softness, it is usually not necessary to consider every actor when creating shadows in 2D. Matching the overall shadow softness and falloff to existing shadows in the footage is usually enough. If the footage does not offer sufficient reference, consider the scale of the light/s in the scene. Large lights produce softer shadows, while small, focused lights produce sharp shadows with a narrow penumbra. Overall shadow softness can be achieved by blurring the shadow's matte using local masks. When the light is coming at a steep angle, the penumbra is fan-shaped, and the falloff also happens gradually along the sides, not just the length.

Breaking up Shadows

The most challenging aspect of creating 2D shadows is matching their shape and deformation to the underlying environment. Easy on a flat, even ground, harder when the shadow falls on an irregular surface or other objects. Simple cheats can be used to break shadows in a convincing way. For example, on a relatively flat but irregular ground like dirt, pebbles, grass, or water, it is often quite effective to break up the shadow matte with some simple noise. Although it is not an accurate representation of the surface, the illusion is usually quite sufficient. This type of treatment is of course not a solution for large surface irregularity (for example, stairs) or when the shadow happens over distinct objects. In such cases, the roto shape of the shadow must be animated to reflect the wide deformations in the shadow's shape, a challenging process, especially when both the occluding and occluded surfaces are moving or deforming.

Shadow Color

Junior compositors often make the mistake of overlaying the shadow as if it was a separate element. This forces a consistent color, when in fact the shadow's color depends on the color of the surface. Color-correcting the footage through a matte is a preferable method, as it preserves the underlying hue. However, simply reducing brightness (gaining down) may push the black values too low, so it is usually necessary to gain down while also slightly lifting the blacks and reducing saturation. The shadow area should be tinted toward the hue of the remaining light/s. In a daylight environment, this would correspond to the sky color, while in nighttime or interior scenes the hue would match the combined color of the remaining lights (such shadows are rarely as cool as daytime exterior). Shadow tinting should be subtle – the slight bluishness of shadowed

A: a palm tree is added to the foreground, B: color is adjusted to match the environment, the bottom of the trunk is darkened a bit and a very subtle proximity shadow added to the ground, C: the tree's alpha is skewed, rotated, and scaled to create the shadow, D: shadow color and softness adjusted.

LIGHTING IN 2D

areas on a clear day is nowhere near as saturated as the blue sky itself. Since our eyes are sensitive to black mismatches, it is important to check the blacks in the created shadows against existing shadows in the footage.

Contact and Proximity Shadows

AO and shadow passes help generate contact shadows for CG elements, but 2D elements require compositors to manually create occlusion areas around the element's points of contact with the footage (or between two separate elements). Contact and proximity shadows can be created by using the element's alpha and slightly dilating and blurring it, or by drawing simple soft mask shapes around the areas. The softness and intensity must be animated to match the action. The closer the elements are to each other, the darker and sharper the shadow. For a walking actor, the ground contact shadow is darker and sharper when the foot is touching it, then gradually softer and lighter as the foot moves up. Similarly, if the composited actor is reaching out to touch an element in the footage, the shadow's intensity and sharpness increases as the hand gets closer to the element. Compositors and matte painters often focus on the obvious contact or near-contact areas and less so on the subtler proximity occlusion. For example, a very soft, very subtle darkening of a wider area underneath the walking actor can truly help the integration of the element in the environment. Such an almost imperceptible occlusion effect can go a long way in improving photorealism.

Case Study: Matte Painting Integration in Film

The Greatest Showman.
© Twentieth Century Fox. VFX by Brainstorm Digital.

Creating photoreal, detailed matte paintings is a challenge, but integrating them into the footage is often an additional challenge. Here are two examples from Brainstorm Digital's VFX work. The first, from *The Greatest Showman*, is a fall-to-winter conversion – done mostly by adding a dramatic sky that changes the entire mood of the shot. The original sky was very bright and flat, and replacing it with a cloudy dark sky required substantial relighting of the shot. Some overall color corrections were used to bring down the tones to match the darkness of the sky, but the mansion façade was tricky: parts of it became too muddy and lost their definition because of the darkening, and additional matte painting was necessary to bring back the detail. Replacing a bright background with a much darker one inevitably causes issues of bright edges around wispy elements, and indeed, some tricky edge reconstruction work was necessary to treat all those twigs and small tree branches.

The second example is from James Gray's film *The Lost City of Z*. In this particular shot, explorer Percy Fawcett heads toward the Royal Geographic Society's headquarters. Gray wanted an exact replica of the historical RGS building in Savile road, but the London parts were in fact shot in Belfast, so we explored several potential locations in the city. Eventually, we ended up choosing an intersection just off the crew's hotel, because of the similarity in layout and proportions to the real location. The green screen was intended to cover all the action, but cinematographer Darius Khondji ultimately went for a wider framing, and additional roto was necessary as some of the action went off the screen.

The Lost City of Z.
© Keep Your Head Company, Amazon Studios. VFX by Brainstorm Digital.

LIGHTING IN 2D

The movie was shot on film with an anamorphic lens, factors that make a difference when integrating matte painting elements: film has heavier and more pronounced grain than digital footage, which makes grain-matching a crucial integration step. Film also has a subtle characteristic softness that is distinctly different from digital media. The anamorphic lens introduces a second layer of softness that is uneven across the frame, and, of course, a very pronounced distortion that must be matched (notice the slanting of vertical lines). Yet the most challenging integration aspect in this shot was the dense atmosphere – several smoke machines were working hard on the set to emulate the thick, soot-filled air of early 20th-century London. Adding or replacing buildings across the frame required meticulous matching of black levels, and adding back blowing smoke, either by keying it over the green screen or recreating it with external elements where it could not be keyed.

Atmospheric Depth

Photorealism strongly relies on an accurate depiction of depth. Our eyes are sensitive to depth mismatches, and digital imagery easily falls apart when aerial perspective is off or inconsistent. In visual effects, atmospheric depth is typically added at the compositing stage. Even if certain atmospheric elements such as fog or smoke are rendered in CG, the final adjustments are done in comp, with interactive control and in the context of the footage and/or final image. The method for generating atmospheric depth depends on the type of elements: for CG rendered elements, the Z depth pass provides an accurate per-pixel representation of the distance from camera and serves as a base for all depth effects. When dealing with 2D elements from footage or still images, compositors and matte painters must rely on their visual skills and keen understanding of distance and depth. In lack of a depth pass, artists also need to manually separate or "slice" different depths in the images by painting masks or rotoscoping. Atmospheric depth is tied to accurate color grading, and the color principles discussed below apply equally to 3D (Z depth pass) and 2D (manual depth separation) workflows.

Referencing the Footage

The first step when integrating an element is to assess its distance from the camera, based on its position in the image (how deep it sits within the footage), and then identify areas in the footage at the same depth as reference for the effect of the atmosphere on color. For example, when adding a building element to a photo of a city, existing buildings which sit at a similar depth in the footage can serve as an indication to the amount of hazing. Look at the blacks first – not just their value (how lifted they are), but also their specific RGB balance (it may be useful to temporarily raise the viewing gamma to see better into the blacks). Matching the subtle, almost imperceptible color detail in the low range is a key step in matching the overall aerial perspective and the effect of atmospheric elements like fog, dust, or smoke.

That said, there are times when the original footage does not provide the necessary depth clues. For example, when the elements are placed deeper than any existing object in the footage (adding mountains in the distance, or a plane high up in the sky), or when the entire scene is a CG render or matte-painting. In such cases, the sky is the best guide. Lifting the color values of distant

The same tree element is placed at three different depths (left). The substantial color changes must be applied to each tree to integrate it into the environment at that particular depth.

The Shelter by Tamas Medve. 3D Studio Max and Photoshop.
© Tamas Medve.

Building Megalopolis II by Benjamin Bardou.
© Benjamin Bardou.

elements toward the color of the sky is a basic way to simulate aerial perspective. As discussed in Chapter 6, humidity, dust, and other aerosols congregate in the lower atmosphere, which affects the sky color at the horizon. Since most distant elements sit near the horizon, these factors affect their color as well. Sometimes (especially with very large distant elements such as mountains) it is not enough to just push the blacks and midtones toward the horizon color. Atmospheric components like low-lying clouds or fog may partially or completely obstruct distant elements, and it is important to show their interaction with the added elements. Low-lying fog, for example, can blanket the foothills at lower altitude, and then dissipate at higher altitude, with the peaks clearer than the base. It is important to treat the sky (whether it already exists in the footage or is added as a sky dome to a CG scene) as a true atmosphere – a three-dimensional volume that engulfs the scene and interacts with it, rather than a 2D background that simply sits behind the scene.

While lifting the low end for atmospheric depth, it is important not to brighten the higher midtones and highlights. Clean air usually leaves highlights intact, while haze may dim them, but highlights never get brighter because of the atmosphere. Therefore, color operations like lift or gamma are a good choice for depth grading. An effective technique for adding atmospheric depth is to grab the sky in the footage, blur it enough to erase any discernible detail, and then subtly screen it over the composited elements. It is important to use a screen merge operation and not an additive (A+B) operation. The screen operation (A+B–AB) protects the top range and prevents highlights from getting brighter, but effectively lifts the low end and lower midtones.

Chapter 18

Lens and Camera Effects

The significance of adding lens and camera characteristics at the compositing stage cannot be overstated. This is not just the icing on the cake – this is the essence of photorealism. Even the most realistic CG render feels somewhat artificial without the appropriate touch of defocus, lens distortion, flares, and grain. Lens effects serve as a final glue that binds all the elements in a matte painting or composite because they strengthen the illusion that everything in the image was physically captured by a camera.

Defocus

Every CG render engine provides the ability to apply 3D depth of field as part of the render. This generally produces the most accurate defocus, without any of the issues associated with Z depth. However, 3D defocus is baked into the render, and cannot be changed or adjusted later in compositing. It also requires higher sampling rates and slows down the rendering. The 2D option is certainly more flexible – the focal point, depth of field, and defocus amount can all be tweaked and adjusted while the results are viewed in realtime. As long as you are aware of the Z depth limitations discussed in Chapter 16 (in particular, issues with transparent and volumetric objects), then 2D defocus can be an efficient alternative to 3D depth of field for CG renders.

Compositing applications offer dedicated tools for applying accurate defocus based on the render's Z depth pass. Non-normalized passes work especially well since they cover an infinite range. The focal point is selected by sampling the Z depth value at the desired focus area, and then the depth of field and defocus intensity are adjusted. Defocus tools usually offer additional features for precisely controlling the look of the bokeh, like setting the number of polygons (to match the number of aperture blades) and adjusting their relative curvature, adding typical highlights bloom with variable threshold, gamma shifting, or changing the defocus aspect ratio (for non-spherical anamorphic defocus). Such features allow the artist to emulate the specific characteristics of any lens and achieve seamless integration with photographed material.

When working with 2D elements, there is of course no Z depth pass. Applying convincing depth of field in a fully 2D workflow requires a good eye and a clear notion of where each element is placed in 3D space. In lack of a depth pass, it is certainly harder to create a smooth transition from

Tweaking defocus in comp. A: depth pass, B: focal point near the back wall, C: focal front moved to the front, D: exaggerated defocus with five-blade aperture, gamma correction, and highlight bloom.

in-focus to out-of-focus. Focus level gradation can be somewhat simulated with soft masks, and although the result is not quite the same as true focal transition, it can nonetheless be an effective cheat. When integrating elements into live-action footage, focus level and bokeh type should be matched to areas at a comparable depth.

Lens Distortion and Chromatic Aberration

Chromatic aberrations are important for integrating elements, and for adding a subtle sense of a lens medium to CG renders. The effect can be easily replicated by slightly offsetting one or two of the RGB channels. An offset of 1–4 pixels (depending on the resolution) is usually enough to create the typical fringing of chromatic aberration, while higher values are used more for pronounced stylized effects. Transverse aberration is stronger toward the fringes of the frame (see Chapter 10), and can be simulated by scaling the selected RGB channels from the center of the frame.

From a technical standpoint, **lens distortion** is an indispensable component of camera tracking. Distortion features vary greatly between different lenses, and although some of these variations are hardly visible to the eye, their precise calculation is crucial for 3D camera tracking. Some lens distortion tools offer elaborate distortion models that mimic real-world spherical and anamorphic lenses, as well as rectilinear and fish-eye projections. But beyond its technical importance, lens

A pronounced chromatic aberration (right) is generated by offsetting the red and green channels in opposing directions.

distortion can add a great deal of realism to fully CG games and even static renders, as long as it is kept within a plausible range that matches the context.

Lens Flares

Lens flares serve a triple purpose: they add visual drama, they give a sense of a physical lens, and they help tie together different elements in the comp. Flares are an important instrument for enhancing the photoreal aspect of digital imagery and serve as a very effective compositing "glue", because they happen over of all the elements in the image. The essential flares characteristics discussed in Chapter 10 need to be implemented in the context of the shot. In particular, the movement and intensity fluctuations should be tied to the movement of the relevant light sources in or around the frame and random disturbances and imperfections must be added to avoid an overly clean and perfect look.

There are essentially two ways to create lens flares: procedural generation and real footage. Most compositing and photo-editing applications provide some procedural tools for designing lens flares, and there are also many third-party flare-creation plugins available. Procedural tools offer the advantage of accurate flare motion and intensity in relation to the light source, and full control over the shape and color of the various flare elements. However, procedural flares are too clean and perfect out of the box, and need to be further degraded and varied through noise or texture modulation. The extra effort can truly make a difference between a tacky effect and believable visuals. Real-world footage, on the other hand, has all the photoreal detail and imperfections built-in. There are quite a few stock libraries that include a wide selection of flares (ideally shot over a clean black background) that cover various lenses and lights. However, it can be difficult to match the motion and interaction between the footage of a full flare effect and a specific shot or CG render. Stock footage of single, isolated flare components is usually the most useful, because it allows the freedom to combine several elements and animate them in context of the particular shot (or use them to enhance procedurally generated flares).

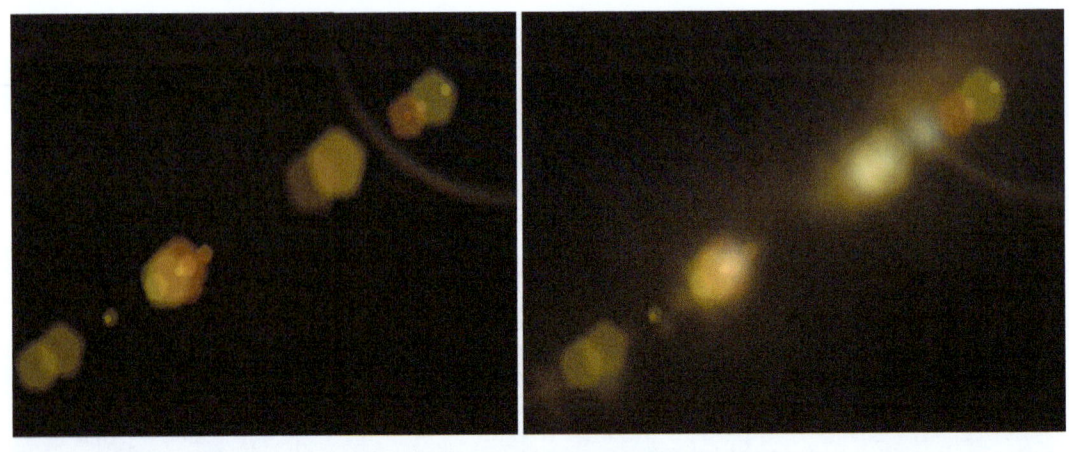

A procedurally generated lens flare (left) looks a bit too clean and perfect. Blurring some parts, adding localized glows, and running the elements through a grunge map helps give it a more natural look.

Motion Blur

3D motion blur is usually rendered as part of the CG scene. However, like defocus, it is baked into the render and cannot be further adjusted in comp, so sometimes it is more practical to add motion blur to CG renders at the compositing stage. This requires rendering a **motion vector** pass along with the beauty. Compositing tools like Nuke's **vector blur** node apply motion blur based on the motion vectors. The advantage of applying motion blur in 2D is not only shortened 3D render times but the ability to fine tune the motion blur based on the context of the footage. However, when motion blur is applied to a complete render, bad edges and artifacts tend to form around areas of overlap between moving and static objects (or between objects moving in different directions and speeds). To avoid this, it's best to render the scene in separate layers.

Adding motion blur to 2D elements is of course limited to two axes, but thankfully, motion blur that happens on the Z axis (towards or away from the camera) is generally less noticeable. 2D vector information can be generated by tracking the motion of the 2D element. When tracking is not possible (or the results not satisfactory), motion blur can be faked with a directional blur. Of course, the exact amount and angle need to be keyframed manually to match the speed and direction of the object. As discussed in Chapter 15, extracted and rotoscoped edges often require added motion blur to match the original footage, and the same techniques (tracking or manual direction blurring) can be used for this type of edge treatment.

Grain

Grain is added last, on top of all the components, and its contribution to the final integrity of a composite image or shot is as crucial as it is subtle. The process of matching and adding grain often also requires removing any previous grain from different elements to prevent mismatched, double, or frozen grain. Grain and noise removal (**degraining** or **denoising**) is often a balancing act between removing as much of the grain as possible, and preserving sharpness and detail. Sometimes the best way to achieve an optimal balance is by experimenting with different tools

Artificially added grain does not show well in the blacks (left), yet in both digital and film mediums, grain is usually stronger in the blacks. It is therefore important to adjust the grain level in the blacks separately (right).

and settings (In addition to native tools in compositing applications, there are plugins that use different algorithms for degraining and denoising). There are several techniques for re-applying grain to footage (such as degraining it first and then using a difference or minus merge operation to extract the grain), but visual grain matching and manual adjustments are often preferable. Grain size and softness should be matched and adjusted separately for each RGB channel, and both dark and bright areas should be examined. Grain in the blacks is particularly important, and most grain tools offer a separate control for that. When adding grain to a fully CG image or shot, the reference for grain should either be the surrounding shots (in VFX), or, in the context of visualization or games, by examining desired camera or film stock characteristics.

Epilogue

The Future

Back in 2017 I wrote an article for the indie filmmaking magazine *NoFilmSchool*. In that article, "How Two Companies Are Drastically Altering the Future of Visual Effects",[1] I highlighted two emerging projects, and explained why I think they will be spearheading visual effects in the near future. One was *Lytro*'s newly developed light-field camera, the other was *Elara* (later called *Athera*), the virtual cloud hub developed by *Foundry* (makers of *Nuke* and *Mari*). Contrary to my enthusiastic forecasts, both projects evaporated shortly after: *Lytro* ceased operations in 2018, and *Foundry* closed *Athera* in 2019. Did I completely miss the mark? Yes and no, I would say. While foundry chose to focus on their software products, extensive cloud services (and in particular virtual workstations) are now offered by the "big ones" (*Amazon*, *Google*, *Microsoft*), and are increasingly used by VFX companies for remote work. Lytro's light-field camera was too expensive and bulky, but other, less accurate depth-detection technologies are already widely used in consumer phone cameras. Eventually, I believe, precise per-pixel depth detection will be available in professional cameras at reasonable costs. The concept of capturing depth in tandem with the color image is just too promising to be ignored.

The point here is that although I was wrong at the micro level (those two projects did not live up to their promise), I was correct at the macro level (the trends still live and flourish). Therefore, this final chapter is in no way an accurate or reliable set of predictions – really, my guess is as good as yours. But I think that it is nonetheless appropriate to end this book with a quick overview of some emerging trends that, I believe, may shape the future of photoreal digital visual content creation.

Realtime Rendering

As I wrote more than once in the book, the potential of realtime rendering is only starting to be exploited, and the rate of technological advancements in the last five years or so leaves little doubt about the future role of realtime technologies and game engines. Epic's unreal Engine 5 (not yet out at the time of writing this book) promises to eliminate much of the shortcomings of realtime rendering, and if global illumination and raytraced reflections can be generated accurately in real time now, it is only logical to assume that other computationally heavy features (like true subsurface scattering) will soon follow. The shift to realtime technologies in visual effects and visualizations is ongoing, and photorealism is a key factor in this shift: until recently, opting for interactive realtime rendering inevitably meant lowering the threshold of realism, detail, and believability, but this is no longer the case.

Realtime rendering does not mean that CG is created on the fly – it still takes time and effort to model, texture, and shade 3D scenes. Neither does it eliminate the need for compositing and matte painting in visual effects. But the advantages of fully photoreal, physically based realtime rendering are vast: on-the-fly layout and lighting adjustments, fast prototyping and design, flexible and fast pre-visualization for film and TV, virtual environments (see below), on-set visualization for directors and cinematographers, reduced need for expensive render farms and long rendering schedules, and believable, photoreal interactive architectural visualizations and immersive games and VR. Looking forward, photorealistic realtime rendering is bound to revolutionize digital visual content.

Photorealism on the Cloud

Microsoft's new flight simulator generated a great deal of hype long before its release in summer 2020, because it offered something that flight simulators could never offer before: incredibly detailed and accurate environments that go on for thousands of miles, populated with thousands of airports and cities. Such amount of detail, so crucial for photoreal environments, cannot possibly be stored on any single consumer system. Instead, Microsoft uses its vast global resources to store the data on the cloud, and that data is retrieved continuously during gameplay. With the ability to use the cloud to store and process massive datasets, future games and interactive visualizations could offer a quasi-unlimited level of detail and stunning photorealism, because they will no longer depend on limited end-user specs. The technology for transferring pixels and screen actions in real time over the internet already exists. It is used, for example, by VFX artists to remotely operate software on powerful virtual workstations. The price of such technologies and their dependency on fast internet connections currently limits them to (mostly) company-level usage. But this is very likely to change, and widespread consumer-level cloud operation could make immensely realistic, detailed realtime environments and characters a household reality in games, VR, and interactive visualizations.

LED Screens and Virtual Environments

While Disney's *The Mandalorian* was not the first production to use LED screens in tandem with realtime game engine technology, it certainly elevated the concept of a virtual set and established new standards for similar workflows. Rear projection (background footage screened behind the actor and captured in-camera) has been used in cinema since the 1930s, but the motion discrepancies between the camera and the screened footage, as well as lighting mismatches often caused scenes to feel very artificial (as is quite evident in numerous driving scenes in the history of cinema). Digital compositing and green screens certainly offer more control over the background during post-production, and enable tracking the background to the camera. But green-screen compositing still suffers from potential lighting mismatches and a slew of edge and integration issues (as discussed in Chapter 15).

In a virtual set workflow, the 3D environments are created in a game engine during pre-production, and then displayed on giant LED screens that partially (sometimes fully) surround the set. The important advantage of an LED screen over rear projections is that it physically lights the set, essentially acting as a real-world sky light (similar to image-based lighting in CG rendering).

Thus, the lighting on the actors matches the virtual environment that surrounds them. The physical camera is connected to the game engine's virtual camera, and the displayed background environment continuously reacts to the physical camera's movement and angle (and even focal changes), so proper perspective and parallax are always preserved. In addition, realtime rendering allows for quick, on-the-spot changes to layout and lighting within the environments, which gives the filmmakers a new level of flexibility on the set. Finally, because everything from the foreground actors and physical set to the virtual background is captured on camera, there are no green screen extractions, no spill, no edge issues, and (potentially) no need for additional VFX work in post.

While this process offers a new and exciting way of extending physical sets, it is important to note its limitations: compared to green screens, LED surround screens are expensive and bulky, and can only be set up in a large indoor soundstage; the virtual environments must be created and completed before the shooting phase starts; and, just like IBL sky domes, environments displayed on LED screens are merely eggshells – actors cannot walk through them or physically interact with them. Yet despite these limitations, it seems like the continuous development of LED screens technology and realtime rendering will contribute to an increased use of virtual sets in a wide variety of production scenarios.

Machine Learning

The power of machine learning algorithms (often discussed under the broader term "artificial intelligence") is in the ability of the algorithm to improve its performance through the continuous sampling of data. Machine learning is being used in a wide variety of fields, and is also getting a foothold in digital visual content creation and manipulation. Take, for example, rotoscoping: a tedious, time-consuming process that is nonetheless an essential task in visual effects. Our natural, instinctive ability to identify and separate objects in 2D footage is in fact an extremely difficult challenge for computers. The more a machine learning algorithm "studies" footage of, say,

The 600-pixel wide photo on the left was enlarged four times its size through an AI algorithm that fills in missing pixels.

humans, the more it is able to accurately identify humans in footage and rotoscope them. We are still far from fully automated rotoscoping – current applications are too crude and inaccurate to replace roto artists – but it is logical to assume that in the future, tasks such as separating an actor from the background could be successfully and accurately done by powerful machine learning algorithms.

Here is another example: there is a current proliferation of online services that can enlarge low-resolution photos to twice or even four and eight times their original size. Such algorithms are "trained" by analyzing thousands of images and are capable of filling in the missing pixels with contextually matching imagery as the resolution is increased – an automated matte painting of sorts. Will they eventually replace matte painters? Probably not. But one can certainly see how, in the future, machine learning would help in creating photoreal content by assisting the artists with many of the time-consuming tasks, like searching and collecting relevant imagery in a matte painting workflow, color-matching in compositing, analyzing footage for lighting, depth sorting 2D material, and more.

Procedural Environments

In Chapter 14 I discussed procedural modeling for natural assets like terrains and trees. But algorithm-driven automation can be also used to generate entire environments populated with terrains, plants, buildings, and even "live" animated creatures and characters. This is an intriguing prospect for the future of photorealism. In 2016, the game *No Man's Sky* was released with the exciting promise of unlimited exploration of an infinite number of entirely procedurally generated worlds. Despite (or maybe because of) the hype, the game was initially received with some disappointment, as players criticized the boring gameplay and repetitiveness of the procedural environments (the game has since gone through several major updates and improvements and is now viewed quite positively).

While the world's best-selling game (Minecraft) is entirely procedural, few photoreal games are currently based on fully automated, purely procedural generation. Most use a combination of pre-built assets and some form of algorithmic distribution. But looking forward, there is much potential in systems that generate entire environments with all their assets from scratch, based only on a set of physical, thematic, and aesthetic rules. Such systems are useful not only for games, but also for VFX, visualizations, and various simulators. The amount of complexity and realism depends only on the quality of the algorithm: how closely it emulates the complex relationship between chaos and order in natural environments, or the function-driven expansion of human dwellings. The idea of realistic, believable jungles, deserts, or cities at the push of a button is not so far-fetched.

Will Photorealism Disappear?

Traditional art gradually shifted from figurative to abstract around the turn of the 20th century. Artists lost interest in recreating reality and instead searched for new avenues of expression. Will photorealism also go out of vogue at some point? Drawing and painting always served a much broader function than just pure art. Historical documentation, family portraits, scientific research, journalism, advertisement, entertainment – for most of these day-to-day uses, photography emerged as a better alternative. Similarly, photorealism serves a wide range of practical purposes,

Procedural forest environment by Robert Berg. Generated in Unreal Engine.
© Robert Berg.

from visualizations to games. It is much less an artistic, aesthetic, or stylistic ideal as it is a functional necessity for immersive experiences. As such, it is very unlikely to lose its importance, but rather the opposite – the immersive experience is bound to be pushed even further. But photorealism as we currently know it is merely an artificial emulation of photography, nothing more than 2D images on screens (even VR is essentially projected moving pictures). Will we ever shift into a new phase of artificial reality, one that is truly three-dimensional and involves the simulation of touch and smell? Such a shift is bound to overtake photorealism in entertainment and games, in the same way photography replaced painting in the late 19th century. The "photo" will then be taken out of "photorealism", because we will no longer emulate photography – we will emulate reality.

Note

1 How Two Companies are Drastically Altering the Future of Visual Effects, Eran Dinur, *NoFilmSchool*, May 24, 2017. https://nofilmschool.com/2017/05/how-two-companies-are-drastically-altering-future-visual-effects.

APPENDIX A

Glossary of Abbreviations

AI	Artificial Intelligence
AO	Ambient Occlusion
AOV	Arbitrary Output Variable (render pass)
AR	Augmented Reality
ArchViz	Architectural Visualization
BRDF	Bidirectional Reflectance Distribution Function (shader model)
BTDF	Bidirectional Transmittance Distribution Function (shader model)
CG	Computer-Generated
CGI	Computer-Generated Imagery
CMYK	Cyan Magenta Yellow Black
CRT	Cathode-Ray Tube (type of monitor)
DEM	Digital Elevation Model
DOF	Depth of Field
DSLR	Digital Single-Lens Reflex (camera)
DXR	DirectX Raytracing
EXR	HDR multi-channel image format (aka OpenEXR)
FOV	Field of View
GI	Global Illumination
GPU	Graphics Processing Unit
HDR	High Dynamic Range
HDRI	High Dynamic Range Imagery
HSV	Hue Saturation Value
HZ	Hertz
IBK	Image-Based Keyer
IBL	Image-Based Lighting
IES	Illuminating Engineering Society
IOR	Index of Refraction
JPG	Joint Photographic Experts Group (image format)
LCD	Liquid Crystal Display (type of monitor)
LED	Light-Emitting Diode
LOD	Level of Detail
N	Normal (facing direction)
P	Position (as in P pass)

PBR	Physically Based Rendering
RGB	Red Green Blue
RTX	Nvidia's realtime raytracing GPU technology
SLR	Single-Lens Reflex (camera)
sRGB	Standard Red Green Blue (color space)
SSS	Sub-Surface Scattering
USGS	United States Geological Survey
UV	The X and Y axes in texture mapping
VFX	Visual Effects
VR	Virtual Reality
Z pass	Depth pass

APPENDIX B

Software list

This list includes only those applications mentioned in the book. It is by no means a comprehensive list.

All-round 3D Software

3D Studio Max (Autodesk)
Blender (open source)
Cinema 4D (Maxon)
Houdini (SideFX)
Maya (Autodesk)

Specialized 3D Software

Sculpting

Mudbox (Autodesk)
Zbrush (Pixologic)

Terrain and Landscape Creation

Gaea (Quadspinner)
Terragen (Planetside Software)
Vue (e-on Software)
World Creator (BiteTheBytes)
World Machine (World Machine Software)

Plant Modeling

Plant Factory (e-on Software)
SpeedTree (IDV/Unity)
Xfrog (Xfrog inc.)

Other Specialized 3D Software

Clarisse IFX (Isotopix)
HDR Light Studio (LightMap)
Marvelous Designer (CLO Virtual Fashion)
Shave and a Haircut (Joe Alter)

Game engines

Unity (Unity Technologies)
Unreal Engine (Epic Games)

Render Engines

Arnold (Autodesk)
Cycles (Blender)
Octane (Otoy)
Redshift (Maxon)
V-Ray (Chaos Group)

Image editing

Photoshop (Adobe)

Compositing

After Effects (Adobe)
Fusion (BlackMagic Design)
Nuke (Foundry)

Texture Authoring

Substance Alchemist (Adobe)
Substance Designer (Adobe)
Substance Painter (Adobe)
Mari (Foundry)

INDEX

The Complete Guide to Photorealism for Visual Effects, Visualization and Games: Index. Locators in *italics* refer to figures.

2D workflows 172–173; color 172–173, 175, *176*, 193; distinction from 3D 20, *21*; edges 176–182; lighting 193–204
3D workflows 20, *21*

abbe number *141*, 141
aberrations 99; chromatic 104–105, *105*, 206–207, *207*; compositing 205; defocus 99–102, *100–101*, 205–206, *206*; distortion *103*, 103–104, 206–207; flares 105–109, *107–109*, 207, *208*; grain 110–111, *111*, 208–209, *209*; monochromatic 99; motion blur 109, *110*, 208
absorption of light 57, 58–59, 72–73
additive color 36
aerial perspective 76–79
albedo 66, 148, 149
albedo passes 191, *192*
ambient light 55–56, *118*, 118–119
ambient occlusion (AO) *119*, 119, 129
ambient occlusion (AO) maps *152*, 152–153
anamorphic lenses 108
animation 2, 14–15
anisotropy 98, 136–137, 139
AOVs *see* render passes
aperture width 100
architectural visualization 25–28; 2D workflows 172; exterior renders *29*, *30*; side by side comparison 67–68
area lights 123–124
artificial lighting 83–86, 131
the atmosphere 71–73; aerial perspective 76–79; moon landing photographs 76
atmosphere layer (color) 34
atmospheric depth 202–204
atmospheric scattering 74–76
axial aberration 104

baked-in lighting 155–156
Bardou, Benjamin 204
barrel distortion 104
base color 33, 148, 149
beauty passes 183–184, *184*
Berg, Robert *214*
bit depth 45–48

blacks: albedo 66; as colors 46–47; shadows 46, 91
blooms 108, *109*; *see also* highlights bloom
blue screens 178
blur 102, 109, *110*, 182, 208
Bokeh 102
BRDF shading model 121, 133–141
brightness (color) 37, *37–38*, 38
bump maps 151–152

camera characteristics: aberrations 99, 103–104; chromatic aberration 104–105, *105*; compositing 205; defocus 99–102, *100–101*, 205–206, *206*; distortion *103*, 103–104, 206–207; flares 105–109, *107–109*, 207, *208*; grain 110–111, *111*, 208–209, *209*; and human vision 16–18; motion blur 109, *110*, 208
camera layer (color) 34
cameras: color 45, *46*; field of view 10–11; and human vision 9–13, *10–11*; image quality 19–20; level of detail 15–16, 17–18
car paint shaders 142
CG characters: light 55–56; "uncanny valley" 14–15
CG imagery: improving 190–192; integrating elements 183; modeling 163–164; photographic texture maps 155; portraiture 144, *144–145*; rendering 114, 115
chromatic aberration 104–105, *105*, 206–207, *207*
clear coat 137–138
the Cloud 211
coat 137–138
color 31–33; 2D workflows 172–173, 175, *176*, 193; absorption of light *58*, 58–59; additive 36; bit depth and dynamic range 45–48; BRDF shading model 139, 140; diffuse color 62; edges 182; hue, saturation, and brightness 37–40; operations 40–45; shadows 91, 198–200, *199*; six-layer approach 33–35; sky light 129; subtractive 35–36

color maps 148, 148–149
color temperature 83
Colorsponge, Carlos 142
complex index of refraction 98
compositing 172; color matching 175, *176*; deep compositing 189–190; lens and camera characteristics 205; with render passes 183–189
conservation of energy 66, 149
contact shadows 93
contrast (color) 149, 191
Cramb, Liam 122
crepuscular rays 76
cryptomatte 188–189

daylight 69; aerial perspective 76–79; the atmosphere 71–73; atmospheric scattering 74–76; natural environment in Clarisse IFX 79–81; physically based renderer (PBR) 128; the sun 69–71
deep compositing 189–190, *190*
deep data 189
defocus 99–102, *100–101*, 205–206, *206*
degraining 208–209
DEM data 165, 167–168
denoising 208–209
dense point cloud 187–188
depth of field (DOF) 100, *101*
detail, level of 15–16, 17–18
dielectric materials 94–96, 148–149, 151
dielectric shaders 135–136, *136–137*
diffraction spikes 106, *106*
diffuse color 62, 148
diffuse reflection 59, *62*, 62–63; BRDF shading model 135, 139–140; dielectric materials 94–95
diffuse roughness 135
diffuse sky radiation 74
diffused light 55
digital media 22; games 24; visual effects 22–24; visualization 25–30
direct illumination 54, *55*, *56*, 155–156
direct passes 183–184
directional light 55, 123
dispersion 141
displacement maps 153, *153*
distortion *103*, 103–104, 206–207
dome light 125

dynamic level of detail (LOD) 15–16
dynamic range 45–48

edge color 182
edges (2D workflows) 176–182, 192
Edwards, David *172*
electromagnetic spectrum *52*
elevation data 165–166
emission 140
environment light 81, 125, 129
erosion simulation 166, 167, 168
exposure: gain 41; for texture photos 156–157

Facing Normal passes 187, 188
facing normals 186
field of view 10–11
Final Fantasy: The Spirits Within 14, *14*
flares 105–109, *107–109, 207, 208*
flat shader 133
flight simulators 211
fluorescent lamps 84–85
focal length 100–101
focal plane 99
focus distance 100
fog color 139
fractal-based elevation 166
frame rates 109
Fresnel effect 95–96, 98, 134, 196
Fresnel Equations/Coefficients 95
Funke, Marvin *171*
fur shaders 143

gain (exposure) 41, *41*
games: digital media 24; realtime rendering 114, 210–211; technological change 24
gamma (color) 42–44, *43*
Gaussian blur 102, 109
glint 106
global illumination (GI) 118
Gouraud model 133
grain 62, 110–111, *111, 208–209, 209*
The Greatest Showman 23, *200, 201*
green screens 178

hair shaders 143
halogen lamps 84
Hannisdal, Terje *166*
haze 77, 79
hazing effect 191
HDR (High Dynamic Range) environments 124, 125, *126,* 126, 128–129
HDR (High Dynamic Range) photography 13
height maps 153, 165–166
Heral, Jeff *165*
highlights: rim highlights 63; specular reflection 61; whites 48
highlights bloom 102, 191
hue (color) 37, *37–38,* 38–39
human vision: and cameras 9–13, *10–11*; imperfections 16–18; level of detail 15–16; "uncanny valley" 14–15
humidity 78

ID passes 188–189
Illuminating Engineering Society (IES) 126–128, *127*
image-based lighting (IBL) 124–125, 126, *127*
image quality 19–20
image textures 154, 158, *159*

imaginary worlds 18
incandescent lamps 84
index of refraction (IOR) 65, 136
indirect illumination 54, *55*
inverse-square law 53
luit, Jose 146, *159*

Kamolz, Aron 80–81
Karimi, Hadi *130*
Kelvin (K) 83

Lambertian reflectivity model 133
lamp types 84–85
lateral aberration 104
LED lights 85
LED screens 211–212
lens aberrations 99, 103–104
lens characteristics 99; chromatic aberration 104–105, *105, 206–207, 207*; compositing 205; defocus 99–102, *100–101,* 205–206, *206*; distortion *103,* 103–104, 206–207; flares 105–109, *107–109, 207, 208*; grain 110–111, *111,* 208–209, *209*; motion blur 109, *110,* 208
lift (color) 42, *42–43*
light: 2D workflows 193–204; absorption 57, 58–59; albedo 66; ambient 55–56; architectural visualization 67–68; direct and indirect illumination 54, *55*; interactions 57, 57–58; modeling for 163–164; as particles 51, 52–53; photons 57; reflection 57, 59–62; refraction 64–65; and rendering 115; scattering 55, 59, 63, *63–64*; transmission (transparency) 57, 64–65; as waves 51–52, *52*; *see also* artificial lighting; daylight; nighttime light
light decay 53–54
light emitters: ambient 55–56, 118–119; artificial lighting 83–86, 131; contemporary 123–128; nighttime light 82; the sun 69–71; traditional 55, 122–123
light-field cameras 210
light fixtures 83, 86, 122, 124, 131
light intensity 84
light modifiers 85–86
light portal 130
light wrap 182, *192*
lighting passes 183–186
longitudinal aberration 104
The Lost City of Z 201, 201–202
Lumens 84
luminaires 83
Lux 84

machine learning 212–213
man-made lighting *see* artificial lighting
man-made objects: detail and imperfections 17, 17–18; modeling 163
material properties 94; dielectric materials 94–96, 148–149, 151; metals 97–98, 148–149, *150,* 151
mattes 188, 195–196, 200–202
Medve, Tamas *203*
mesh lights 124
metallic maps 150–151
metallic shaders 135–136, *136–137*
metals 97–98, 148–149, *150,* 151
Mie scattering 74, *75,* 75, 78
modeling 163; for lighting 163–164; procedural 164–169

monochromatic aberrations 99
Monte Carlo approach 121
motion blur 109, *110,* 208
Munsell color system 37

natural environment in Clarisse IFX 79–81; *see also* daylight
neon lights 85
nested shadows 92
nighttime light 82
Normal passes 187, 188
Nuke 188, 189

offline rendering 23
offset (color) 42
opacity maps 153–154

P passes 187, 188
Panayiotou, Luke *194*
Pandhi, Dax 167–168
particles, light as 51, 52–53
path tracing 120–121
Patiphan, Maxchill 144, *144–145*
Phong model 133
photogrammetry models 161
photographs: 2D and 3D workflows 20; bit depth 45; detail and imperfections 16–18; human vision and cameras 9–13; product visualization 28–29; shooting and prepping for texturing 155–157, 161
photometric lights 126–128
photon mapping 120
photorealism: definition 9; future of 213–214; image quality 19–20
physically based rendering (PBR): path tracing 120–121; strategies for PBR lighting 128–131; texturing *147,* 147–154
pincushion distortion 104
plant modeling 168–169
point lights 122, *123*
Point Position passes 187, 188
The Polar Express 14, *14*
procedural environments 213, *214*
procedural modeling 164–169
procedural textures 157–158, *159,* 160
product visualization 28–29
Purkinje Effect 82

quadratic decay of light means 53
quadratic rate 53–54
QuadSpinner 167–168

racking focus 99
radiosity 119–120
radius 140
rasterization 116
Rau, Raphael *28, 117,* 164
Rayleigh scattering 74, *75,* 77
raytracing *116,* 116–117
realtime rendering 114, 210–211
red, green, and blue (RGB) 36; bump maps *151*; hue, saturation, and brightness 37–40; rendering 115
reflection of light 57; diffuse 62–63, 94–95, 135, 139–140; Fresnel effect 95–96; six-layer approach 34; specular 59–62, 94–95, 136; sunlight 72–73
reflections: 2D workflows 193–196, *197*; "highlights" 48; metals 97
refraction of light 64–65, 98
refractive index 65
render channels *see* render passes

render elements *see* render passes
render passes 183–189
render resolution 191
rendering: biased vs. unbiased 121–122; CG imagery 114; compositing with render passes 183–189; computing power 115; contemporary light emitters 123–128; deep compositing 189–190; and lighting 115; lighting passes 183–186; realtime 210–211; from scanline to path tracing 115–121; strategies for PBR lighting 128–131; traditional light emitters 122–123; utility passes 168–169; *see also* BRDF shading model
resolution 155
Righi, Massimo *143*
rim highlights 63
roughness: diffuse 135; specular 136; transmission 138, *138*
roughness maps 150, *150*

Sadokha, Julian *29*, *113*
sampling 121; *see also* Monte Carlo approach
sampling rate 121
saturation (color) 37, *37–40*, *39–41*, *44–45*, 149
scale 128
scanline 116
scatter anisotrophy 139
scattered light: diffuse reflection 62, 63; glow 106; specular reflection 59–60; subsurface scattering 63, *63–64*, 139–140; transmission scatter 139; as type of ambient light 55
Schindelar, Christopher 114, *129*, *155*
Scionti, Pasquale *25*, *27*, *67*, 67–68, *131*, 131–132
Scruggs, Sarah 160–162
shaders: BRDF shading model 133–141; car paint shaders 142; evolution of 133; hair/fur shaders 143; volumetric shaders 142–143

shadow matte passes 186, *187*
shadows: 2D workflows 197–200; blacks 46, 91; "cast" and "ambient" 87–88; color 91, 198–200, *199*; contact 93; daylight and absence of *70*, 70–71; nested 92; overlapping 92; softness 88–89, *89*, *90*; utility passes 186
sheen 141
six-layer approach (color) 33–35
sky light 81, 125, 129
skylight 74
sodium-vapor lamps 85
specular balance 94–95
specular intensity 136
specular reflection 59–62, *60*, *61*; BRDF shading model 136; dielectric materials 94–95
specular roughness 136
SpeedTree 160–162
spill suppression *178*, 178
spot lights 122, *123*
starburst 106
subsurface scattering 63, *63–64*, 139–140
subsurface scattering color 140
subtractive color 35–36
the sun 69–71; *see also* daylight
sun beams 76
surface curvature *34*, 60–61, *61*, 62, 160
surface normal 59

technological change: computing power 115; games 24; machine learning 212–213; photorealism 213–214; procedural environments 213; realtime rendering 210–211; virtual environments 211–212; visual effects 210
terrain filters 166
terrain modeling 165–166
texturing 146–147; image textures 154, 158, 159; physically based renderer (PBR) 147–154; physically based rendering (PBR) *147*; procedural textures 157–158, 159, 160;

shooting and prepping photos 155–157, 161; SpeedTree example 160–162; workflows 154, 158, 159–160
thin-film interference 141
tiling 157, 159
translucent materials 64
transmission amount 138
transmission color 139
transmission depth 139, *139*
transmission roughness 138, *138*
transmission scatter 139
transmission (transparency) 57, 64–65
transmission weight 138
transparency 57, 64, 138–139, 185–186
transparency maps 153–154
transverse aberration 104

"uncanny valley" 14–15
the unreal 18
utility passes 186–189

V-number 141
video games *see* games
view factor 119–120
virtual environments 211–212
visual effects: digital media 22–24; games 24; technological change 210
visualization: architectural 25–28, *29*, 30, 67–68, 172; digital media 25–30; product 28–29
volumetric light 76, *76*
volumetric shaders 142–143

Wainstein, Javier *120*
wave-particle duality of light 51
waves, light as 51–52, *52*
whites 47–48, *48*
workflows: 2D compared to 3D 20, *21*; texturing 154, 158, 159–160; *see also* 2D workflows

Z buffer 116
Z depth 186, 189, 205

INDEX

221

Taylor & Francis eBooks

www.taylorfrancis.com

A single destination for eBooks from Taylor & Francis with increased functionality and an improved user experience to meet the needs of our customers.

90,000+ eBooks of award-winning academic content in Humanities, Social Science, Science, Technology, Engineering, and Medical written by a global network of editors and authors.

TAYLOR & FRANCIS EBOOKS OFFERS:

- A streamlined experience for our library customers
- A single point of discovery for all of our eBook content
- Improved search and discovery of content at both book and chapter level

REQUEST A FREE TRIAL
support@taylorfrancis.com

For Product Safety Concerns and Information please contact our EU representative GPSR@taylorandfrancis.com Taylor & Francis Verlag GmbH, Kaufingerstraße 24, 80331 München, Germany

Printed and bound by CPI Group (UK) Ltd, Croydon, CR0 4YY